THE STRAITS OF WAR

Gallipoli Remembered

Introduction by Sir Martin Gilbert

SUTTON PUBLISHING

First published in 2000 by
Sutton Publishing Limited · Phoenix Mill
Thrupp · Stroud · Gloucestershire · GL5 2BU

British Library Cataloguing in Publication Data
A catalogue record for this book is available from the British Library

ISBN 0-7509-2408-X

Typeset in 10.5/13pt Photina.
Typesetting and origination by
Sutton Publishing Limited.
Printed in Great Britain by
MPG Books, Bodmin, Cornwall.

CONTENTS

Plates 1–14 appear between pp. 136 and 137

CONTRIBUTORS

General Sir Hugh Beach was awarded the Military Cross while serving in the Royal Engineers in 1944. After a succession of senior appointments, he retired in 1981 as Master General of the Ordnance, becoming Warden of St George's House, Windsor Castle, for five years, and a member of the Security Commission. From 1986 to 1989 he was Director of the Council for Arms Control. He has written and lectured widely on questions of defence and disarmament, including particularly the morality of nuclear weapons.

The Rt Hon. Sir Edward Heath, who earned a mention in despatches while serving in the Royal Artillery during the Second World War, has been a Member of Parliament since 1950 and is now Father of the House of Commons. After serving as Government Chief Whip from 1955 to 1959 he entered the Cabinet and held a number of ministerial appointments before becoming Prime Minister from 1970 to 1974. He also achieved international recognition as a yachtsman and as an orchestral conductor, and his publications reflect these interests as well as politics.

His Royal Highness The Duke of Edinburgh served as an officer in the Royal Navy from 1939 to 1952. He is obviously able to view the military campaigns of Britain, her allies and the Commonwealth from a very commanding viewpoint.

The Rt Revd and Rt Hon. Lord Runcie served in the Scots Guards during the Second World War and was awarded the Military Cross in North West Europe in 1945. He took Holy Orders in 1950 and became Principal of Cuddesdon Theological College 1960–9, Bishop of St Albans 1970–80 and Archbishop of Canterbury 1980–90. He has written widely on theological topics.

John Grigg served in the Grenadier Guards between 1943 and 1945, and subsequently made a career as a political commentator and historian. He has established a particular reputation as a biographer of David Lloyd George, with special reference to the political role of that statesman before and during the First World War.

Professor Robert O'Neill served in the Australian Army 1955–68, and was mentioned in despatches in the Vietnam War. Embarking upon an academic career as a strategic analyst and historian, he became Director of the International Institute for Strategic Studies from 1982 to 1987, since when he has been a Fellow of All Souls College, Oxford, as Chichele Professor of the History of War. He is also a Member of the Commonwealth War Graves Commission, and has written numerous books and articles on strategic and military questions.

Osman Olcay is a distinguished Turkish diplomat. A former Minister of Foreign Affairs, he has also been Deputy Secretary General of NATO and has served as Ambassador of Turkey in Finland, in India, at the United Nations and in NATO.

Field Marshal Sir Nigel Bagnall was commissioned into the Green Howards in 1946 and served in Palestine and in Malaya, where he was awarded the Military Cross and Bar. He subsequently commanded the 4/7 Royal Dragoon Guards and rose to become Commander-in-Chief, British Army of the Rhine and Commander, NATO Northern Army Group (1983–5), and Chief of the General Staff (1985–8). A keen student of military history, his book *The Punic Wars* was published in 1990.

The Rt Hon. J. Enoch Powell became Professor of Greek in Sydney University in 1937, but in 1939 returned to Britain to enlist as a private soldier in the Royal Warwickshire Regiment. By 1944 he had reached the rank of brigadier, and after the war entered politics, serving as a Member of Parliament from 1950 to 1987. His publications range from classical scholarship through theology and lyric poetry to political economy, and include a biography of Joseph Chamberlain. He died in 1998.

Lieutenant General Sir Leonard Thornton was commissioned into the New Zealand Army in 1937, and during the Second World War served in the Middle East and in Italy, earning two mentions in despatches. His subsequent military career led him to be Chief of the General Staff in New Zealand from 1960 to 1965, and Chief of the Defence Staff from 1965 to 1971. After retiring from the Army he was New Zealand's Ambassador in South Vietnam and the Khmer Republic from 1972 to 1974, and later was actively involved in the production of a television documentary on Gallipoli. He died in 1999.

Sir Martin Gilbert is a Fellow of Merton College, Oxford, and one of the foremost authorities on the history of the twentieth century. In addition to succeeding Randolph Churchill as official biographer of Sir Winston, where he was personally responsible for volume 3 which covers the Gallipoli campaign, he has written comprehensively on various aspects of both world wars, on the Holocaust and on the Arab–Israeli conflict.

Professor Jean-Charles Jauffret is Professor of Modern History and Director of the Military History Centre at Université Paul Valéry, Montpellier. He is also a Professor at the Military School at St Cyr where, from 1983 to 1991, he was Maître de Conférences. He has published widely on French military history, specialising particularly in the war in Algeria and in the social structure of the French Army and its officer class.

Professor Sir Michael Howard served in the Coldstream Guards during the Second World War, and was awarded the Military Cross. Embarking subsequently upon an academic career, he successively held Chairs as Professor of War Studies at King's College, London; in Oxford as Chichele Professor of the History of War and later Regius Professor of Modern History; and at Yale as Lovett Professor of Military and Naval History. He was a co-founder, and is now President, of the International Institute for Strategic Studies. His numerous writings include the volume on Grand Strategy in the *Official History of the Second World War*, an authoritative study of the Franco-Prussian War and (as co-editor) a definitive English edition of Clausewitz's *On War*.

Professor Michael Stürmer has, since 1973, been a Professor of Medieval and Modern History at the Friedrich-Alexander-Universität, Erlangen-Nürnberg. From 1988 to 1998 he was Director of the Stiftung Wissenschaft und Politik (a research institute for international affairs) at Ebenhausen in Bavaria, and in 1988–9 he held a Chair at Johns Hopkins University, Bologna, Italy. He is a specialist in the history of the nineteenth and twentieth centuries, and his writings include *The Restless Empire: Germany 1866–1918*.

Admiral of the Fleet Sir Julian Oswald joined the Royal Navy in 1947. After a succession of appointments ashore and afloat, including command of Britannia Royal Naval College, Dartmouth, he became Commander-in-Chief, Fleet, and Allied Commander-in-Chief, Eastern Atlantic and Channel, from 1987 to 1989, and Chief of Naval Staff and First Sea Lord from 1989 to 1993.

The Rt Revd Richard Harries served as an officer in the Royal Corps of Signals from 1955 to 1958. He took Holy Orders in 1963 and, in 1981, became Dean of King's College, London, before appointment as Bishop of Oxford in 1987. He is well known as a writer and broadcaster on theological questions; his publications include *Christianity and War in a Nuclear Age*. He is also President of the Council on Christian Approaches to Defence and Disarmament.

North Sea

BRITAIN

SWEDEN

DENMARK

Baltic Sea

BORKUM

Kiel

London

Stettin

HOLLAND

Berlin

Warsaw

RUSSIA

GERMANY

BELGIUM

Paris

River Danube

AUSTRIA-

Vienna

Budapest

Odessa

FRANCE

SWITZERLAND

HUNGARY

River Danube

ROUMANIA

Trieste

Bucharest

Marseille

Belgrade

ITALY

Adriatic Sea

Cattaro

SERBIA

BULGARIA

Black

Rome

MONTENEGRO

Sofia

Sea

ALBANIA

THRACE

TURKEY

Salonika

GREECE

Mediterranean Sea

Strait of Otranto

Aegean Sea

ANATOLIA

| 0 | kilometres | 400 |
| 0 | miles | 250 |

© Martin Gilbert 2000

RHODES

BULGARIA

Constantinople

Black Sea

Caucasus

RUSSIA

Kars

Caspian Sea

Salonika

GREECE

Chanak

ANATOLIA

OTTOMAN

Aegean Sea

Marmarice

Alexandretta

PERSIA

RHODES
(ITALIAN)

CYPRUS
(BRITISH)

Baghdad

EMPIRE

Mediterranean Sea

Haifa

Basra

Fao

Persian Gulf

Jerusalem

Alexandria

Suez Canal

EGYPT
(BRITISH)

Akaba

Suez

| 0 | kilometres | 500 |
| 0 | miles | 300 |

© Martin Gilbert 2000

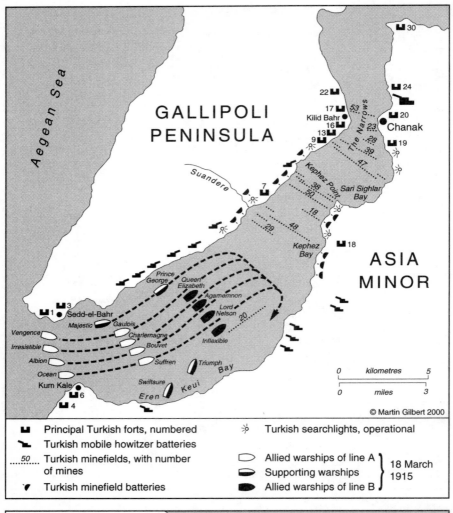

Principal Turkish forts, numbered

Turkish mobile howitzer batteries

.....50.... Turkish minefields, with number of mines

Turkish minefield batteries

Turkish searchlights, operational

Allied warships of line A

Supporting warships

Allied warships of line B

18 March 1915

© Martin Gilbert 2000

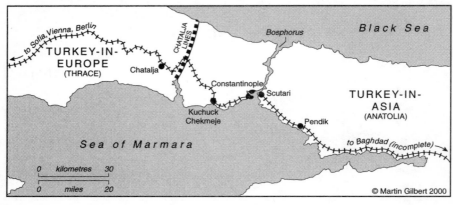

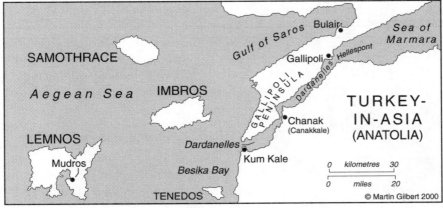

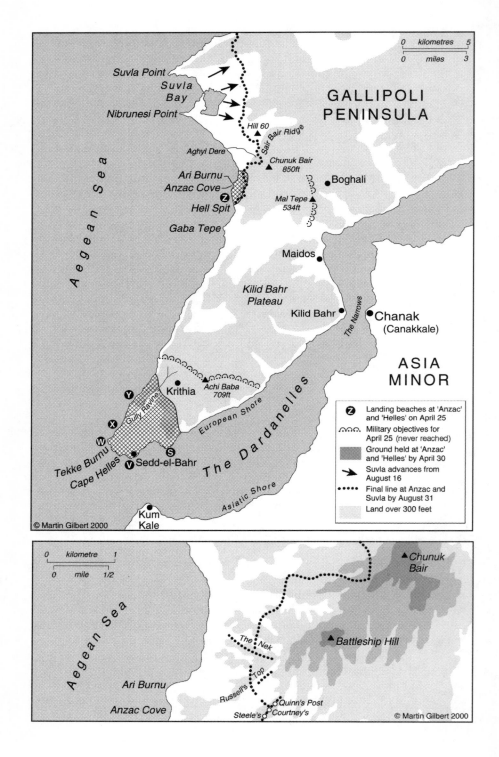

Suvla Point

Suvla Bay

Nibrunesi Point

Aegean Sea

GALLIPOLI
PENINSULA

0 kilometres 5
0 miles 3

Hill 60

Sari Bair Ridge

Aghyl Dere

Chunuk Bair
850ft

Ari Burnu
Anzac Cove
Z
Hell Spit

● Boghali

Mal Tepe
534ft

Gaba Tepe

Maidos ●

Kilid Bahr
Plateau

Kilid Bahr ●

The Narrows

● Chanak
(Canakkale)

ASIA
MINOR

Achi Baba
709ft

Y
Krithia ●

Gully Ravine

X

W

Tekke Burnu
Cape Helles

S

V Sedd-el-Bahr

European Shore

The Dardanelles

Asiatic Shore

© Martin Gilbert 2000

Kum
Kale ●

Z Landing beaches at 'Anzac'
and 'Helles' on April 25

⌒⌒⌒ Military objectives for
April 25 (never reached)

▓ Ground held at 'Anzac'
and 'Helles' by April 30

→ Suvla advances from
August 16

•••• Final line at Anzac and
Suvla by August 31

░ Land over 300 feet

0 kilometre 1
0 mile 1/2

Aegean Sea

▲ Chunuk
Bair

The Nek

▲ Battleship Hill

Russell's Top

Quinn's Post

Courtney's

Steele's

Ari Burnu

Anzac Cove

© Martin Gilbert 2000

INTRODUCTION

Martin Gilbert

The Anglo-French naval attack on the Dardanelles in March 1915, and the Allied military landings that April on the Gallipoli peninsula, followed by the fighting on the peninsula that ended with the evacuation of the Allied forces almost nine months later, constitute one of the most recounted episodes of the First World War.

From the moment Turkey entered the war with her naval bombardment of Odessa on 29 October 1914, as an ally of Germany, the defeat of Turkey became a war aim of the Entente Powers. British hostilities against Turkey were authorised by the Foreign Office two days later, and communicated to the Admiralty. British naval action followed almost immediately at five different points of the Ottoman Empire. On 1 November an armed Turkish yacht was sunk in Smyrna harbour by two British destroyers. On the 2nd British sailors landed at Akaba at the northern end of the Red Sea (the sailors returned to their ship after a few hours). On 3 November the outer forts of the Dardanelles were bombarded (from a distance of seven miles) and the arsenal at Sedd-el-Bahr blown up. On 7 November an Indian Army force, on the orders of the Viceroy Lord Hardinge, landed at Fao, at the mouth of the Persian Gulf, and captured Basra with hardly any opposition. On 18 December another British force landed at Alexandretta on the eastern shore of the Mediterranean (it withdrew three days later, having cut the railway line from Anatolia to Suez).

These five actions raised the alluring spectre of defeating Turkey, and of using Turkey-in-Europe as a springboard for an attack deep into Austria-Hungary and even Germany itself, having, by a military victory, persuaded Greece, Bulgaria, and even Italy – each of which had territorial designs against Turkey – to enter the war on the side of the Entente.

As the trench warfare on the Western Front emerged by the end of 1914 as the main feature of Britain's war against Germany, any talk of a sustained assault on Turkey was denounced by the 'westerners' as a diversion and a sideshow, too costly in men and munitions to be worth risking the stability of the front in France and Flanders. To the First Sea Lord, Lord Fisher, who had proposed the defeat of Turkey using a substantial force of Greek, Bulgarian and British troops, the First Lord of the Admiralty, Winston Churchill, replied on 4 January 1915: 'I would not grudge 100,000 men because of the great political effects in the Balkan peninsula: but Germany is the foe, and it is bad war to seek cheaper victories and easier antagonists.'

That Turkey would be an 'easier' antagonist seemed clear from the successful landings at Akaba, Fao and Alexandretta, particularly the last-named, where the British force had remained ashore unchallenged for three days. During the Dardanelles Commission of Enquiry in 1916, Churchill told the commissioners that the landing at Alexandretta 'is not without its significance, because it helped to form the opinion in our mind as to the degree of resistance which might in all circumstances be expected from Turkey. What kind of Turk was this we were fighting?'

Since the earliest weeks of the war, Churchill himself had been attracted to the idea of a swift blow against Turkey. On 4 September 1914, two months before Turkey had entered the war, he had informed Admiral Mark Kerr, the British commander of the Greek Navy: 'The right and obvious method of attacking Turkey is to strike immediately at the heart.' At that time Churchill was attacted to a plan to use a Greek army 'to seize the Gallipoli peninsula' under the superiority of naval predominance. This Greek seizure of Gallipoli would, Churchill envisaged, 'open the Dardanelles, admitting the Anglo-Greek fleet to the Sea of Marmara, whence the Turco-German ships can be fought and sunk, and where, in combination with the Russian Black Sea Fleet and Russian military forces, the whole situation can be dominated'. What Churchill did not then know was that Constantinople, the annexation of which was the main inducement to Greek participation, had already been promised by Britain in utmost secrecy to Russia, by the Prime Minister, Asquith, and the Foreign Secretary, Sir Edward Grey.

The 'Greek' plan was the first of a dozen different war plans put forward by Churchill and other British politicians and senior serving officers to break the stalemate on the Western Front. The search for another theatre of war was continuous. On 29 December 1914 Churchill wrote to Asquith: 'Are there not other alternatives than sending our armies to chew barbed wire in Flanders?' His proposal, then, was for a British amphibious landing on the German North Sea coast, followed by the capture of the Kiel canal, British naval dominance of the Baltic, and a Russian military advance on Berlin. Lloyd George, then Chancellor of the Exchequer, wanted a British military assault launched from Salonika, to help Serbia. He also wanted to land 100,000 men in the Turkish province of Syria, to capture Palestine ('territory which appeals to the imagination of the people as a whole'), in order to force Turkish troops away from the Caucasus front, where they were in the process of pushing back the Russians.

Help for Russia was a dominant theme of ministerial discussion in the early weeks of 1915. On 2 January the Secretary of State for War, Lord Kitchener, wrote to Churchill: 'I do not see that we can do anything that will seriously help the Russians in the Caucasus. . . . We have no troops to land anywhere. . . . ' Kitchener added: 'The only place that a demonstration might have some effect in stopping reinforcements going East would be the Dardanelles.' This was particularly so, Kitchener told Churchill, if it could be shown, as had been suggested by the Russian Commander-in-Chief, 'that Constantinople was threatened'. As for 'anything big' in that region, Kitchener commented, Britain would not be ready for that 'for some months'.

Kitchener's reference to 'a demonstration at the Dardanelles' had lit the fuse. As the idea of such a demonstration gathered impetus, several plans were put forward. Envisaged was not just the bombardment of the forts at the entrance to the Dardanelles, as had taken place in November 1914, but a dash through the narrows and into the Sea of Marmara by a combined British and French fleet; and not necessarily just a naval dash, but a combined naval and military assault which would enable the Entente to occupy the Gallipoli peninsula. The goal in each case would be for the Entente warships to enter the Sea of Marmara, secure their lines of communication, and bombard Constantinople.

In my Gallipoli Memorial Lecture (1995) I set out the evolution both of Churchill's thought and the proposals which others contributed to the debate. This process culminated in Asquith's instruction to the War Council on 13 January 1915, 'That the Admiralty should also prepare' – in addition to an attack which Asquith authorised on the Austro-Hungarian port of Cattaro in the Adriatic – 'for a naval expedition in February to bombard and take the Gallipoli Peninsula, with Constantinople as its objective.' In this instruction Asquith made no reference to the participation of the army or the involvement of the War Office and Lord Kitchener. Yet to 'take the Gallipoli Peninsula' could hardly be done by ships alone, however successful they might be in pushing past the Turkish defences at the narrows.

At each subsequent meeting of the War Council the question of whether troops would be used, and if so which troops, was at the centre of the discussions. On 16 February 1915 Kitchener agreed to use the 29th Division, which was then in England. Three days later he opposed the idea. That morning British warships bombarded the outer forts of the Dardanelles. The fuse lit by Kitchener's 'demonstration at the Dardanelles' had begun to blaze. When, at the War Council of 24 February, Asquith asked whether Australian and New Zealand troops were 'good enough' for an important operation of war, Kitchener replied that they were 'quite good enough if a cruise in the Sea of Marmara was all that was contemplated'.

At each successive meeting of the War Council, different Cabinet Ministers saw merit, and considerable advantage to Britain, in Asquith's War Cabinet conclusion to 'take the Gallipoli Peninsula'. The defeat of the Turks, even the prospect of their defeat, was a great attraction. It seemed to offer Britain, France and Russia the prospect of drawing other, hitherto neutral, nations into the war on the side of the Entente. Indeed, four weeks after the Gallipoli landings had taken place, Italy concluded that Turkey would be beaten, and joined the Entente. Greece and Bulgaria continued to sit on the fence of neutrality, but each stood to gain territorially from the defeat of Turkey, as did Italy (which was promised considerable territorial gains, including control of southern Anatolia).

For the governments in London and Paris, the prospect of a naval victory at the Dardanelles at the time of the naval attack of 18 March 1915 was a high point of hope. The prospect of a land victory on the peninsula after 25 April 1915, when troops were finally put ashore, under Kitchener's ultimate responsibility, despite his initial reluctance, created high expectations. The hope and the expectation were both dashed. The naval attack of 18 March – following the loss of three of the ten Entente battleships to Turkish mines, and the deaths of 47 British and 620 French sailors – was not renewed. The troops, coming ashore on 25 April, and fighting their way inland, assisted by the massive firepower of the British naval guns, failed to reach their first day's objectives, the high ground from which they could sweep down to the shore of the Sea of Marmara. Nor were they to reach those first day's objectives in the weeks and months ahead, despite coming several times very close indeed to success, and despite several renewed offensives, including a new landing at Suvla Bay in August, and almost nine months of continuous fighting.

More than half a million men were in action on Gallipoli in the Entente ranks. Of these 37–8,000 British and Empire soldiers, and 13–14,000 French soldiers, were killed. More than 150,000 Allied troops were wounded. The Turkish death toll was at least 86,000 (the official Turkish figure).

Tens of thousands of letters were written from the Gallipoli peninsula. Those that have been published can often speak with a greater directness than any historical summary. One such letter, written by an Irishman and a poet, Lance Corporal Francis Ledwidge – who was killed by a shell on the Western Front in 1917 – described his experiences at Suvla Bay on 15 August 1915: '. . . a man on my right who was mortally hit said: "It can't be far off now", and I began to wonder what it was that could not be far off. Then I knew it was death and kept repeating the dying man's words: "It can't be far off now". But when the Turks began to retreat I realized my position, and, standing up, I shouted out the range to the men near me and they fell like grass before a scythe, the enemy. It was Hell! Hell! No man thought he would ever return. Just fancy out of D Company, 250 strong, only 76 returned.' Ledwidge added – he was writing to a friend and fellow-poet – 'By Heavens, you should know the bravery of these men: Cassidy standing on a hill with his cap on top of his rifle shouting at the Turks to come out: stretcher-bearers taking in friend and enemy alike. It was a horrible and a great day. I would not have missed it for words.'

The events at the Dardanelles and on the Gallipoli peninsula within the space of nine months have been described by many historians. The complexity of their task might appear almost overwhelming. It was two writers in 1917, Acting Commander A.T. Stewart RN and the Revd C.J.E. Peshall, Chaplain RN, both of whom were serving in HMS *Cornwallis* at the V Beach landing on 25 April 1915, who summed up the dilemma of all authors seeking to illuminate the campaign when they wrote in *The Immortal Gamble*: 'The tremendous episode of the great landing blazes at you from so many facets, is so crowded in every one of its glowing hours with heroic deeds, pathetic incidents, and unflinching purpose, that it is necessary to hold all records of it at long arm's length to grasp even one aspect of the majestic drama.'

One of the first to seek to grasp not one but many aspects of the Gallipoli campaign was Brigadier Aspinall-Oglander, in his two *Gallipoli* volumes of the British official military history of the First World War. He had been a member of General Hamilton's staff, and had gone ashore after the landing at Suvla Bay in August. In later decades, those who had not been present, and in due course those who had not even been born when the naval guns first opened fire against the Dardanelles defences in November 1914, were to write about the campaign. Each was to be caught up in some way or other, not only in the hardships and setbacks, but in the epic nature of the struggle – what a Second World War soldier, John North, author of *Gallipoli: The Fading Vision*, called 'the mystique of Gallipoli'. Alan Moorehead and Robert Rhodes James, both with a clear eye for all that was wrong, inept and reprehensible, likewise understood and reflected that mystique.

Moorehead's assessment of the campaign, written in 1956, the year when another Anglo-French amphibious enterprise was launched in the eastern Mediterranean, may stand the test of time. He writes of how, as the years passed, 'the Gallipoli adventure was seen, not in isolation, but as part of the general strategy: not as a sideshow, but as an alternative to the fearful three years of slaughter in the trenches in France and Flanders, to the long campaign against the Turks in Mesopotamia, and to the expedition to Salonika.' Moorehead adds: 'It was even perhaps not too much to say that if the Allies had succeeded in penetrating the Dardanelles in 1915 or 1916 the Russians would not have signed a separate peace, and that the revolution might not have followed, not at all events so soon, or possibly so drastically.' It was to help Russia, then being hard pressed by the Turks in the Caucasus, that Kitchener had originally suggested 'a demonstration' at the Dardanelles.

Literary men who were present at Gallipoli added their powerful voices, heard most expressively in two novels, A.P. Herbert's *Secret Battle* and Ernest Raymond's *Tell England*, and in Compton Mackenzie's *Gallipoli Memories*. Churchill wrote in 1919, in the foreword to A.P. Herbert's book: 'It was one of those cries of pain wrung from the fighting troops by the prolonged and measureless torment through which they passed; and like the poems of Siegfried Sassoon should be read in each generation, so that men and women may rest under no illusion about what war means.' Ten years later, in 1929, L.S. Amery noted in his diary a remark by Churchill about the Dardanelles: 'Talking of the series of mischances which just prevented our getting through, he said jestingly that his only consolation was that God wished things to be prolonged in order to sicken mankind of war, and that therefore He had interfered with a project which would have brought the war to a speedier conclusion.'

Fierce criticisms of the conduct of the campaign were also voiced in print while the campaign itself was still bring fought. In his book *The Uncensored Dardanelles* Ellis Ashmead-Bartlett angered many contemporaries when he recalled watching the approaching flames of a scrub fire and the crawling figures who were caught between the flames and the Turkish snipers and the bursts of shrapnel. When the fire had passed, Ashmead-Bartlett wrote, 'little mounds of scorched khaki alone marked the spot where another mismanaged soldier of the king had returned to mother earth'. Reviled by many for his reports from the battlefield, Ashmead-Bartlett was praised by the official Australian war historian, Dr C.E.W. Bean, as 'the most brilliant of the war correspondents' on the peninsula. Criticism of the campaign had begun while the campaign itself was being fought.

'Wars are not won by evacuations' had been Winston Churchill's comment in 1940 after the Dunkirk evacuation. Prince Philip, in his Gallipoli Memorial Lecture (1987), reflected on the evacuations that took place from Anzac and Cape Helles in December 1915 and January 1916: 'The ultimate irony was that the evacuation turned out to be the most successful operation of the whole campaign. Every single soldier and virtually every horse, mule and weapon was taken off the peninsula at the cost of one man slightly wounded.'

The fascination of the Dardanelles and Gallipoli campaigns remained strong throughout the interwar years, and survived the dramatic events of the Second World War. The Gallipoli Memorial Lectures, inaugurated 1985 – on the seventieth anniversary of the landings – and continued annually until the year 2000, are a symbol of this fascination. The lectures were held at the Holy Trinity Church, Eltham, where a Gallipoli memorial chapel was established in 1917, and where an annual memorial service had been held from 1917 until 1984. The lectures formed part of a shortened memorial service. Each lecturer contributed a special facet to the recounting of the story, a tribute to the tenacity of the impact which the nine-month struggle had on subsequent years, and indeed on subsequent generations.

Year by year, lecturers have cast their personal glow of thought on the campaign and its aftermath. Archbishop Runcie (in 1988), after listing the many errors of the campaign, remarked: 'Yet Gallipoli was not a madcap adventure. It was part of a total vision of Churchill's, born out of the failure of the navy to force the Dardanelles. There were good grounds for thinking that if we had broken through to Constantinople, where so much of the Turkish armaments industry was located, and Turkey was taken out of the war, a decisive blow would have been dealt to Germany from the rear.' Thirty-four years earlier, in 1954, Clement Attlee, a former Prime Minister and leader of the Labour Party, who had fought at Gallipoli as a 32-year-old captain, told Churchill, during a public tribute, that the Dardanelles was 'the only imaginative strategic idea of the war. I only wish that you had had full power to carry it to success.'

The number of men who, like Attlee, fought at Gallipoli and later rose to prominence, was considerable. Mustafa Kemal became President of Turkey. He was succeeded as president by another veteran of the campaign, Ismet Inönü. Admiral Keyes was serving as Director of Combined Operations in 1940. The future careers of three soldiers who had fought on the peninsula were mentioned in his lecture by a New Zealander, Lieutenant General Sir Leonard Thornton (1994), who said: 'I would like to think that there was significant military profit in the presence on Gallipoli of three young officers who later came to fame, and did better than their predecessors.' He was referring to Field Marshal Slim, the future victor over the Japanese in Burma, Field Marshal Harding, who served as a lieutenant general in the post-D-Day advance from Normandy to the Rhine, and the New Zealander Lord Freyberg, who in 1941 commanded the Allied – including Anzac – forces on Crete. 'I do know,' said General Thornton, 'that the New Zealanders were to be grateful in the Second World War for General Freyberg's insistence on sound planning and co-ordination, his enthusiasm for night operations rather than daylight attacks, and his reliance on ample and skilled medical services. All of these sprang in the first instance from his own experiences at Gallipoli and helped make him the outstanding and respected field commander he was.'

In his lecture, Professor J.-C. Jauffret (1996) noted the failure of the French High Command between the wars to learn the lessons of combined operations 'at a time when French military thought became ossified in the concept of a continuous front'. Professor Robert O'Neill (1990) also dwelt on the combined operations lessons. Recalling 1940, he wrote: 'After the evacuation from Dunkirk, Churchill's mind turned to the problems of landing a force to liberate the European continent: his Dardanelles experience stood him in good stead. Combined Operations Command was established in 1940 and Churchill pressed for the development of the ships and landing craft needed to put a huge army back into a strongly defended Europe.'

Professor Sir Michael Howard (1997) emphasised the forging of Australian nationality, quoting Charles Bean's conclusion in *The Story of Anzac*: 'In no unreal sense it was on the 25th of April 1915 that the consciousness of Australian nationhood was born.' Sir Michael added: 'The same of course can be said of New Zealand.' Professor Michael Stürmer (1998) noted that the precariousness of the Turkish position at Gallipoli drew the German military planners to the view that 'Turkey had to be saved through an offensive on Serbia': Bulgaria was brought into the war as a Central Power, and the offensive launched, with German, Austrian and Bulgarian divisions, in the early autumn of 1915. To meet this threat, British and French troops were landed at Salonika on 5 October 1915. For the future of the Gallipoli campaign, it was a fatal diversion of troops. In addition, Serbia was crushed.

The German contribution to the battle itself was considerable. A German general, Liman von Sanders, commanded the Turkish 5th Army on the peninsula, and was assisted by several German artillery specialists. German aircraft, based at Chanak, provided the Turks with aerial reconnaissance. In his lecture on the naval contribution to the campaign, Admiral of the Fleet Sir Julian Oswald (1999) noted the early use at Gallipoli of British aerial reconnaissance, as well as the way in which minesweeping 'found itself catapulted into the twentieth century', not with the happiest of results, he reflected. And he noted a parallel between the Turkish minelaying successes, which effectively ended the attempt to defeat the Turks by ships alone, and the North Korean minelaying off Inchon in the Korean War four decades later, though in the end the Inchon landings proved a success for the American planners.

Russian warships also participated in the campaign. 'We watched with special interest the Russian cruiser with five funnels demolish the village of Yeni Shehr on the Asiatic side,' wrote the Revd O. Creighton in his diary as his ship approached Cape Helles. In 1916 he published his diary in his eyewitness account of the British forces, *With the Twenty-ninth Division in Gallipoli: A Chaplain's Experiences*.

Edward Heath, a former prime minister, who had seen active service in the Second World War, spoke in his lecture (1986) of the coming of war in 1914, stressing his conviction that 'the collapse of international stability and the breakdown in managed relations between the imperial powers before the First World War has a vital lesson for us today'. War could be more easily avoided and international tensions defused in a world which had seen 'the determined integration of Europe', itself a reaction to the two world wars.

Enoch Powell, whose father-in-law had been invalided from Gallipoli to Cairo during the campaign, reflected (1993) on Britain's traditional closeness to the Ottoman Empire before 1914, and reflected that it was 'remarkable that so staggering a disaster inflicted upon British arms neither created at the time nor left behind it a rooted hostility such as our most successful encounters with other opponents have left behind'. In his lecture Field Marshal Sir Nigel Bagnall (1992) spoke of 'The Human Story'. He quoted from Christopher Pugsley the words of an Australian soldier at the forward position at Quinn's Post: 'As the Turkish line was only a fifteen-second dash away, the front and support trenches on and immediately below the crest were always crowded to repel an attack. Casualties were heavy, there were mangled bodies of our own men and the Turks everywhere, and the stench was nearly unbearable. The heat was intense and the flies swarmed in their millions, you couldn't drink your own tea or eat your stew without them flying in and out of your mouth.'

John Masefield, in one of the first books written about the campaign, *Gallipoli*, published in September 1916, commented: 'Men in Gallipoli in the summer of 1915 learned to curse the sun as an enemy more cruel than the Turk. With the sun and the plague of flies came the torment of thirst, one of the greatest torments which life has the power to inflict.' As for the Turks, Masefield added, 'They had always more water than we, and (what is more) the certainty of it.'

Field Marshal Bagnall recalled one of the least remembered of the Allied units at Gallipoli, the Gurkhas, who formed 'the single largest contingent from the Indian Army which fought at Gallipoli'. Also fighting on the peninsula was the first all-Jewish military force to be in action for more than two thousand years: the Zion Mule Corps. Its five hundred members had been recruited in Egypt from Jews expelled from Palestine by the Turks. With their own Star of David insignia, eight Jewish and five British officers, including their commander, Lieutenant-Colonel J.H. Patterson, they were in the fiercest of the actions. Patterson wrote in his book *With the Zionists in Gallipoli*, published in 1916: 'Many of the Zionists, whom I had thought somewhat lacking in courage, showed themselves fearless to a degree when under heavy fire.'

Egyptian and Greek labourers built roads on the peninsula under continual Turkish shellfire. Black Senegalese troops fought at Cape Helles from the first day. Sikhs were in action as part of the Indian Army. Among those killed by the frequently misdirected British naval shellfire (now known as 'friendly fire') was a South African VC, Captain Shelley. The New Zealand forces included Maori soldiers. British troops – whom several lecturers urged us not to forget amid the recounting of diverse nations – were in action everywhere. Scottish soldiers were responsible for the name of Aberdeen Gully, at Cape Helles. One of the landing beaches at Cape Helles, W Beach, is better known as Lancashire Landing. In his study of the campaign, entitled *Gallipoli*, Captain Eric Bush, who served as a midshipman at the landings, wrote of the landing at W Beach, and of those watching it from on board ship: 'Gallantly led by their officers, the Lancashire Fusiliers hurled themselves ashore. Many were hit in the sea, and many who gained the beach were mown down immediately. Eye witnesses, anxiously watching, asked each other, "What are they resting for?" But they were dead.'

An Irish officer who fought on the peninsula, Major Bryan Cooper, wrote in *The Tenth (Irish) Division in Gallipoli*, published in 1917: 'Death had made strange bedfellows: in one little cemetery high up at the Chailak Dere behind Rhododendron Ridge there lay side by side Private John Jones, Royal Welch Fusiliers, and Sergeant Rotahiru of the Maoris. From the two ends of the earth Christian and Buddhist and Sikh had come to fight in the same cause, and in death they lay together.'

The former Turkish Foreign Minister, Osman Olcay (1991), spoke of the human side of the struggle, reflecting that much of Alan Moorehead's *Gallipoli* was 'devoted to the description of scenes which we would nowadays be tempted to consider surrealistic and which, I believe, are unique in the annals of warfare; men helping each other in the middle of opposite trenches full of utterly exhausted and nervous sharpshooters to carry wounded and bury dead while exchanging gifts, jokes and compassionate greetings, even good wishes and calling cards with inscriptions such as "Profession – student in Poetry" before returning to their respective sides to continue their murderous daily business.'

The Turkish minister also quoted, as did several other lecturers, the words of Kemal Atatürk inscribed on the memorial above Anzac Cove, and at the Atatürk Memorial Garden in Australia:

There is no difference between the Johnnies and Mehmets to us where they lie side by side here in this country of ours. You, the mothers, who sent their sons from far-away countries, wipe away your tears; your sons are now lying in our bosom and are in peace. After having lost their lives on this land, they have become our sons as well.

The individual experiences of those sons are an integral part of the history of the campaign, which had its origins in Cabinet rooms and embassies. In his reflections on the different natures of the two world wars, John Grigg (1989) also quotes from a letter from a soldier sailing from Liverpool to Lemnos: 'Fancy, 80 stokers deserted before we sailed and a guard with fixed bayonets had to be placed on the remainder.' This episode, Grigg notes, is not in the official histories: 'Who knows how many other such incidents have gone unrecorded?'

In the first of the Gallipoli Memorial Lectures (1985), General Sir Hugh Beach began with quotations from those who had fought on the peninsula, and those who had witnessed the fighting there, among them H.W. Nevinson, whose book *The Dardanelles Campaign* was first published in November 1918. 'Every kind of store of arms', Nevinson wrote of Anzac Cove, 'has to be dragged or "jumped" up these ant-hills of cliffs and deposited at the proper hole or gallery. Food, water, cartridges, shells, building timber, guns, medical stores – up the tracks all must go, and down them the wounded come.' Nevinson added: 'The domestic virtues which constitute the whole art of war are exercised with a fortitude rarely maintained upon the domestic hearth.' General Beach commented with incredulity: 'The "domestic *virtues* which constitute the whole art of war"? It seems to me . . . that there had been translated into the Gallipoli Peninsula *all* the domestic *horrors* of trench warfare in Flanders – modulated only by the quite exceptional Asiatic heat of the summer of 1915.'

The final speaker (in the year 2000), Richard Harries, Bishop of Oxford, also begins his lecture with an eyewitness account. 'We are quite old hands at the game now,' wrote William Wilson, a young chaplain with the 8th Scottish Rifles, on 16 June 1915, to his mother, 'though I confess that I had the "Jumps" yesterday and so did we all – but it is perfectly wonderful how soon one gets used to it; we only duck now when we actually hear the whiz of a shell coming, and are getting to know the sound where they will burst.' As for Nevinson, so for Williams, there is the domestic aspect. On 10 October 1915 he wrote home: 'My servant considers that I have a pair of boots worth polishing! Could you send out a tin of polish – but I don't want any unless you can get some *dark* stain – polish – mahogany or dark red!' The bishop ends his lecture with the words from 1 Corinthians 15, 'Therefore, my beloved brethren, be steadfast, immovable, always abounding in the work of the Lord, knowing that in the Lord your labour is not in vain', and he comments: '"Not in vain". That is our hope even though the way in which that hope is fulfilled goes out in mystery.'

The question of faith which the Bishop of Oxford raises has wide resonance. The Crosses, and also the Stars of David, on the Commonwealth

War Graves at Gallipoli, must give each visitor cause for reflection beyond the day-to-day scenes of battle. The bishop quotes from Ernest Raymond's novel *Tell England* (Raymond had been a chaplain at Gallipoli). The book, first published in February 1922, was reprinted fourteen times in that one year. In it, Padre Monty speaks of how, but for the war, two friends, one of whom was killed on Gallipoli, would not have been brought together. 'But, as it is, the war held you in a deepening intimacy till – till the end. It's – it's perfect.'

This lecture series ends. But the recounting of the saga of Gallipoli will continue. Its successes and failures, bravery and cowardice, savage incident and sublime courage, will call forth the skills of many more writers and historians during the twenty-first century.

Merton College, Oxford
21 January 2000

ONE

THE MURDEROUS RESPONSIBILITY

Hugh Beach

24 April 1985

I strayed about the deck, an hour, tonight
Under a cloudy moonless sky; and peeped
In at the windows, watched my friends at table,
Or playing cards, or standing in the doorway,
Or coming out into the darkness. Still
No one could see me.

I would have thought of them
– Heedless, within a week of battle – in pity,
Pride in their strength and in the weight and firmness
And link'd beauty of bodies, and pity that
This gay machine of splendour'ld soon be broken
Thought little of, pashed, scattered . . .

Only, always,
I could but see them – against the lamplight – pass
Like coloured shadows, thinner than the filmy glass,
Slight bubbles, fainter than the wave's faint light,
That broke to phosphorus out in the night
Perishing things and strange ghosts – soon to die
To other ghosts – this one, or that, or I.

That was Rupert Brooke, the first and perhaps the most famous of the Gallipoli expedition to perish – written not long before he died in a French hospital ship, off Skyros, of blood-poisoning from an insect bite. 'He died at 4.46, with the sun shining all round his cabin, and the cool sea breeze blowing through the door and the shaded windows. No one could have wished a quieter or calmer end in that lovely bay shielded by the mountains and fragrant with sage and thyme.'

He was buried that evening in an olive grove above Trebuki Bay. At the grave were Denis Browne (who wrote that description of his death and was to die himself on 4 June), Bernard Freyberg (who won his first DSO at Bulair 48 hours later and went on to win three bars to it – and a VC), Charles Lister, Clegg Kelly, Patrick Shaw Stewart, Arthur Asquith, Johnny Dodge. Sir Ian Hamilton felt the loss keenly: 'Death grins at my elbow. I cannot get him out of my thoughts. He is fed up with the old and sick – only the flower of the flock will serve him now, for God has started a celestial spring cleaning, and our star is to be scrubbed bright with the blood of our bravest and our best.' He was right about the blood, but not about *his* star. Within six months he had been dismissed and was never to command again. Did he guess – that night? 'Watchman of the milky way, shepherd of the golden stars, have mercy upon us . . . thy will be done. *En avant* – at all costs – *en avant.*'

'Nature was so beautiful' – a young officer of the Lancashire Fusiliers writing of this evening all those years ago on the cruiser *Euryalus* off Tenedos – 'a dead flat calm, an oily sea, a silent beautiful rock-crowned island, with its replica in the bay beneath, no sound or movement in water or in air, no signs of the prodigious eruption of metal and men which was to greet the dawn.' He was in the assault on W Beach. But Gallipoli in the late spring *is* beautiful.

'It was a beautiful day.' This is Major Mure, with the 29th Division at Helles:

I think it was the most intensely blue of all the vivid blue days I saw at Gallipoli. The air danced and shimmered as if full of infinitely small dust of blue diamonds. Butterflies swam through it; a thousand wild flowers perfumed it. Always there in the radiant days of the brief early summer our eyes saw great patches of bloom except where they beheld only desolation, aridity, death and blood. Achi Baba, ever the most prominent mark in view, loomed like a lump of awkwardness in the near distance, so shapeless that its very ugliness was picturesque. The sun went down in glory and in rainbows of fire as we worked, and the guns a little further inland – the never ceasing guns – belched out a venomous requiem and a reiterated threat.

And so – we buried the dead.

At Anzac, as Colonel Skeen wrote to his wife, 'There has been a succession of beautiful days ever since we landed – the sea like glass and the hillsides covered with flowers and trees . . . some of the flowers are really beautiful – a thing just like a white wild rose grows all over the hills and in a field in front of the trenches is a mixture of marguerites and poppies which we must imitate in our next garden.' So throughout May, and then the heat increased until by August it was unbearable. 'The sea was like glass – melted', Hamilton again, 'blue green with a dull red glow on it; the air seems to have been boiled.' The flowers and then the grass withered and vanished. In their place came dust, covering everything, horribly pungent; enormous flies, green and loathsome, and with them the Gallipoli gallop, a highly debilitating form of dysentery. Here is A.P. Herbert – the peninsula seemed to be thick with poets, or at least versifiers:

> This is the fourth of June.
> Think not I never dream
> The noise of that infernal noon
> The stretchers' endless stream
> The tales of triumphs won
> The night that found them lies
> The wounded wailing in the sun
> The dead, the dust, the flies.
>
> The flies, oh God, the flies
> That soiled the sacred dead
> To see them swarm from dead men's eyes
> And share the soldiers' bread!
> Nor think I now forget
> The filth and stench of war
> The corpses on the parapet
> The maggots in the floor.

A.P. Herbert was at Helles. At Anzac the whole Corps – 20,000 men or more – were crammed into an area that you could cover with the top-joint of your finger on a 1-inch map: a tangle of steep ravines, washaways and cliffs cascading down the west flank of the peninsula to the Aegean. Ashmead-Bartlett, war correspondent, wrote: 'The whole scene at Anzac beach reminded one irresistibly of a gigantic shipwreck. It looked as if the whole force and all the guns and ammunition had not been landed but had been washed ashore.' Orlo Williams, Clerk to the House of Commons turned Chief Cipher Officer, was reminded of 'the cave dwellings of a large and prosperous tribe of savages who live on the extremely steep slopes of broken sandy bluffs covered with scrub'. As to *why* they were there, more later. Robert Rhodes James, who has walked the course with care, writes: 'On the beach there were mounds of stores, men hanging about waiting for orders, casualties awaiting embarkation, pyramids of tinned meat and biscuits which also served as shelter from the shrapnel, trains of mules standing in rows being loaded with water cans or ammunition, fatigue parties laying telephone wires or setting off for the front line with supplies, while above, in the cliffs, hundreds of dugouts were perched crazily like some extraordinary rookery.' By night – this is a New Zealander, C.B. Brereton – 'the Anzac position looked for all the world like a great foundry, working strenuous overtime, sparks flying everywhere, and when shells were bursting great fiery showers flew in all directions like a heavy blow on red-hot metal. This was accompanied by a clanging and cracking that made the likeness complete.'

'So here the Anzacs live' – this is Henry Nevinson – 'practising the whole art of war. Amid dust and innumerable flies, from the mouths of little caves cut in the face of the cliffs they look out over miles of sea up to the precipitous peaks of Samothrace and the grey mountains of Imbros. Up and down the steep and narrow paths the Colonials arduously toil, like ants which bear the burdens of their race. . . . Every kind of store and arms has to be dragged or "jumped" up these ant-hills of cliffs and deposited at the proper hole or gallery. Food, water, cartridges, shells, building timber, guns, medical stores – up the tracks all must go, and down them the wounded come.

So the practice of the simple life proceeds, with greater simplicity than any garden suburb can boast, and the domestic virtues which constitute the whole art of war are exercised with a fortitude rarely maintained upon the domestic hearth.'

The domestic *virtues* which constitute the whole art of war?

It seems to me – but I am certainly no expert – that there had been translated into the Gallipoli peninsula *all* the domestic *horrors* of trench warfare in Flanders, modulated only by the quite exceptional Asiatic heat of the summer of 1915.

At Helles, though the ground is flatter, the congestion was almost as intense. The whole Corps area was never larger than a postcard – on a scale of 1 inch to a mile!

There is a small ravine on the western side where 10,000 Turks were killed in a week, and piles of skulls are to be found to this day. The Turks never buried their dead. If one attacked, one was lucky to get beyond the first Turkish trench. And then, as one young soldier wrote, 'the bottom of the trench was choked with dead bodies, friend and foe, and slippery with their life-blood. Corpses had been built into the parapet, the dead then affording protection to the living. Wherever one looked there was death in some ghastly form, arms and legs and decapitated bodies sprawling around in all manner of horribly grotesque postures. To me that scene was the personification of stark naked horror.'

After one attack Corporal Riley, whose letters are in the Imperial War Museum, wrote: 'Some of the 7th Manchester were lying, wounded, about 25 yards in front of their trench; and there they lay all day in the hot sun, not daring to move until night, when some of them might be able to crawl slowly and painfully back to our lines . . . It is impossible to describe how men in the trenches were living. Tall men slouched, thin, round-shouldered, bandaged over their septic sores, dirty, unshaven, unwashed. Men were living like swine, or worse than swine. About those crowded trenches there hung the smells of latrines and of the dead. Flies and lice tormented men who had hardly enough strength to scratch or fan the flies off for a few seconds. The August sun scorched us for there was no shade. No photograph could show the misery of those trenches, that Saturday afternoon.'

Back at Anzac, there is a vivid description of the Wellington Battalion, having attacked at dawn, holding off a series of counter-attacks. 'By early afternoon the forward trench was so choked with bodies that it had to be abandoned and another scratched immediately behind it. The Wellingtons seemed to rise up, each time, from nowhere and the Turks were hurled back.'

When darkness came, reinforcements were moved up. 'Sergeant Pilling led a platoon and was appalled by the ranks of dead and wounded, the cries for water. The shattered remnants of the attacking force were withdrawn. Their uniforms were torn and drenched with sweat and blood; they were caked in dust; they could hardly walk; most of them had had no sleep for more than 48 hours; none had had any water since dawn; they spoke in whispers and they trembled violently; some broke down and wept. Of the 760 New Zealanders who had advanced so confidently at first light only 70 were unwounded.'

Major Allanson, commanding 1/6 Gurkhas, after a brilliant action, needing medical attention, describes the journey back to Anzac Cove; 'The nullahs on the way back were horrible, full of dead and dying, Maoris, Australians, Sikhs, Gurkhas and British Soldiers, blood and bloody clothes, the smell of the dead now some two days old . . . I left that battlefield a changed man; all my ambitions to be a successful soldier have now gone; knowing all I now know, I feel the responsibility, *the murderous responsibility*, that rests on the shoulders of an inefficient soldier, or one who has passed his prime to command.'

And this brings me towards the centre of what I want to say. That the Gallipoli campaign was *murderous* is clear beyond all doubt. Total Allied casualties were probably about 250,000, of whom nearly 50,000 died. Turkish casualties were probably higher – bringing the total of killed and wounded on both sides to over half a million. The Allies never achieved even their *initial* D-Day objectives, though they held on for 8½ months and were never thrown back into the sea. It was a desperately close-fought campaign which ended – you could say – in a tactical draw. You could also say, though it is a backhanded way of looking at things, that if the divisions at Gallipoli had not been fighting there they would have been getting killed or wounded somewhere else – the Baltic, Salonika, Syria, Egypt – or more likely Flanders. You could say that the stakes were high enough to justify the attempt; that instead of the short route to Constantinople via Gallipoli, the Allies were forced to take the long and weary road via Mesopotamia and Palestine. You can speculate upon the effects in Russia if the campaign had succeeded. The Prussian Pasha Kannengiesser (= tubthumper!), writing ten years later, said: 'The year 1915 had already proved a disastrous year for Russia and now came this shattering blow to their morale. They were finally cut from their Allies. *Without Gallipoli they would probably have had no revolution.*' As Churchill said: 'the terrible "ifs" accumulate'. But look at it how you will, for the Allies it was *strategically* a major disaster.

The value of a lecture of this kind is, at least in part, to keep green the memory of those (on both sides) who suffered, so that their heroism, their humour and their endurance shall not yet be forgotten. It is in that spirit that I have been trying to evoke some aspects of the human condition.

But to leave it at that would be a terrible cop-out. Because more than any other campaign of which I've read Gallipoli seems to scream with the question 'Why?' Nor is there any shortage of suggested answers. The bibliography is enormous, and ever-increasing. Churchill, Fisher, Lloyd George, Asquith, Hamilton, Keyes, Guépratte, Wemyss, von Sanders and umpteen others have written personal accounts: there are huge collections of papers available, not least Kitchener's, Birdwood's and Hamilton's. (Only Hunter-Weston seems not to have contributed; I doubt if writing was his strong suit.) There are the *Dardanelles Commission Report* and the *Official History*. There are regimental histories galore. What can one add to all this?

It seems to me quite clear, however, that the key to nearly everything that went wrong was *cybernetic* – by which I understand myself to mean a failure of the *steering gear*. This seems to me the common thread that runs from top to bottom and is worth illustrating at the various levels: at the level of planning and higher direction; at the level of organisation; at the level of execution. Allow me a little time in each area.

The *strategic* ingredients of the decision to go for Gallipoli included: pressure from the Russians, British naval reverses, and disenchantment with the Western Front. The Russians were asking for help as early as the end of 1914. Their autumn campaign in Prussia had disastrously failed with over a million casualties. A Turkish Army had advanced into the Caucasus in December and came close to scoring a huge success – failing only when 30,000 of them literally froze to death. The Grand Duke Nicholas appealed to the British government for a *demonstration* against the Turks to draw part of their army away from Russia. Secondly, there was disenchantment with the prospect of a war of attrition in France – which was the best that the French and Joffre seemed able to offer. An attack upon Turkey would have the appeal of neutralising one of Germany's most important allies, opening a sea-route for support of the Russians, and drawing the neutral Balkan countries, Greece, Roumania, Bulgaria, into the Entente. Meanwhile the Royal Navy was also having a bad war: three cruisers lost to submarines off Holland, *von Spee* dominating the South Atlantic and *Emden* the Indian Ocean, the dreadnought *Audacious* sunk and the Royal Naval Division failing to avert the loss of Antwerp. A success was badly needed *somewhere*. All this led, by the turn of the year, to pressure, mainly by Churchill, for an attempt to 'force the Dardanelles'.

For at least a month, until mid-February 1915, the Dardanelles operation was seen as purely naval, with at the most two Marine battalions to demolish the fortress artillery. Fisher, throughout this period, regarded the operation as unjustifiable, but could not carry against Churchill's enthusiasm. Then, bit by bit, through February, Kitchener found himself agreeing to the commitment of troops *somewhere* in the Eastern Mediterranean; 29 Division, the Australian and New Zealand Army Corps, the Royal Naval Division, and then a French Division chipped in. Rear Admiral Wemyss was sent off to Lemnos – 'without instructions, staff or means, to establish a base 3,000 miles from Britain; 700 from Malta, 575 from Alexandria, whose only asset was the huge but exposed natural harbour of Mudros. There was only one tiny pier, no depot ship or supplies, no accommodation on shore and wholly insufficient water resources.' No one, at this stage, even knew what the expeditionary force was *for*. Then, on 19 February, came the first naval bombardment of the Dardanelles forts. Militarily it was quite ineffective, but diplomatically a *succès fou*. The Bulgarians broke off negotiations with the central powers; the Greeks offered three divisions; the Russians spoke of attacking Constantinople from the east; the Italians made friendly noises; and in Constantinople itself there were signs of panic. After this there could be no going back. Kitchener telegraphed to Egypt firmly allocating the Australian and New Zealand Corps 'to occupy any captured forts' and 'to give cooperation'. But as he then clearly explained: 'It would not be a sound military undertaking to attempt landing in force on the Gallipoli peninsula *until* the naval operations for the reduction of forts have been successful and the passage has been forced.'

So the next phase consisted of the attempt, by purely naval means, to do just that. A fresh bombardment of the outer forts on 25 February met with some success, but once the warships entered the straits difficulties increased. Mobile howitzer batteries opened up and could not be spotted. Some of the ships and crews were less than first class. 'Some were green,' Admiral Brodie wrote, 'mostly with age.' Seaplanes from *Ark Royal* were unreliable. A series of Marine landings at the entrance forts did well at first, but as they were repeated over a ten-day period resistance grew. Bombardment of the coast artillery seemed to be having little effect. Above all, the minesweepers – small trawlers with civilian crews from the north-east ports of England, which could barely make three knots against the Dardanelles current – repeatedly failed to sweep any mines. The combination of searchlights, howitzer shells, and the mines themselves was simply too much for them and from 1 to 13 March, despite almost nightly attempts, they achieved nothing.

Over the same period an attempt by Admiral Hall (Director of Naval Intelligence) to buy the Dardanelles for £4 million also foundered – mainly because the British side could not guarantee to leave Constantinople in Turkish hands! And so, on 18 March, there followed the grand naval assault upon the narrows: eighteen battleships, with an armada of cruisers and destroyers, 'it looked as though no human power could withstand such an array of might and power'. It was the nearest equivalent, in all history, to a naval cavalry charge, and it was a decisive failure. The Turks fired off most of their ammunition, but their guns remained largely intact. The battleships blundered into an uncharted row of mines, laid only a few nights earlier. The minesweepers, as usual, wavered and fled. Three battleships were sunk and three more crippled. The force withdrew. Although there was much talk of reorganising and trying again, in fact nothing of the kind ever happened.

What *did* happen was a complete change in the complexion of the plans. When Hamilton was first appointed, and then briefed, by Kitchener on 13 March, the military operation was still to be undertaken 'only in the event of the Fleet failing to get through after every effort has been exhausted'. Kitchener hoped to get through without it.

On 22 March, *after* the naval failure, when Hamilton and de Robeck, the new naval Commander-in-Chief, first got together, the latter said at once that he could not get through without the help of the troops. The crucial decision was then taken to proceed on the basis of a joint operation. London was told and had to make the best of it. It was decided also to send the Army back to Alexandria to reorganise, thus making a postponement till after mid-April inevitable. The extra warning time thus given to the Turks for digging, wiring, laying minefields, camouflage and above all training were – in von Sanders' words – indispensable. Hamilton assumed, and indeed de Robeck promised, that in the meanwhile a vigorous offensive on the forts, reconnaissance, and sustained and determined sweeping operations would continue. In the event the fleet effectively disappeared. Hamilton assumed that the operations eventually to be undertaken by the Army would be in conjunction with another major naval assault on the Dardanelles. In fact de Robeck had decided that the Navy would never again attack the forts until the Army had occupied the Gallipoli peninsula. Nor did they.

Why – and this is the crucial question – did things drift in this way until an operation emerged for which there had been no planning, no training, no intelligence, totally inadequate logistical preparation, and on the major outline of which the naval and land forces commanders-in-chief continued to have totally incompatible conceptions? Partly, I suppose, because nothing of this kind had ever been attempted before. Partly, I suspect, it was due to the inadequacy of the Whitehall planning machinery. The War Council did not meet regularly, nor forward its conclusions to the Cabinet. It kept its proceedings in manuscript, received few departmental memoranda, did not work to an agenda, and met only when the Prime Minister summoned it. So ministers tended to move off in differing directions. As Sir William Robertson put it: 'The Secretary of State for War was aiming for decisive results on the Western Front; the First Lord of the Admiralty was advocating a military expedition to the Dardanelles; the Secretary of State for India was devoting his attention to a campaign in Mesopotamia; the Secretary of State for the Colonies was occupying himself with several small wars in Africa; and the Chancellor of the Exchequer was attempting to secure the removal of a large part of the British Army from France to some Eastern Mediterranean theatre.'

As was well known, the First Sea Lord (Fisher) saw eye to eye with his boss on almost nothing, particularly on the Dardanelles, while the CIGS (James Wolfe Murray) saw himself simply as Kitchener's Chief of Staff to give advice and information when asked. Kitchener, quite out of touch with the new General Staff created by the Haldane reforms, never asked him! Only Hankey seems to have had any premonition of disaster. As early as 19 March he was attributing the naval fiasco to 'inadequate staff preparation' and advocating a technical naval and military committee – the first germ of the Chiefs of Staff. Not long afterwards he put his finger on the fundamental flaw in the whole Gallipoli concept. 'Up to the present time,' he wrote, 'no attempt has been made to estimate what force is required to make sure of success. We have merely said that so many troops are available and they ought to be enough.' When he told Churchill that the landings would be 'of extraordinary difficulty', Churchill said that he could see no difficulty at all. On 12 April Hankey sent to Asquith a memorandum that concluded: 'The military operation appears, therefore, to be to a certain extent a *gamble* upon the supposed shortage of supplies and inferior fighting qualities of the Turkish Armies.' He was right.

The War Office estimate of casualties for the landing and capture of the whole peninsula was only about 5,000. 'At the outset' – this is the finding of the Dardanelles Commission – 'all decisions were taken and provisions based on the *assumption* that, if a landing were effected, the advance would be rapid and the resistance slight.' But there was little hard evidence in support of this assumption and no lack of warnings: the fighting in the Caucasus, on the Canal, at Basra and at the Dardanelles forts. But these were disregarded, and in their absence plans and assumptions were allowed to feed on each other, and to spread outwards and downwards via GHQ to the whole force. 'I only hope I may be able to nip over and have a look at Troy,' wrote Patrick Shaw Stewart. 'I don't think this is going to be at all a dangerous campaign – we shall only have to sit in the Turkish Forts *after* the Fleet has shelled the unfortunate occupants out of them.'

So in Whitehall there was neither grip nor vision but considerable disarray lit by one, brilliant, strategic idea.

And much of the same was true at the level of the Force Headquarters. There was never one man in overall command: it was Hamilton and de Robeck jointly. There was never a joint headquarters. During the preparation Hamilton was at Alexandria, in *Arcadian* or at Lemnos. Later he set up his headquarters on Imbros. De Robeck was at sea. During the actual landings Hamilton joined him in *Queen Elizabeth*, but this meant his staff being incarcerated in gun turrets and other clanging recesses where they were quite useless. And, which was perhaps much worse, proper use was never made of the administrative staff. Hamilton was obsessed with the virtue of a small headquarters and had an antipathy for administration. The AQ staff were appointed late; then left in Alexandria; then kept on a separate ship at Mudros and left in no doubt that they were regarded as a tedious encumbrance. Not till Hamilton was superseded were the general and administrative staffs brought together; and it may be that the efficiency and success of the final evacuations owed much to just that fact. Communications were always difficult, and it is tempting at times to ascribe almost the whole cause of the fiasco to the absence of any efficient form of combat net radio. But that was nothing new, and applied to both sides equally – so as an explanation it is not particularly helpful!

Let me tell a few more stories on the theme of cybernetic failure: the first quite literally. The Anzacs were to land, in forty-eight rowing boats, towed in by pinnaces and then cast off 50 yards out, spread out over a mile of beach giving easy access to the hinterland. They actually landed, completely intermingled, on a tiny stretch of coast only a few hundred yards wide, about a mile too far north, giving directly on to a steep rise, or almost sheer cliffs. This upset every plan. Not only was the movement inland far slower than it ought to have been, but units became (and remained) inextricably mixed up, and Anzac Cove became instantly, and long remained, an administrative shambles, thus slowing down the build-up perhaps fatally. The bridgehead remained, for the full eight months that it was occupied, the literal cliffhanger that I earlier described, which it need never have been.

And yet, the sea that night was a dead flat calm; the battleship *Triumph* was anchored – as far as is known correctly – to mark the rendezvous and assess the current; and three more battleships, *London, Prince of Wales* and *Queen*, were to lead the 'tows' to within a mile of their landing places. What can have gone wrong? The official account is that an unexpected northerly current pushed the tows off course and that Lieutenant Commander Waterlow, leading the right wing, then misidentified a headland in the dark and steered still further to the north. But Commander Dix, on the other flank, says that seeing the right wing coming across (as *he* knew wrongly) he steered under their stern, thus closing the whole array like a concertina. Why, if Dix knew where they were, did Waterlow not? There is also evidence that the battleships themselves were too far north. The *legend* is that Turkish soldiers, seeing a marker buoy the day before, swam out and moved it, but this is quite incredible. One theory is that Rear Admiral Thursby, in *Queen*, made a last-minute change of plan, but could not signal to *London*, so Dix did not know. This would explain almost everything. There *had* been a change of landing site, though in the opposite, southerly direction, not long before. Thursby did report that the southern tow had landed within a hundred yards of its assigned position. But why, if there was a further change of plan on Thursby's part, did this never come out in the subsequent investigations? We shall never know the truth. What is certain is that a navigation error took place, on a coastline that had been closely reconnoitred, not short of distinctive landmarks, clearly visible from 1,000 yards out, on an almost perfect night, where there was no enemy opposition whatsoever. One cannot say that if the Anzacs had been correctly landed by the Navy their mission would have succeeded. One can say that from that moment their chances of *initial* success were greatly lessened, and that from this mishap the whole expedition never really recovered.

An even odder episode, though probably with less far-reaching consequences, was the operation at Y Beach, a landing detached from the rest of those at Helles, about 5,000 yards up the west coast. It had been decided upon late on in the planning, by Hamilton himself, to make use of a small beach, and a pathway up the cliff, where there were known to be no Turks. The troops concerned were the KOSB, a company of South Wales Borderers and the Plymouth Battalion of Marines – some 2,000 all told. Lieutenant Colonel Koe of the KOSB thought he was in command, but at a conference four days earlier it was discovered that Lieutenant Colonel Matthews of the Marines was senior. He had been put in command, but Koe was away sick at the time and no one remembered to tell him. He had no orders at all; Matthews was told only to advance 'some little distance inland', capture a gun and attract reserves. Later he was to contact the main body and join it for the march north.

The landing was entirely uneventful. Fighting patrols found only four startled Turks. Two companies of the KOSB went inland as far as the deep ravine – barely marked on their maps – where the 10,000 Turks were to die in a week, two months later, and the piles of skulls are still to be seen. On that day it was quite deserted. Koe, still thinking he was in command, appealed to Divisional HQ for information and advice but got no reply. Matthews, with his adjutant, walked across to the village of Krithia – also deserted. He was the last British soldier ever to get there! It was a beautiful day, but the officers began to feel uncomfortable. They all went back to the 'camp' which was sprawled along the cliff top. At 3 o'clock in the afternoon they decided to dig in but it was too late. Before 6 p.m. the Turkish counterattack had started and by nightfall they were in a state of siege. In fact the Turks were always outnumbered, but they pressed their attacks through the night: by dawn Koe was dead, there had been heavy casualties, and many of the men had shot all their ammunition away. Matthews, whose conduct was impeccable, beat off a final attack at the cliff top and the Turks then withdrew out of sight of the warships' guns. Matthews, once it was apparent that the Turks had gone, inspected his position, and to his amazement found much of the force had *gone*, abandoning its equipment. What seems to have happened is that some men had drifted down to the beach. A young officer asked for help and the Navy promptly re-embarked him. Other officers, seeing this, and thinking that an order had been given, followed suit. By 7 a.m. several hundred men were either back on the warships or waiting on the beach while puzzled and then frantic messages passed to and fro. Matthews by now had had no message of any kind from Divisional Headquarters for 29 hours and seeing the evacuation proceeding rapidly also assumed that they had ordered it.

At this point Hamilton himself, having failed to persuade Hunter-Weston to take any interest in Y Beach, ordered some reinforcements to go there, off his own bat, and proceeded to go there himself in *Queen Elizabeth*, arriving at 9.30 a.m. What he saw amazed him. 'I disliked and mistrusted the look of those aimless dawdlers by the sea. There was no fighting; a rifle shot now and again from the crests where we saw our fellows clearly. The little crowd and the boats on the beach were right under them and no one paid any attention or seemed to be in a hurry. Our naval and military signallers were at sixes and sevens. The *Goliath* wouldn't answer; the *Dublin* said the force was coming off and we could not get into touch with the soldiers at all.' Hamilton, by now, had made the same assumption, that the evacuation had been ordered. The whole contingent re-embarked. That afternoon Adrian Keyes was sent ashore to make certain there was no one left behind. The battlefield was utterly deserted!

I will tell one more story of cybernetic breakdown. The time was early August when, in synchrony with new landings at Suvla Bay, there was also to be a wide flanking attack out of Anzac, moving first north close to the coast and then east up a steep valley, the Aghyl Dere, then south-west to the summit of the central spine of the peninsula. The left-hand column, to be led by guides, was composed mainly of Indian and Australian troops, the latter under a Brigadier Monash. He was an Australian Jew, an engineer by profession, deeply interested in the art of war, a brilliant officer who did better the higher he went; he was later to become a Corps Commander and be described by Lloyd George as the 'most resourceful general in the British Army'.

But on the night of 6/7 August 1915 resourceful he was not. Things started badly, but not *that* badly. Assembling the units in the ravines at Anzac took far longer than expected. It was pitch dark. A few men panicked and ran back, causing confusion. The guides took a dud short cut where there were snipers. By 2 a.m., instead of approaching the ridge, the soldiers were only just reaching the Aghyl Dere. The moon rose. Casualties were seen 'throwing themselves about'. The General (Cox) arrived slightly wounded, having lost his column and his headquarters! The brigades pushed on; there were more snipers; at daybreak they were exhausted, still entangled in the foothills, and had not started to move towards the objectives they should have reached four hours earlier. The leader of the guides was killed at dawn. Allanson, commanding 3/6 Gurkhas, who had made much the best progress, was then put by Cox under Monash's command and went to report to him. This is what he found:

A lot of shooting seemed to be going on, and there were some wounded lying about, but what I mostly saw were men hopelessly exhausted, lying around everywhere, all movement and attempt to advance seemed to have ceased. This is not surprising to me now . . . it had been a most exhausting night march and the sun was terribly powerful. But what upset me most was that Monash himself seemed to have temporarily lost his head, he was running about saying 'I thought I could command men,

I thought I could command men', those were his exact words. I went up and told him that my battalion had been placed in reserve at his disposal but he said to me 'What a hopeless mess has been made of this, you are no use to me at all.' I said nothing more but got back to my battalion as soon as I could . . . I thought that the best thing I could do was to start up the hill on my own . . . I was anxious to get away from Monash as quickly as I could as I felt thoroughly upset by what I had seen.

In the fighting that followed, Allanson's Gurkhas did brilliantly and in the end got up and over the ridge, though being on their own the position could not be sustained. Allanson was put up for a VC and got a DSO. Monash's Australians, by contrast, having made an attempt upon the ridge from the north, were shot to bits by well-concealed machine-guns and, for the first time in the campaign, broke and ran. It is hard not to blame him. He was an excellent officer, but in the wrong job and at the wrong time. It must have been at least partly with him in mind that Allanson wrote of 'murderous responsibility'.

In speaking of *cybernetic* failure, has one said anything at all, apart from importing a word from the new jargon? I think so. Whitehall, as it seems to me, was in the grip of a brilliant strategic idea that was simply too big for it to handle. The techniques of command and control in joint operations took decades more to develop. What happened more recently in the Falklands leads one to suspect that neither in Whitehall coordination nor at Task Force level are we yet anywhere near perfection. Within the Force itself, perhaps the main problem was that the whole machine had been too rapidly expanded. George Lloyd, an MP serving in Gallipoli, wrote to his wife at the end of July from GHQ on Imbros: 'the one thing that hits one in the face the whole time is the very small number of men who are efficient. What is the cause of it? Is it our system of education, is it something in the character we are breeding? It is the one thing – *the one thing* – that has struck me over and over again.'

I wish I had found that quotation before I finished a recent report on the Army's 'system of education'. Actually I think that the British Army today is highly efficient, and that an excellent system of education has much to do with it – of which the 'character that we are breeding' is a most important ingredient.

Let me finish with one more anecdote that is in one sense a parable. At Helles, in late June, to assist identification, the men had small metal triangles sewn on their backs. As the bombardment lifted the ground was suddenly filled with thousands of sparkles of glittering metallic light, as though, in Hamilton's words, 'someone had quite suddenly thrown a big handful of diamonds on to the landscape'. In the attack of 6 August Corps

Headquarters told HQ 29th Division that the Turkish front line was definitely captured, as their observation officers could see the metal discs on the soldiers' backs in the enemy trenches. Their wearers, however, were all dead.

Patrick Shaw Stewart, who was killed later on the Western Front, wrote:

> Was it hard Achilles
> So very hard to die?
> Thou knowest and I know not –
> So much happier I.
>
> I will go back this morning
> From Imbros over the sea;
> Stand in the trench Achilles,
> Flame-capped, and shout for me.

TWO

DEFENCE: FACE THE FACTS

Edward Heath

24 April 1986

The horrors and confusions of the Gallipoli campaign are known to us all. To those who were not there, the account of events has come from the history books. To those who were, the memories of those weeks will ever be fresh and vivid, printed on their minds as they affected them each in different ways.

No textbook can do justice to the individual acts of courage that some of you will recall, nor to the personal tragedies that will never be reported. I have no wish to intrude on private memories or reopen old wounds.

Many have since tried, with the benefit of hindsight, to apportion responsibility for what occurred and to construct what should have happened. This is not my task. The lesson I wish to draw from Gallipoli is not from the mistakes of the campaign itself, but from the international crisis which led to the outbreak of the First World War and, indirectly, to the Allied attempt to take the Dardanelles.

The background to the First World War was one of escalating crisis between the great powers of the day, provoked by German expansionism. The growth in Russian strength at the expense of the declining Austro-Hungarian Empire, and of Germany's determination to expand her power in the face of the Triple Alliance, created an explosive situation which the final clash of interests in the Balkans ignited.

The potential for a similar conflict today is much reduced, largely as a result of the determined integration of Europe which was the reaction to the two world wars. The formation of the Atlantic Alliance and later the European Community, which together created political stability and economic growth in the West, set the international scene for a prolonged period of detente with the Soviet Union and her allies. This has kept the world at peace since 1945.

But the 1980s have again seen a crisis in many aspects of our international relations. The Soviet Union, like Germany before the First World War, has reached the point where she perceives the balance of economic and military power to be tipping steadily and perhaps inevitably in favour of her opponents. All the signs are that the feeling is growing in the Soviet Union that the crunch is coming: that Russia must hold her own now or slip forever into political and military decline.

That is why the Soviets are so keen to get an arms agreement, but one that does not leave them at a disadvantage with the west: that is why the Soviet leadership is making renewed efforts to increase division within the Atlantic Alliance and establish stronger links with individual European nations; and that is why the Soviet Union is so alarmed at the prospect of Star Wars.

These attitudes on the part of the Soviets and the reactions of the West raise international tensions and increase the chances of the technological arms spiral reaching the point where something goes wrong.

They also increase the likelihood that a localised conflict of interests – as in the Balkans all those years ago– will develop into an international clash between the superpowers. Communications technology, for example, has obviously been transformed from what it was seventy-one years ago, but recent events have shown that sophisticated technology does not necessarily mean successful communication in times of crisis.

Today the problem is not restricted to continental Europe. Rapid technological development has led to the potential globalisation of conflict. The growth of Soviet ability to project power all round the world, and the similar American flexibility to switch its defence capability wherever it is needed, have significantly added to the potential regional theatres of war. The Middle East is the most obvious such theatre, as the United States' plans for a rapid deployment force suggest. The Pacific Basin and Central America are clearly others.

And as Soviet strength has grown, so has American concern about Soviet interventionism and with it a belief that the Soviet Union has sought to develop the ability to disarm the United States with a swift first strike. This seems to have led the Reagan administration to a determined bid for military superiority and to a lessening on both sides of a serious desire for successful talks on arms reduction.

Differences between the United States and her European allies have become more marked and are more openly disputed. In Europe, millions of people have taken to the streets to protest against the deployment of American missiles which had been requested by their own governments. In the United States, there is an increasingly impatient feeling that Europe should shut up or put up more for its own defence.

This volatile international situation must not be allowed to continue.

We in Europe must face up to the present dilemma and play our part in resolving it.

First, we must recognise the need for a strong, self-reliant European role within the Atlantic Alliance and take direct steps to integrate European defence policy and practice. Second, we must recognise the connection between the enormous economic costs of the arms race and the dangerous instability that it produces, and seek substantial quantitative and qualitative verifiable reductions in nuclear weapons. Third, we must seek a return to a new détente that will allow the peaceful resolution of regional differences throughout the globe, based on a practical understanding of the legitimate strategic interests of the superpowers.

The disproportionate responsibilities in the present alliance are largely the result of Europe's dependence on the United States in the years following the Second World War. The United States chooses weapons, decides deployment, conducts arms control negotiations, and dominates East–West diplomacy and relations with the Third World.

It also bears the burden of providing most of the West's nuclear strategic defence, and plays the leading role in defending western interests outside Europe. The United States spends 6.9 per cent of its Gross National Product (GNP) on defence, while only Britain among her allies spends more than 5 per cent of GNP. The United States has been increasing its defence spending by about 7 per cent per annum but even in Britain real growth in defence spending is now under 3 per cent.

The United States is therefore understandably concerned about this imbalance, and not only for financial reasons. Their concern goes to the heart of the US/European strategic relationship. For when the US nuclear guarantee was first extended to Europe to compensate it for its conventional inferiority, the Soviet nuclear arsenal involved no danger to the United States itself. But the advent of the intercontinental ballistic missile changed the position completely.

The failure of a credible conventional defence of Europe against a Soviet invasion would now confront the United States with a choice between the defence of its troops and using nuclear weapons: and the ultimate price of a nuclear escalation is tens of millions of civilian casualties on the American mainland.

It has therefore been a consistent aim of American defence policy since the early 1960s to persuade Europe to invest enough in conventional defence to sustain the doctrine of flexible response. That requires sufficient conventional force to hold any attack for long enough to negotiate its de-escalation if it is accidental, or in the event of an intentional attack on Europe, long enough for the West to signal its determination to go nuclear and give the aggressor a chance to back down.

It must now become an aim of European defence policy to establish a European identity and responsibility for the defence of Europe which will enable her to speak to the United States on equal terms, contribute more to the formulation of defence policy, and at the same time inspire greater legitimacy among the European public for defence arrangements.

There is no reason why the 320 million people of Europe, with tremendous industrial resources and long military experience, should be unable to organise an effective military coalition to defend themselves against 280 million Russians, who are contending at the same time with over 1,000 million Chinese on their eastern flank.

Practically speaking, there should be no constraints through lack of resources on the development of a fuller European defence policy. In 1982, American Defence Secretary Weinberger estimated the combined GNPs of the European members of NATO at $2.7 trillion against $2.3 trillion for the whole Warsaw Pact. What holds us back is our political fragmentation and military vulnerability.

The elimination of duplication in research, development and deployment would add up to an estimated 30 per cent to procurement budgets. Conformity of armaments and interchangeability of stockpiles would improve operational effectiveness. There are, for example, five different types of tank. This alone would create problems with supply in times of war and so delay the effectiveness of a conventional response. If Europe can achieve a coordinated approach to procurement, she can strengthen her defence without necessarily increasing overall government expenditure or diverting resources from public welfare.

But such an approach for defence procurement will only work if we can realise closer coordination at the political level in the formulation of our defence and foreign policy. We must reconcile our different views and reduce the multiplicity of mechanisms of consultation within Europe if we are to talk to the United States, and face our opponents, with one voice.

Lord Carrington, the then Secretary-General of NATO, observed that the political integration of Europe would be a major contribution to its cohesion. The alternative is a disunited Europe speaking in a babble of discordant voices to Washington and Moscow, with frustration and suspicion the result. It is surely right that the best way to serve the Atlantic Alliance in the 1980s is to be European.

The second major area in which we must move is arms control. The cost of defence, including the nuclear build-up, to both sides is overwhelming. The Soviet Union spends 14–16 per cent of its GNP on defence. It has to do so to keep pace with the United States, which, with a GNP more than twice that of the Soviet Union, spends nearly 7 per cent. So long as the nuclear powers continue the competitive race to achieve a decisive margin of superiority, whether by numbers of weapons or in the development of a decisive technology, this level of spending can only increase.

When societies divert their economic resources into needless military competition to the detriment of other pressing demands on their expenditure, the social balance of those societies is at risk. In addition, public disquiet increases as social services are perceived to suffer while money pours into apparently fruitless defence projects. This causes political instability which worsens the atmosphere in which international relations are conducted.

So for both moral and political reasons it is time for a serious effort to halt and, if possible, reduce current levels of defence expenditure.

Competitiveness has reached the point where it has gained a destabilising momentum of its own. Arms control negotiations have failed to achieve the purposes of cooperation: stable nuclear armouries and an end to their growth.

When the SALT process started in 1972, the intention was clear. It was to establish constraints on the quantity of nuclear arms by limiting the number of missile launchers. However, it was always recognised that there would have to be several further treaties to limit the quantitative growth of nuclear weaponry by other means. It was also intended to stabilise nuclear armouries by eliminating those capabilities which could be used in a first strike and by encouraging a switch to those weapons which would survive a hostile action and could logically only be used to respond to, and not to initiate, an attack.

Since 1972, the only progress that has been made is the unratified 1979 SALT 2. The consequences of this failure are deeply disturbing. The SALT 1 constraints have been circumvented by the growth of warheads and payloads. The USA now has 10,174 warheads each with an average missile payload of 2 million kg. The USSR has 10,223 warheads but with an average missile payload of 6 million kg.

More alarming still, new developments threaten both sides with what is commonly acknowledged to be the worst possible configuration of nuclear deterrents: one in which each believes the other to have, or to be developing, a first strike capacity.

Nuclear armouries became dangerously unstable with the addition of multiple warheads to missiles in the mid-1970s. This had a multiplier effect, since its warheads themselves were targets. There were now much greater advantages in a first strike to destroy the multiple warheads before they could be launched.

This danger would only be reduced if both sides knew *either* that there was a high probability that a surprise attack was impossible because the defender would be able to launch his reply before being struck *or* that sufficient of the enemy's capabilities would survive the surprise. But it is here that new developments in weapons technology threaten us with further destabilisation.

Quick release weapons launched either from adjacent land or from submarines just off the coast can smash the military infrastructure, and especially the command and communications facilities of an opponent, within 3–6 minutes of being launched. This would prepare the way for a surprise attack on the principal missile fields, which would very probably fail to receive intelligence of the incoming attack or any instructions concerning it.

Such a result would be made even more probable by the development and deployment of space weapons, thus undermining the agreement that, in the interests of stability, space should remain a safe reserve for satellite intelligence-gathering, so removing any opportunities for surprise attack. The important point here is that instability arises from the fears of both adversaries about the possibility of first strikes, and that these fears are given substance by the increasing technological sophistication of weaponry and the failure of arms control to contain it.

A return to successful arms control therefore requires a political and philosophical rethink of our objectives and the methods we use to achieve them. We can then turn to practicalities.

A significant problem in our present thinking is the attention given to numerical differences over general stability. Logically it matters little if one side has fewer weapons than the other, so long as it is known to have enough to prevent an aggressor defeating it in a first strike. Even the proposed 50 per cent reductions of 5,000 warheads would give both superpowers the ability to destroy the world many times over. Politically and psychologically, however, the overall numbers are of immense significance.

The search for numerical balance in each subcategory of nuclear firepower needlessly complicates negotiations. Each side feels that its geopolitical position, or the technical features of its armoury, demands special advantages in particular dimensions of nuclear power, and that as a result absolute symmetry is simply not negotiable. In any case, the two sides are far from agreeing what represents a genuine balance. SALT 1 recognised all this, and sought a broad, asymmetrical balance known as equivalent security. This involves eliminating those weapons which give a major incentive to strike before being struck.

In the present competitive atmosphere, however, technology has tended to lead to deployment, thus making qualitative control impossible. Anything technically feasible is quickly developed into a new capability, however destabilising, for fear that unilateral restraint will only allow the other side to go ahead and develop that capability for itself.

The new capability is then unashamedly deployed in order to increase the bargaining position of its owner. As both sides are always at different points in the development cycle, the superpower with new projects about to reach fruition has had an interest in slowing down negotiations. And so the posturing goes on.

It is time for the theatrical summitry of the last few years to make way for the continuous quiet management of international stability by the relevant governments. In this way, understandings can be reached to make significant reductions in multiple warheads, missile payloads, and all quick release weapons with the capacity for the destruction of command and communication facilities. To make such reductions effective, we must also seek the termination of further innovations in technology.

This brings us to Star Wars. The danger of the Strategic Defence Initiative (SDI) is that it pushes the armaments competition to new heights of technological sophistication which the Soviets at present cannot match. The Soviets do not believe that Star Wars will provide the complete defence that is being promised to the US public. No system, human or mechanical, can ever be 100 per cent foolproof. But they are concerned that it would give the United States an adequate defence against the Soviet reply to a missile-launched first strike. This would enable the United States to attack the USSR with comparative invulnerability. We may believe that the USA will never use this capacity for a first strike against the Soviet Union, but the latter do not see it that way.

Inevitably, if the Soviets fail to get an arms deal, they will attempt to counter SDI with many more intercontinental ballistic missiles, new types of decoy, jamming and interference mechanisms, false image projections, and missiles which spin in the boost phase. Space mines and other anti-satellite weapons could be developed, putting satellites crucial to surveillance and arms control at risk. And of course Star Wars would be no defence against tactical nuclear missiles which could easily slip under the 'defence shield'.

A Pentagon report has estimated the total cost of SDI at \$250–\$500 billion. These funds are much needed to strengthen ailing conventional defences. Star Wars will not free the world from nuclear weapons. It would be disastrous if an attainable arms reduction agreement was thrown over for a probably unworkable, dangerous and vastly expensive system which would further destabilise the superpower relationship and increase the insecurity of the Atlantic Alliance.

I hope that the force of these arguments will be recognised by the leaders of the nuclear powers and that we will soon see a return to a more practical and realistic understanding between East and West. I hope that we will achieve a lasting agreement on arms control and return to a period of stable détente.

Only against such a background of stability in international relations can effective, practical steps be taken to defuse tensions in areas of conflict outside Europe, such as the Middle East. A failure to understand each side's legitimate strategic interests has characterised the superpowers' policies towards this vital area. With so many potential trouble spots in the world, we must have a more responsible attitude among the great powers.

All this may seem a long way from Gallipoli. The world has changed much since then. Countries have come and gone, new alliances have been forged, and the weapons of war have become ever more destructive. But although the map and the means of war have changed, the ambitions and attitudes in the minds of presidents and generals may not be so very different. In the dealings among nations, history all too often repeats itself. I have tried to show how the collapse of international stability and the breakdown in managed relations between the imperial powers before the First World War have a vital lesson for us today.

If we heed this lesson, we will serve well the memory of those who died in the landings at Gallipoli.

Postscript

Since I delivered the Gallipoli Lecture in 1986, the world has undergone a period of dramatic change. In 1986 the Berlin Wall remained erect as a symbol of the ideological divide between East and West and Mikhail Gorbachev's policies of *perestroika* and *glasnost* were still in their infancy. The underlying weakness of the economy in the USSR always posed a danger to its political institutions, but the pace of change in the former Soviet Union came as a great surprise to me, and to most people.

Despite the historic changes to our continent since 1986, I still believe that the best way to serve the Atlantic Alliance is to be European. We now live in a world of five superpowers – the USA, China, Japan, Russia and the European Union – and for the foreseeable future the associations and the rivalries that are going to matter are those between these five political and industrial power blocks. As we approach the next century it is only by being in Europe – and by taking a lead in Europe, instead of trailing along behind – that we can remain a serious presence on the world stage, where, with our proud heritage, we undoubtedly belong.

But I hope my 1986 lecture retains some historical interest and I am delighted to send my support once again to the Gallipoli Memorial Lecture Trust.

THREE

ENDS AND MEANS

Prince Philip
Duke of Edinburgh

7 May 1987

I have to confess that when I accepted the invitation to give this address, I had little detailed knowledge of the campaign. I knew the whereabouts of the Dardanelles, in fact The Queen and I were shown over the battlefield during a state visit to Turkey. I knew that it was fought with the greatest gallantry on both sides and that the heroism of the Australians and the New Zealanders had become a legend among their countrymen. I knew that it ended with a miraculous evacuation, and that it took place in 1915. But that was patently not sufficient, so there was nothing for it but to read it up.

I started my research with *Gallipoli*, by Captain Eric Bush RN, for the simple reason that he had sent me a copy when it was published in 1975. Captain Bush was a midshipman in HMS *Bacchante* which formed a part of the naval force during the campaign. It is a fascinating account, particularly of the naval operations, and made all the more compelling by the fact that he was an eyewitness to many of the dramatic events in that remarkable campaign.

When I had read the book, I thought it might be an idea to look up his list of references with a view to going into it all a bit more deeply. I was somewhat chastened when I counted something like forty-five books on the list.

As a first step I thought I would have a look to see what was available at Windsor. To my astonishment, I found no fewer than five books touching on the subject in the bookcase in my own room. They all had King George V's book-plate in them. These were *The World Crisis, 1915* by Winston Churchill; *Lord Fisher* by Admiral Bacon; *The Naval Memoirs of Admiral of the Fleet Sir Roger Keyes; The History of the Great War*, by John Buchan and *The Dardanelles Campaign* by H.W. Nevinson. I must add that I was also greatly assisted by Martin Gilbert, Sir Winston Churchill's biographer, who by chance stayed at Windsor.

Needless to say, there was no dispute between the authors about the salient facts. Some gave greater emphasis to certain aspects than others, but the descriptions of the events were substantially the same. There the similarity and the consensus ended. Motives, opinions, views, priorities, strategic concepts, assessments of personalities; in fact in every respect other than the bald facts the authors each painted sharply different pictures.

So it seemed to me that rather than go through yet another account of the astonishing story of the campaign, it might be more interesting to try to trace the influence of the personal views and attitudes of the main actors during the period leading up to the fateful decision to undertake the attack on the Dardanelles forts.

The problem was to know where to begin because, in so many cases, strategic concepts and opinions had already been formed long before the war broke out. Ever since Nelson's day, the Navy abhorred the idea of ships attacking forts, but on the other hand Admiral Duckworth had led a fleet through the narrows and nearly reached Constantinople in 1807, although he just managed to get out again.

As might be expected, a great deal of thought had been given to the strategic problems that would arise in the event of war breaking out with Germany. There were two principal issues to be considered: the role of the Navy and the employment of the British Expeditionary Force, which meant, to all intents and purposes, the Regular Army. Perhaps the most vivid illustration of this divergence of views is contained in an account of a meeting of the Committee of Imperial Defence in 1909. Fisher was the First Sea Lord, and Asquith the Prime Minister.

> During the Morocco crisis the French Government was within an inch of war with Germany, and insisted on 120,000 British troops being sent to the French frontier. The Cabinet agreed. At a meeting of the Defence Committee, where the military plans were set forth by General Nicholson, Fisher remained silent, seated opposite to Mr Asquith at the end of a long table. The only question put to Fisher was 'Whether the Navy could guarantee transport', to which he answered 'Yes'. Mr Asquith then asked him if he had anything to say; and he replied that he had nothing to say that anyone present would care to hear.

Mr Asquith pressed him; then a scene took place. Fisher told the committee that if 120,000 English were sent to France, the Germans would put everything else aside and make any sacrifice to surround and destroy the British, and that they would succeed. Continental armies being what they are, Fisher expressed the view that the British Army should be absolutely restricted to operations consisting of sudden descents on the coast, the recovery of Heligoland, and the garrisoning of Antwerp.

He pointed out that there was a stretch of 10 miles of hard sand on the Pomeranian coast which is only 90 miles from Berlin. Were the British Army to seize and entrench that strip, a million Germans would find occupation; but to despatch British troops to the front in a continental war would be an act of suicidal lunacy arising from the distorted view of war produced by Mr Haldane's speeches, and childish arrangements for training 'Terriers' after war broke out. Fisher followed this up with an impassioned diatribe against the War Office and all its ways, including conceit, waste of money, and ignorance of war. He claimed that the British Army should be administered as an annex to the Navy and that the present follies should be abandoned.

At this point Mr Asquith said, 'I think we had better adjourn'. This was done, but for some months onward the Defence Committee never considered, nor did the soldiers propose, any plan for helping the French by means of an Expeditionary Force to take part in the main land fighting.

Anyone who has read anything about Fisher will recognise his inimitable style. He was recalled as First Sea Lord at the end of 1914 by Churchill, who had then become First Lord. Throughout his second spell in that office, Fisher never really changed his mind and kept coming back to these two points: the landing of a Russian army on Germany's Baltic coast and the occupation of the Belgian coast by the British Army. It is perhaps ironic that the Monitors and the landing-craft, or 'Beetles' as they came to be known at the Dardanelles, were designed by Fisher for use in the Baltic or on the Belgian coast.

As far as operations on the Belgian coast were concerned he saw eye to eye with Churchill. In his book, *World Crisis*, there is a series of letters on this subject between himself and Sir John French, the British Commander-in-Chief in France. He sets out the general scene in the following passage:

. . . in November 1914, Sir John French wished to make an advance in conjunction with the Belgian Army along the sea coast from Nieuport towards Ostende and Zeebrugge . . . it appealed very strongly to Lord Fisher and Sir Arthur Wilson [Wilson had succeeded Fisher as First Sea Lord when the latter retired at the end of 1909]. The Admiralty War Staff were increasingly apprehensive of the dangers of a hostile submarine base developing at Zeebrugge from which our cross-Channel communications would be continually harassed. I had always wished to see the British Army with its left hand on the sea, nearest to its home, and with its left flank guarded by the Navy. I saw in this the prospect of close and effectual cooperation between Fleet and Army out of which the amphibious operations in which I was a believer might develop.

Neither Lord Kitchener nor the War Council were opposed to these ideas. On the contrary, they united British opinion – professional and political, naval and military, War Office and General Headquarters. General Joffre, however, did not think well of the plan . . . The French Government also on political grounds showed themselves strongly opposed to allowing the British armies to occupy the sea flank, or to acquire a close association with the Belgian forces.

It turned out that this extraordinary attitude of the French was based on their fear that Britain might remain in occupation of Belgium after the war. Similar damaging jealousies between the Allies were to have an important influence on the Dardanelles project.

A point worth noting from the account of the Fisher 'scene' is that Fisher only gave his opinion when pressed by the Prime Minister. You will appreciate its importance when we come to the decision by the War Council to undertake the naval attack on the Dardanelles.

There are two other major strategic factors to be considered before getting to the origins of the Dardanelles campaign. In the first place it is quite evident that the main theatre of the war was Europe. Germany could only be defeated by the invasion of her territory. That was generally accepted, but the problem was how to achieve it. Unlike any previous wars, the front lines of the antagonists had become a continuous line of entrenchments from the coast of the North Sea to the Alps.

Out-flanking, in the accepted military understanding of that term, was therefore impossible. This was at least partly the reason that so much futile effort and so many lives were expended in frontal assaults. While out-flanking was not possible in the land battle, it was still possible in the grand strategic sense. Fisher's Baltic project would have had the effect of turning Germany's right flank. Other than the Adriatic coastline of Austria–Hungary, which Lloyd George wished to attack, the nearest thing to a left flank was Turkey which, after much assiduous wooing by Germany, had thrown in her lot with the Central Powers.

Within the higher Allied councils of war there were two principal factions: those who wished to concentrate everything in the main theatre with a single thrust at the enemy's heartland, and those who wished to turn the enemy's flank, on one side or the other. This division of opinion was further complicated by the natural desire of the Admiralty to bring the German High Seas Fleet to a decisive action. It was believed by the more aggressive elements that this could only be achieved by some provocative act such as seizing the island of Borkum. On the other hand there were those, such as Jellicoe, the Commander-in-Chief Grand Fleet, and later Fisher himself, who held that all the Navy needed to do was to maintain command of the seas by keeping a superior force in home waters to prevent the enemy from doing any mischief outside the North Sea.

The possibility of taking some action in the Near East had been under general consideration since the outbreak of the war. As early as 26 August 1914, the British adviser to the Turkish Navy, Rear Admiral Limpus, suggested a landing between Smyrna and the Dardanelles. However, in the very first days of 1915, three events conspired to concentrate the minds of the members of the War Council on the advantages to be gained by directing a threat at Constantinople. The first was the declaration of war by Turkey.

The second was a paper, dated 28 December 1914, by Maurice Hankey, Secretary of the Council, who drew attention to the great benefits to be derived from forcing Turkey out of the war. Russia was getting desperately short of artillery ammunition and rifles for her armies, her economy was under serious pressure owing to the fact that she could not export her wheat surplus and she was also having to fight both the Germans and the Turks at the same time.

It was confidently expected that the opening of the Dardanelles and the arrival of an Allied fleet at Constantinople would solve all these problems and, furthermore, it would have the effect of persuading Greece and Bulgaria, the two neutral Balkan states, to join the Allies against the Central Powers. In Hankey's view, if Bulgaria could be induced to join the Allies – by the offer of the Greek province of Thrace – '. . . there ought to be no insuperable obstacle to the occupation of Constantinople, the Dardanelles and Bosphorus.' It would, in fact, constitute a serious out-flanking movement on the Germans.

The third event was the receipt of a telegram, on New Year's Day, from the Russian Commander-in-Chief, the Grand Duke Nicholas, to the effect that he was being sorely pressed and that any demonstration which suggested a threat to Constantinople would be very much appreciated. This appeal was all the more difficult to resist as in August 1914 the Grand Duke had responded to an appeal from the French and British for a Russian offensive to relieve pressure on the Western Front. The Russian offensive had just ended in the disastrous Battle of Tannenberg.

On receiving the Grand Duke's telegram, Kitchener wrote to Churchill: 'The only place that a demonstration might have some effect in stopping reinforcements going East would be the Dardanelles. . .' On 2 January, Kitchener sent a telegram to Petrograd assuring the Grand Duke that '. . . steps will be taken to make a demonstration against the Turks'. However, it so happens that in the previous November Churchill, with Fisher's approval, had signalled to Admiral Carden, then Commander-in-Chief in the Mediterranean: '. . . without risking the ships demonstration is to be made by bombardment on the earliest suitable day by your armoured ships and the two French battleships against the forts at the entrance to the Dardanelles at a range of 14,000 to 12,000 yards.'

The bombardment took place on 3 November 1914, the day before Britain's declaration of war on Turkey. Although this demonstration alerted the Turks to the need to strengthen the defences at the entrance to the straits, they did little work on them for some time.

Hankey's paper had an electrifying effect on Fisher. On 3 January 1915, he put his thoughts on paper in a letter to Churchill in which he made a number of important points.

I've been informed by Hankey that War Council assembles next Thursday, and I suppose it will be like a game of ninepins! Everyone will have a plan and one ninepin in falling will knock over its neighbour! I CONSIDER THE ATTACK ON TURKEY HOLDS THE FIELD! – but only if it is IMMEDIATE! However it won't be! Our Aulic Council will adjourn till the following Thursday fortnight! (NB When did we meet last? and what came of it???)

We shall decide on a futile bombardment of the Dardanelles . . .

What good resulted from the last bombardment?

Did it move a single Turk from the Caucasus? . . .

This is the Turkey plan:

1. Appoint Sir W. Robertson the present Quartermaster-General to command the Expeditionary Force.

2. Immediately replace all Indians and 75,000 seasoned troops from Sir John French's command with Territorials, etc., from England (as you yourself suggested) and embark the Turkish Expeditionary Force ostensibly for the protection of Egypt! WITH ALL POSSIBLE DESPATCH at Marseilles! and land them at Besika Bay direct with previous feints before they arrive with troops now in Egypt against Haifa and Alexandretta, the latter to be a REAL occupation because of its inestimable value as regards the oil fields of the Garden of Eden, with which by rail it is in direct communication, and we shove out the Germans now established in Alexandretta with an immense Turkish concession – the last act of that arch-enemy of England, Marschall von Bieberstein.

3. The Greeks to go for Gallipoli at the same time as we go for Besika, and the Bulgarians for Constantinople, and the Russians, the Serbians and Roumanians for Austria (all this you said yourself)

4. Sturdee forces the Dardanelles at the same time with 'Majestic' class and 'Canopus' class! God bless him!

But as the great Napoleon said, 'CELERITY' – without it – 'FAILURE!'

The suggestion that the Greeks might go for Gallipoli was vetoed by the Russians, who would not countenance the Greeks anywhere near Constantinople, particularly as the British Foreign Secretary, Sir Edward

Grey, had already promised the city to the Russians in the event of the defeat of Turkey.

Churchill replied by letter to this typical piece of Fisher prose in these words: 'I would not grudge 100,000 men because of the great political effects in the Balkan peninsula: but Germany is the foe, and it is bad war to seek cheaper victories and easier antagonists.'

Many years later Churchill was to have a slightly different recollection of his views. He wrote in *World Crisis*:

> Lord Fisher's third paragraph about the Greeks, Bulgarians, Serbians and Russians expressed exactly what everybody wanted. It was the obvious supreme objective in this part of the world. The question was, How to procure it?
> This was the root of the matter. It was in connection with this that Lord Fisher's fourth paragraph made its impression on me. Here for the first time was the suggestion of forcing the Dardanelles with the old battleships.

On the same day that he received the letter from Fisher, he sent the following signal to Vice-Admiral Carden:

> Do you consider the forcing of the Dardanelles by ships alone a practicable proposition?
> It is assumed older battleships fitted with mine-bumpers would be used, preceded by colliers or other merchant craft as mine-bumpers and sweepers.
> Importance of results would justify severe loss.
> Let me know your views.

On 4 January there was a further exchange of letters between Churchill and Fisher, in which Fisher commented: 'The naval advantages of the possession of Constantinople and the getting of wheat from the Black Sea are so overwhelming that I consider Colonel Hankey's plan for Turkish operations vital and imperative and very pressing.'

In a further letter to Churchill, on the morning of the meeting of the War Council on 28 January, Fisher again emphasised the importance he attached to military cooperation: 'I make no objections to enter Zeebrugge or Dardanelles if accompanied by military cooperation *on such a scale* (as to secure) our permanent military occupation of the Dardanelles Forts pari passu with the Naval bombardment.'

In view of the fact that Fisher was later to say that he had always been against the Gallipoli project and of the fact that he resigned over the issue, these two letters of his, and Churchill's understanding of them, need some explanation.

I have come to the conclusion that there must have been a serious misunderstanding. As far as the need for the 'Turkey operations' was concerned, they were obviously both in complete agreement. However, it also seems obvious that Fisher understood them to include the whole plan as outlined in the four paragraphs of his letter, or that any bombardment would be accompanied by military action on a sufficient scale. It would appear that it was never his intention to suggest a solely naval attempt to force the Dardanelles. Indeed, he had written, 'We shall decide on a futile bombardment of the Dardanelles'.

Furthermore, his plan for the Baltic landings and his advocacy of bringing the British Army to the Belgian coast so that the Army and Navy could operate together, make it reasonably clear that Fisher always envisaged joint operations.

Churchill seems to have missed this point in his eagerness to get on with some sort of offensive action. Judging by his signal to Carden, it looks as if Churchill took Fisher's fourth paragraph out of context and assumed that Fisher would support the naval bombardment part of his plan as the only element of the 'Turkey operations'. If that view is accepted, then the rest of the developing argument between Churchill and Fisher over the Dardanelles issue falls into place.

On 5 January Churchill received the reply from Carden. As Churchill commented, 'It was remarkable'. 'With reference to your telegram of 3rd instant, I do not consider Dardanelles can be rushed. They might be forced by extended operations with large number of ships.'

Although the message was slightly equivocal, it clearly answered Churchill's question; at any rate it was quite sufficient to encourage him to pursue the idea, and he asked Carden to prepare an outline plan.

Meanwhile the subject of 'Turkey operations' was discussed at the War Council meeting on 8 January. The dominating personality on the Council was Lord Kitchener, the Secretary of State for War. It is quite evident that nothing was decided about the higher conduct of the war without his approval, and on this occasion, as Churchill reports:

Lord Kitchener expressed an opinion in favour of an attack on the Dardanelles. He told the Council that the Dardanelles appeared to be the most suitable military objective, as an attack there could be made in cooperation with the Fleet. He estimated that 150,000 men would be sufficient for the capture of the Dardanelles, but reserved his opinion until a close study had been made. He offered no troops and made it clear that none were available. His contribution was therefore, and was meant to be, purely theoretic.

Churchill may have thought the contribution was 'purely theoretic' but in fact it meant quite clearly that Kitchener had ruled out a combined operation. This was understandable as he was heavily engaged in the formation of the 'new armies' which the Army assumed would be used in France. Furthermore, it meant that he did not wish to see the troops currently defending Egypt to be used for any other purpose. It so happens that a Turkish attack on the Suez Canal had, only recently, been repulsed. So it must have been fully evident to Fisher that his 'Turkey' plan in its entirety stood no chance of being accepted. This may well have been the beginning of his disillusionment with the Dardanelles plan.

Kitchener evidently considered that his undertaking to the Grand Duke Nicholas would be met by some sort of naval action at the Dardanelles, whether it was a bombardment or an attempt to force the narrows.

Churchill, in his anxiety to get something started, apparently failed to notice Fisher's growing apprehensions about the way things were developing. As Fisher pointed out later on, he did not feel that he should attempt to veto the project since a bombardment of the forts by the old ships in the Mediterranean could do no harm, provided the action could be broken off if no progress was made and provided it did not draw scarce resources from home waters. He continued to believe that the Dardanelles operation should be concerted with some other military action either at Gallipoli or a descent on Alexandretta.

On 12 January Fisher wrote to Sir William Tyrrell at the Foreign Office: '. . . If the Greeks land 100,000 men on the Gallipoli peninsula in concert with a British naval attack on the Dardanelles I think we could count on an easy and quick arrival at Constantinople . . .' Matters eventually came to a head at a meeting of the Council on the next day, 13 January. Churchill had circulated Carden's plan and the minutes concluded:

The Admiralty were studying the question, and believed that a plan could be made for systematically reducing all the forts within a few weeks. Once the forts were reduced the minefields would be cleared, and the Fleet would proceed up to Constantinople and destroy the 'Goeben'. They would have nothing to fear from field guns or rifles, which would be merely an inconvenience.

Lord Kitchener thought the plan was worth trying. We could leave off the bombardment if it did not prove effective.

That the Admiralty should prepare for a naval expedition in February to bombard and take the Gallipoli peninsula with Constantinople as its objective.

It was at this meeting that Fisher and Wilson sat silent throughout the proceedings and consequently gave the impression that they approved of the decisions. For this they were subsequently criticised by the Dardanelles Commission. But there is no record of the Prime Minister, or anyone else, having asked for their views.

Unless Fisher had suddenly changed his mind and had come to accept a solely naval operation, he must have assumed that Churchill (who, as First Lord, was a member while they were not) appreciated the importance which they attached to a joint operation. Both assumed that the political reasons for going ahead with the project outweighed their professional reservations. It is tempting to think that the Prime Minister remembered the last time he had asked for Fisher's views and determined not to risk another scene.

The wording of the last paragraph of the minutes – a wording devised by Asquith – is interesting for a number of reasons. Nothing had ever been said, up to this point, about 'taking' the Gallipoli peninsula by a naval expedition; in fact all naval professional opinion was against anything other than a piecemeal destruction of the forts. It seems to have been assumed that, once this had been achieved, the need to occupy the peninsula, in order to secure the communications of whatever fleet managed to penetrate into the Sea of Marmara, would have become self-evident.

It is difficult to believe that anyone could seriously contemplate sending a fleet into the Sea of Marmara without being certain of getting it out again. Duckworth's exploit may have shown that it was possible to get a fleet through the defended narrows, but it also showed that the fleet only had a very limited time to achieve its objective before it became trapped.

Admiral Sir Henry Jackson, who had been charged with the job of evaluating the Carden plan, went no further than to suggest the approval of the bombardment of the outer forts as soon as possible, '. . . as the experience gained would be useful in the subsequent attacks on the narrows'. In his evidence to the Dardanelles Commission, he said that he did not consider that an attempt by the Fleet alone to get through the Dardanelles was a 'feasible operation'; he thought that 'it would be a mad thing to do'.

In a letter to Jellicoe on 21 January, Fisher again referred to a military operation: 'I just abominate the Dardanelles operation, unless a great change is made and it is settled to be made a military operation, with 200,000 men in conjunction with the Fleet.'

Four days later Fisher sent a memorandum to Churchill with the following covering note: 'I have no desire to continue a useless resistance in the War Council to plans I cannot concur in, but I would ask that the enclosed may be printed and circulated to its members before the meeting.'

The memorandum then recapitulates Fisher's views on the employment of the Navy. He emphasises the prime importance of bringing the enemy fleet to action and states that any subsidiary operations, such as the bombardment of the Dardanelles, are only justified if they help to induce the enemy fleet to put to sea. He goes on to say that the first function of the British Army is to assist the fleet in obtaining command of the sea and suggests that this might be accomplished by joint operations against the Turks in the Dardanelles, or an attack on Zeebrugge. He ends with the words 'The English Army is apparently to continue to provide a small sector of the allied front in France, where it no more helps the Navy than if it were in Timbuctoo.'

The next meeting of the Council took place on 28 January, after Fisher had made his opposition to the Dardanelles project quite clear to both Churchill and the Prime Minister, but Asquith so strongly supported the Dardanelles plan that he refused to allow Fisher's memorandum to be printed for the War Council. Asquith was probably strengthened in his resolve to pursue the Dardanelles plan by the arrival of a second appeal from Grand Duke Nicholas, which had just reached the Foreign Office.

Fisher may not have known about this telegram since, when the subject of the Dardanelles came up at the meeting, he remarked that he had not known that it was on the agenda and left the council table in a huff. Kitchener got up and had a word with him and Fisher reluctantly returned to his seat. The final, apparently unanimous, decision to go ahead with the Dardanelles project was then taken.

A somewhat similar situation arose during the Suez crisis in 1956. The then First Sea Lord, Lord Mountbatten, made it very clear to the Prime Minister, Sir Anthony Eden, and to the First Lord, Lord Hailsham, that he was most unhappy about the use of force under the circumstances and, in effect, asked to be relieved. However, he was told by the First Lord to remain at his post and carry out his instructions, which he then did to the best of his ability.

Following the Council, there was a long meeting between Fisher and Churchill at which Fisher was persuaded to give the plan his support. As he told the Commission, 'When I finally decided to go in, I went the whole hog, totus porcus.' This was quite true, until he saw the campaign becoming a drain on naval resources and realised that the longer it went on, the less chance there was of his Baltic project being accepted.

In many ways I feel that Fisher only had himself to blame. To Churchill, with his single-minded determination, it must have seemed that Fisher was always changing his mind. One moment he seemed to be strongly in favour, the next he was counselling caution or was actively opposed.

Fisher was at least consistent in two respects. 'CELERITY OR FAILURE', as he put it, and he never wavered in his insistence on the need for a joint operation. He was proved right in both cases. The trouble seems to have arisen because, while he and Churchill agreed about the ends of the 'Turkey operations', they were completely at odds about the means.

The rest of the story followed like some inevitable Greek tragedy. The success of the bombardment of the outer forts suggested that all was going to be all right. Then things started to go seriously wrong. The attack on the inner forts resulted in the loss of several ships to mines.

Out of sixteen battleships, three had been sunk and four disabled. The ships, particularly the mine-sweeping trawlers manned as they were by their peacetime fishermen crews, found the tidal stream and the constant shelling by mobile field batteries not to their liking. German submarines made their appearance and their success forced the major units of the fleet to retire to Mudros and Tenedos. Admiral de Robeck, who had succeeded Carden, became even more reluctant to renew the attack on the inner forts. This was probably the moment to call off the whole operation.

However, it was at this point that Kitchener finally agreed to send a military expedition under Sir Ian Hamilton, but instead of the 150,000 men he originally estimated would be needed, only about 70,000 were available for the landing, and this after some three months' warning to the Turks and their German allies.

Then the departure of the regular 29th Division was delayed from 10 March to 16 March, and when it got to Mudros it was decided to send it to Alexandria so that the loading of the transports could be reorganised for a landing. The whole force only assembled at Mudros in the middle of April and the landing eventually took place on the 25th, nearly five months after the first bombardment.

During this long period of vacillation the Turks had not been idle and, but for the outstanding courage and tenacity of the Allied troops, the landing could never have succeeded. All the beaches were covered by artillery and rifle fire, all open ground was wired, and the landing force was always fighting uphill against a well-entrenched enemy.

The situation soon developed into a stalemate, both on land and at sea, and the continuous drain on naval resources eventually led Fisher to resign rather than countenance sending any more ships and men out to the Dardanelles. His resignation led to the formation of a Coalition Government, and to Churchill's removal from the Admiralty. However, the campaign continued and, on 5 July, Kitchener told the War Council that the war would be over '. . . as soon as the Gallipoli peninsula was captured . . .'.

A month later, on 6 August, Hamilton made a valiant attempt to break the deadlock with a new landing at Suvla, but that went sadly wrong. The new Territorial Divisions, which were committed to the Suvla landings, lacked battle experience and many of their senior officers were not equal to the task.

Kitchener seems to have started by assuming that the Navy would have no difficulty in forcing the straits, and when that failed his decision to send a military force was too late to retrieve the position. The original expeditionary force was too small and subsequent reinforcements were not adequately trained and arrived too late.

De Robeck, who had led the original assault on the forts before he succeeded Carden, became less and less enthusiastic about attempting another assault on the inner forts, in spite of persistent urging by his Chief of Staff, Roger Keyes.

Maurice Hankey was sent out to report on the situation and suggested that evacuation should be considered. He was followed by Kitchener himself who quickly appreciated the hopelessness of the situation, but decided to send General Monro to take over from Hamilton. Monro, who came from the war in France and believed that every effort should be concentrated in that area, recommended evacuation.

The ultimate irony was that the evacuation turned out to be the most successful operation of the whole campaign. Every single soldier and virtually every horse, mule and weapon was taken off the peninsula at the cost of one man slightly wounded.

Estimates vary, but Captain Bush reckons that the total Empire (British, Australian, New Zealand, Indian and Newfoundland) casualties for the whole campaign amounted to 205,000 (115,000 killed, wounded or missing and 90,000 evacuated sick); those of the French, 47,000. The official Turkish estimate of their casualties was 251,000, but some Turkish authorities put it as high as 350,000.

John Buchan begins his account of the campaign with these words: 'The Dardanelles campaign is one of the most pitiful, tragic and glorious episodes in British history.'

He concludes his account like this: 'Had the fashion endured of linking the strife of mankind with the gods, what strange myth would not have sprung from the rescue of the British troops in the teeth of the winter gales and uncertain seas! It would have been rumoured, as at Troy, that Poseidon had done battle for his children.'

FOUR

THE GOD OF BATTLES AND THE FIGHT FOR FAITH

Robert A.K. Runcie

19 April 1988

The Aegean and the Black Seas are fairly well known to me as a classical scholar and Hellenic traveller. Many times I have sailed past Gallipoli and through the Dardanelles. I have experienced the chatter of a cruise ship conjuring up the ghosts of history and the drama of those waters – the stories and myths of Leander and Xerxes, in sight of the mound of Troy where Hector and Achilles fought and died. Then I have experienced the tribute of silence that descends as we have passed the memorial-marked peninsula of Gallipoli pointing almost accusingly like a finger into the tranquil Aegean, hummocked with the isles of Greece – a silence prompted not least by the presence on board of veterans of the campaign itself.

I have some experience of war as a combatant. Gallipoli was the most ambitious amphibious operation in the annals of history until the Normandy invasion. Those of us who fought in the Normandy campaign were aware of the preparations made for it and could not fail to be heartened by the thought that Winston Churchill – at forty, the daring architect of the 1915 adventure – was determined that close on 30 years later the mistakes would not be repeated. Perhaps those of us who survive owe a strange debt to the shadow of Gallipoli.

Yet I believe you have asked me to contribute as an Archbishop and not as an historian or a soldier. For that reason I intend to speak to you against the backcloth of Gallipoli on the God of Battles and the Fight for Faith.

> Go and may the God of battles
> You in his good guidance keep
> And if he in wisdom giveth
> Unto his beloved sleep
> I accept it nothing asking,
> Save a little space to weep.

'I accept it, nothing asking . . .'. So wrote W.N. Hodgson, the 21-year-old son of the Bishop of St Edmundsbury and Ipswich, in August 1914 at the onset of the First World War. The voice of Christian acceptance is here tinged with the patriotism of Kipling. His was but one of many voices which were silenced for ever in the ensuing conflict – in Hodgson's case, on the first day of the Battle of the Somme. Yet his verse may stand for the general sentiment about the war which long endured at home, despite the carnage at the front. Not just Christian acceptance, but positive encouragement to enlist and fight was the message heard from thousands of pulpits. Bishops, clergy of the Established Church and Free Church ministers and leaders – many of them felt it their patriotic and Christian duty to assist the work of recruitment.

None was more enthusiastic than Bishop Winnington-Ingram, Bishop of London for the first thirty-nine years of this century. He declared his pride that there had been such an 'exodus of young men from Church Choirs, the Church Lads' Brigades, the Church Scouts and the ranks of the servers' in response to 'an appeal to fight a duty to God as well as to the country'. Winnington-Ingram did not confine his activities to the men alone. He urged a rally of 2,000 women in October 1914 to say to their men, 'Go, and go with my love and blessing'. The Mothers' Union assisted the cause in the year the war began by producing a pamphlet entitled *To British Women, How They Can Help Recruiting*. Alan Wilkinson's vivid account, *The Church of England and the First World War*, records the enthusiasm with which the Church generally greeted the war and the subsequent disillusion which this ensured would be the consequence.

> Now God be thanked who has matched us with this hour.

The words are Rupert Brooke's – as also the better known:

> If I should die, think only this of me
> That there's some corner of a foreign field
> That is forever England.

Rupert Brooke's words, like Hodgson's earlier, were written before any experience of war. They are brave, patriotic words, often quoted by those who have never known the reality of war or forget the appalling and undignified suffering it creates. The glorification of war could not last at the front, and the questioning soon began. No doubt Rupert Brooke's style would have changed, had he survived. He died on the way to Gallipoli in 1915 of blood poisoning following a mosquito bite.

Brooke would have been fortunate if he had survived Gallipoli, the carnage was so great. In part it is that carnage which occasions our remembrance. It would be, however, insensitive and superficial to omit any consideration of the strategy and tactics which dictated the campaign. Even though I want to address the impact of war and the experience of war upon faith and the human spirit, I believe we should not neglect to recall what prompted a campaign such as Gallipoli. To attribute it to mere adventurism or to engage in easy denunciations of the military planners' disregard for the value of human life would be cynical and rash. I am suspicious of unconsidered, sweeping judgements. Human beings are more often mistaken than callous and my own experience of battle taught me how seriously strategies are considered and how protective officers are of the men in their charge.

Gallipoli was a campaign that failed. This has been its chief disadvantage in any subsequent assessment made of the motives which prompted it. It was hastily and badly organised. Intelligence was out of date. Maps were inaccurate and sparse. Communications were primitive and chaotic. There were insufficient shells and few mosquito nets. There was bad security in Alexandria. The tactical objectives do not seem to have been coordinated into the overall strategic plan. The execution of the operation was flawed. Such is the general judgement. War in the Levant was not curtailed as a result and, if anything, the impasse on the Western Front was made the more politically intractable because of the Gallipoli failure.

There is no gainsaying much of this judgement. History is not made on what might have been but what actually happened. Yet Gallipoli was not a madcap adventure. It was part of a total vision of Churchill's, born out of the failure of the Navy to force the Dardanelles. There were good grounds for thinking that if we had broken through to Constantinople, where so much of the Turkish armaments industry was located, and Turkey was taken out of the war, a decisive blow would have been dealt to Germany from the rear. The precarious character of the Tsarist regime in Russia led to pessimistic assessments of that country's ability to maintain the war effort unless something was done to bring them relief and assistance.

I say all this because I do not want us to be callously cavalier in judging the motives of military leaders when we think of the impact of the carnage of Gallipoli.

We should also consider the scale of Gallipoli in its romantic anticipation. To this place the British brought an imperial army. The soldiers bore themselves, said John Masefield, like kings in a pageant; their Commander, the gentle and civilised Scot, Ian Hamilton, as he sailed to his battle station, wrote that the 'Aegean seems like a carpet of blue velvet stretched out for Aphrodite'. The gifted young men of that generation in our countries seemed to be gathered together – future statesmen, writers, prime ministers – as well as amazing relationships from W.G. Grace's son to the Australian journalist, Keith Murdoch, who was to be such a thorn in the side of the British leadership and whose son Rupert was to have such a commanding influence on the international news media of today. There were contingents of Sikhs, Punjabis, Gurkhas, the Ceylon Planters' Rifles, and the Zion Mule Corps whose badge was the shield of David, whose orders were given in Hebrew and in English, and who were said to be the first Jewish military unit to go into action since the Fall of Jerusalem in AD 70. Above all, they included the Anzacs, the Australian and New Zealand Army Corps. All this seemed to give a larger scale to the disaster which followed. It was Gallipoli and its quarter of a million casualties which prepared the ground for the acceptance of war deaths on a hitherto unprecedented scale. The Somme and Passchendaele had this terrible precursor.

The scale of Gallipoli, the romantic dreams, the losses, the suffering, the extraordinary conditions the men met with, had their own special impact on those who survived. It was, it seemed, more searing than Flanders for those who returned there and more memorable than Egypt for those who fought thereafter in the Near East. Most of all, the intensity of the experience was felt by the Anzacs. This was the blooding of the Australian and New Zealand nations, just as Vimy Ridge was for the Canadians. I have been privileged to speak in both Australia and New Zealand at the dawn service on Anzac Day and have seldom been so moved by what was clearly an act of national recollection and religious dedication. A campaign like this created that sense of identity and solidarity essential to national pride. The conviction that war on such a scale must have a meaning on the same grand scale has been doggedly clung to by many. There was at Gallipoli a certain nobility of the human spirit but to strain that out we need to look searchingly at the underside of the story.

For those on the beaches and in the trenches the depths of degradation and misery were soon reached. A.P. Herbert, in retrospect, captured in verse something of the nature of Gallipoli which makes the word 'blooding' appropriate not just for the Anzacs but for all who took part.

> This is the Fourth of June
> Think not I never dream
> The noise of that infernal noon,
> The stretchers' endless stream,
> The tales of triumph won,
> The night that found them lies,
> The wounded wailing in the sun,
> The dead, the dust, the flies.

> The flies! Oh God, the flies
> That soiled the sacred dead.
> To see them swarm
> From dead men's eyes
> And share the soldiers' bread!
> Nor think I now forget
> The filth and stench of war,
> The corpses on the parapet,
> The maggots on the floor.

What was true of Gallipoli was reflected elsewhere in the experience of war. A cause in which millions died must be potent with symbols of Good fighting Evil. Or so the soldiers were told. How else could these sacrifices and sufferings make sense? Though that remained an orthodox conviction at home, it gradually grew less and less convincing at the front. And even patriots faltered. Kipling, usually so stirringly patriotic in tone, began, after the death of his only son at Loos in 1915, to question his conscience.

> If any question why we died
> Tell them, because our fathers lied.

There can be no doubt that, to many who fought, the world seemed to have gone mad. Yet from the theatre of war, particularly the First World War, springs some of the most enduring poetry in the English language. In many cases it seems to have been forced from the minds of authors by the unspeakable experiences of trench warfare. Theirs were often minds which never, in the normal course, thought to express themselves in verse. Now they stuttered and exploded into unconventional and, to some, crude and unacceptable 'poetry'.

The sentimental outpourings, inspired by the idea of combat, were all gone, leaving spirits raw and exposed. A compulsion was driving many frustrated soldiers to words, not to eloquent stirring verses, but to 'staccatoed, frantic expression of the truth' that was facing them.

One of the best, arguably *the* best, of the poets to materialise during this time was Wilfred Owen. He was not new to the expression of life in words but had led a fairly sheltered and sedate existence before 1914. Owen was only one of many writers and chroniclers of the war years who felt moved to express the truth as he saw it in words, no matter how horrific the end product looked in black and white.

This process of expiation by composition was already well under way at Gallipoli. Two of the most vivid contemporary accounts were written by chaplains. Oswin Creighton, son of Mandell Creighton, Winnington

Ingram's predecessor as Bishop of London, wrote *With the 29th Division in Gallipoli*. And W.H. Price, another chaplain, set down his reflections in *With the Fleet in the Dardanelles*. The Revd Henry Hall, who established the Gallipoli Memorial Chapel in this church at Eltham, was also a chaplain in the campaign. He wrote to his wife: 'The landing was awful – men and officers shot down in shoals, caught in the wires, killed, wounded and drowned.'

The desire to share something of that experience was deep but Hall's words are an inadequate expression of the horror. While others resorted to poetry as their only means of stammering out fractions of the truth, Hall gave expression to his remembrance in the Chapel here, another form of eloquent testimony and one in which God's share was assumed and unspoken. Hall was invalided out and returned to his parish not long after the campaign ended. Many of the chaplains at Gallipoli, however, like the other men, did not survive to keep remembrance.

The war soon shattered facile notions of providential purpose. Victorian and Edwardian fantasies about progress were also devastated. A sense grew up that there was an element of divine judgement in all this. That sense led the Church of England into organising in mid-war the ill-fated National Mission of Repentance and Hope. But the war did not lead to the religious revival which some observers, then as now, always thought they glimpsed. Rather, at home, stories of German atrocities were increasingly accepted uncritically and this had a negative impact on the country's spiritual health. Responsibility for the war fell on Germany alone. She became its sole cause. The war effort was directed at ridding the world of Prussianism, this incarnation of evil.

Basil Bourchier, an Army Chaplain and later Rector of St Anne's, Soho, said:

> We are fighting not so much for the honour
> of the country, as for the honour of God.
> Not only is this a Holy War,
> it is the holiest war that has ever been waged.

It was remarkable that humour sometimes laced the cynicism of the war poets. Siegfried Sassoon was the most capable of combining the two, as in this extract from 'To Any Dead Officer':

> Goodbye, old lad! Remember me to God,
> And tell him that our politicians swear
> They won't give in till Prussian Rule's been trod
> Under the heel of England . . . !

Sassoon and others felt increasingly the division between those who were fighting in the trenches and those left behind in England, unaware of the unmeetable demands patriotism was making on their fellow countrymen.

But you did not have to be a pacifist to possess a conscience and a faith strained to breaking point. It was sometimes the breaking of faith which seemed to allow some men to retain their conscience. Jackson Page, who died only in April 1987, was the son of a Methodist manse who had been taught in a Methodist school but, upon enlisting, there was a searing question which his faith could not answer 'Can anyone ask Jesus Christ to help them fire a machine-gun?' He concluded that only a negative answer was possible and proceeded to remove Jesus Christ from his mind and consciousness. For him the experience of war removed his belief, held from childhood, that God is Love. Yet Jackson Page, despite a shattered faith, was deeply moved by the work of the chaplains in the war and felt that justice had never been done to their heroism.

Some fell victim to cynicism. One chaplain, though, made a noted breakthrough to many men, not only through the heroism of his ministry but also through poetry. Geoffrey Studdert Kennedy, known affectionately as Woodbine Willie, was probably the best known chaplain of the First World War. Only Tubby Clayton, the founder of Toc H, achieved a similar degree of fame as a household name. Kennedy's own ministry among the men was extended in scope by his excursions into poetry. His verse was rough-hewn. Much of it was intended for the men themselves. His dialect poems, published as *Rough Rhymes*, achieved popularity not because they were good verse – they were not – but because they addressed the dilemmas the men felt deeply but which were too awesome for them to express in words.

Studdert Kennedy knew the feeling experienced by the men. It was not only distance that separated them from their loved ones. In his rhyme 'What's the Good?' Kennedy has a soldier pondering what he had done to his so-called enemies, who remind him even of his own son at home:

> There's a young 'un like our Richard,
> And I bashed 'is 'ead in two,
> And there's that ole grey-'aired geezer
> Which I stuck 'is belly through.
> Gawd, you women, wives, and mothers,
> It's sich waste of all your pain!
> If you knowed what I'd been doin',
> Could yer kiss me still, my Jane?

> When I sets dahn to tell yer
> What it means to scrap and fight,
> Could I tell ye true and honest,
> Make ye see this bleedin' sight?
> No, I couldn't and I wouldn't,
> It would turn your 'air all grey;
> Women suffers 'ell to bear us
> And we suffers 'ell to slay.

Wilfred Owen found outlets for this spiritual dilemma in the compassion of his poetry which was often focused on the enemy with whom he was in combat. His conscience was haunted by the enemy, as in his poem 'Strange Meeting', found among his papers after his death from machine-gun fire in November 1918. It represents a kind of poetic nightmare in which the dead Owen is united with his enemy.

> . . . 'Strange friend', I said, 'Here is no cause to mourn',
> 'None' said the other 'save the undone years,
> The hopelessness. Whatever hope is yours,
> Was my life also'.

But British poets did not have a monopoly on conscience, as this extract from 'Requiem for the Dead of Europe' by a German, Yvan Goll, shows:

> Before sticking your bayonet into his groin did not one
> Of you see the Christ-like look of his opponent?
> Did not one of you notice that the man
> Over there had a kingly heart full of love?

These were the profound questions of war. The search after its purpose eluded many of the fighters, but many turned to God for answers, for hope, and often in angry despair.

God was, indeed, on trial. Where did this terrible degradation of mankind fit into God's purpose? How did those who poured their inner beings into words come to terms with it all? For many there was no justification. God had deserted them. Yet Owen, writing again to his mother, makes an interesting revelation from his experience. This was written in February 1918 (the year he died). Harold and Colin are his brothers.

> If I do not read hymns, if Harold marks no Bible, nor Colin sees no life-
> guide in his Prayer Book, it is no bad sign. I have heard cadences of

harps not audible to Sankey, but which were strung by God: and played by mysteries to him and I was permitted to hear them.

There is a point where prayer is indistinguishable from blasphemy. There is also a point where blasphemy is indistinguishable from prayer.

Somehow it was a particular gift of Studdert Kennedy's to see this point which Owen expresses so forcefully. The horror, death and devastation – a blasphemy against the image of God in man – paradoxically drew men into God's presence. The crucifixion became a controlling image for the religious feelings of those who felt themselves being crucified.

Studdert Kennedy's theology was shaped by this experience. He could only believe in a God who suffered with the men. It was not enough that Jesus suffered and died on the Cross at a moment in history, and not even enough that the act should be of timeless significance. He believed all this, but God could only be God at the front if he suffered now. Kennedy was in revolt against an idea that God could only be experienced in serene and sublime detachment from his world. He satirised it in his poem 'A Sermon':

> Seek not to know the plans of God,
> But pray upon your knees
> That you may love with all your heart,
> With all your soul and mind,
> This perfect God you cannot know,
> Whose face you cannot find.
> You have no notion what He's like,
> You cannot know His Will,
> He's wrapped in darkest mystery,
> But you must love Him still.

This is but part of a long poem consisting of a sustained caricature of sublime religion. It ends with a typical Studdert Kennedy refrain centring all upon the Cross.

> O, by Thy Cross and Passion, Lord,
> By broken hearts that part
> For comfort and for love of Thee
> Deliver us from cant.

And it is the Cross which made, for Studdert Kennedy, a nonsense of the unknowable, transcendent God of the beyond. His theology knew no system but a great deal of pain. He could only express it in verse and in sermons because these were interpretations of life's experience.

The more enduring war poetry from men like Owen and Sassoon is sometimes criticised as unrepresentative of the soldiers' feelings. It is, of course, the mark of a great poet to perceive in the present moment significance which normally only future reflection might reveal. We should not be surprised therefore if poets are also prophets, without honour among their colleagues and kinfolk. But Studdert Kennedy did not suffer from neglect during his time. His work was intended for an immediate audience. He was on the soldiers' level, and he did communicate this sense of God mixed up in the senselessness of war.

Back in England preachers continued to describe the war as a fight for God, country and religion. Studdert Kennedy – and many other chaplains – soon ceased to believe that simple verity. They might not doubt the rightness of the cause – most could be as patriotic as the sternest anti-Prussian zealot – but it was the facile assumption that this was a fight for God and religion which could not survive the carnage. Gradually Studdert Kennedy came to believe that the soldiers were entering into God's nature in this conflict, a nature revealed most fully in the Cross. For a religion which proclaimed a crucified Lord might be peculiarly able to cope with revealing divinity even in horror and bloodshed.

Robert Graves's poem 'Recalling War' suggests that there was much anguished God-directed thought, even among those who could scarcely be described as devout:

> Even there was a use again for God –
> A word of rage in lack of meat, wine, fire
> In ache of wounds beyond all surgeoning.

Perhaps this was so, that such depths and abysses were the prerequisites of a new and further spiritual understanding.

Even in the bitterness there seemed to be faith. The language of faith seemed inescapable whether in anger or in mockery: 'For fourteen hours yesterday I was at work – teaching Christ to lift His cross by numbers, and how to adjust His crown . . . I attended His supper to see that there were no complaints . . . with maps I make him familiar with the topography of Golgotha'. That was Wilfred Owen.

In this lecture I have juxtaposed the idealism and the adventure of war so frequently expressed by those who are distant from its realities, with the heart-rending anguish of those who experienced its devastating effect on the human spirit of the combatants.

The Roman poet Horace fled from the battle of Philippi and war never entered his life or his poetry again. English poets who fought at Gallipoli and in the wars that followed created some of the finest poetry in our language. It may lack the harmony and facility of a Horace but it has the dimension of depth. Among them were those who ceased to believe that war could be the will of the Christian God. Yet they seem convinced that, if He exists, He never deserts us but works through the predicaments created by our history, our ambitions, and even our mistakes.

The time has come to attempt some concluding reflections. I state them succinctly but I hope not too obscurely.

Professor Michael Howard has expressed clearly the moral dilemma which war must create in the human mind:

> Wars do not come simply from militarism and muddle. They may come, and indeed usually have come, from a deliberate intention on the one side to use armed force as an instrument of state and on the other a determination to resist.
>
> The hard fact is that wars are caused as much by our virtues, our sense of justice, our belief in the difference between right and wrong, our loyalties, our readiness to defend a way of life.

That is why I cannot myself accept the pacifist option. Yet I believe that wars should only be fought with a pain in the mind. That is why I have no hesitation in supporting my friends in the Forces and recruiting chaplains to serve them. It should be remembered that it is not the military who create wars. Indeed the activities of our Forces today are palpably deployed in attempts to prevent wars rather than to win them.

Christ was kind to soldiers. The people He was tough with included the clergy as well as the politicians and publicity seekers of the day. To soldiers He was unfailingly sympathetic.

Furthermore, loyalty to a regiment, a ship or a squadron, like loyalty to a country, is a natural human feeling. Jesus the Jew wept in affection over His native Jerusalem, thereby consecrating such natural feelings and loyalties. Patriotism is not enough but it is a kind of nursery for loyalties which need to be deepened as well as extended in scope.

The Second World War, in which I fought, was surrounded by far fewer romantic dreams than the First and was not merely the product of thoughtless patriotism. We had learned something from the earlier world war but not enough. There is no time to explore this now, but simply to state my own belief baldly that war is always the result of failure, even if the Second World War had a sense of inevitability about it. It was a final resort.

I like the verse of Cecil Day Lewis, reflecting his own attitude to the Second World War.

> It is the logic of our times
> no subject for immortal verse
> that we who've lived by honest dreams
> defend the bad against the worse.

If it produced no heroic poetry, many of my friends died in it. I do not believe that they died in vain and I do not believe they would think so either. A war which closed down Belsen and Buchenwald was worth fighting. Personally, I find it difficult to believe in the God of battles, the miracle of Dunkirk, the angel of Mons. For me faith is not believing impossible things. It is trusting that the promises of Christ never fail. It is not hoping the worst will not happen but believing there is no human tragedy which cannot be redeemed – that is, turned to good effect to increase the total output of goodness in the world. In Shakespeare's great war play *Henry V*, the king says:

> there is some soul of goodness in things evil,
> would men observing distill it out.

War is an evil, messy business but even shared anguish can be a bridge of understanding and ultimate reconciliation. When I attempted to preach on this subject at the service following the Falkland Islands campaign, my subsequent correspondence revealed that it was not the combatants but the commentators who wanted to hear more about the God of battles and less about the fight for faith.

So I leave you with my favourite Gallipoli anecdote – it is sentimental, but why not? On 25 April 1965, the fiftieth anniversary, a group of veterans from Australia and New Zealand landed in small boats on the original bridgehead. This time, they fell into the arms of Turkish veterans who had been their enemies. Their welcoming embraces were laced with laughter and with tears.

Some words from William Blake to close:

> Man is made for Joy and Woe
> And when this we rightly know
> Through the world we safely go
> Joy and woe are woven fine
> A clothing for the Soul divine.

FIVE

BRITAIN'S NOBLER WAR?

John Grigg

27 April 1989

My subject takes the form of a question which I should begin by explaining. I am asking which of the two world wars of this century (and no other century has had a war on the global scale) was the nobler, so far as Britain was concerned. By 'Britain' I mean not just the United Kingdom, but the British Empire and Commonwealth which participated in both wars from start to finish.

In the first war no episode, of course, is more symbolic of the contribution from overseas than the Gallipoli campaign, in which (it has been rightly said) Australia and New Zealand came of age as nations. Yet, while always remembering and honouring Anzac prowess at Gallipoli, we should not forget that a large number of men from the United Kingdom also served there – including the Revd Henry Hall, who later started the commemoration of Gallipoli at Eltham – as well as a substantial French force. Nor should we forget that Australian and New Zealand troops later fought with equal valour on the Western Front and, like the Canadians, were particularly prominent in the final stages. The title of one of the most vivid of all first-hand accounts of that war, Alexander Aitken's *Gallipoli to the Somme: Recollections of a New Zealand Infantryman*, is enough to show that Gallipoli was only one of the battlegrounds on which Anzac forces won renown between 1915 and 1918, though it will always be the most distinctive.

What do I mean by 'nobler'? Among various definitions of the word 'noble' in the *Shorter Oxford Dictionary*, the applicable one is this: 'Having high moral qualities or ideals; of a great or lofty character; proceeding from, characteristic of, indicating or displaying, greatness of character or moral superiority.' I shall, therefore, be discussing which of the two world wars was waged, on Britain's part, in the more idealistic spirit and with the higher regard for moral values.

There is, I think, a broad consensus or conventional wisdom in Britain today to the effect that the First World War was one in which the country became involved for old-fashioned 'balance of power' reasons, that it was a singularly nasty and costly war, and that it served no good purpose; whereas the Second World War was a genuine crusade against evil, fought not only more intelligently but also more humanely, and that it may have succeeded, where the earlier war certainly failed, in making the world, or at any rate some parts of it, safe for democracy. Another notion that became fashionable in 1940, and has remained so ever since, is that the second war was, for Britain, a 'people's war', whereas in the first the people's true interests were not at stake, though their emotions were worked on to produce a mood of 'thoughtless patriotism' (as Dr Runcie put it in his lecture; see p. 47). A classic statement of this view, in a book which helped to establish it in the public mind, is the following passage from Francis Williams's *War by Revolution*, published in November 1940:

> This war is a revolutionary war. If it is fought as a national war for the victory of Britain and the established interests of Britain it will in the end be lost. If it is fought as a war of democratic revolution in Europe it can be won. Let no one doubt its revolutionary nature. This is not a struggle between national interests, a battle to decide the balance of power within an established and accepted order of world society. It is a civil war within Western Civilization and upon its issue depends the total shape of the future.

We can see there all the ingredients in what was to become a powerful myth: that Britain was not fighting a war in defence of its own vital interests, but a revolutionary war on behalf of democracy; that the idea of a balance of power was obsolete and discredited; and that the old international order based on nation-states would have to give way to something entirely new.

In postwar Britain nothing, perhaps, has done more to propagate and perpetuate an unfavourable view of the First World War than the musical *Oh What a Lovely War*, which was turned into a highly successful film. The message there is similar to that of Francis Williams's book, though with a more explicitly Marxist flavour; and it is conveyed to the beguiling accompaniment of First World War songs. The process of myth-making has been further assisted by a growing ignorance of history, affecting not only the general public but, more critically, the rulers of the country, in whom at least a modicum of historical knowledge used to be normal. (The extent to which politicians are now ignorant of the past is, surely, one of the most disturbing features of our time. When the state is run by people who know no history, it becomes like an individual without memory – but with this difference: that whereas everybody recognises personal amnesia as a terrible handicap, few seem to be aware that the same is true of collective or institutional amnesia.)

It may already be apparent that I regard the popular view of the First World War, and of Britain's role in it, as historically flawed. And it is probably no less apparent that I am sceptical of any attempt to describe the second as different in kind and morally superior. I shall, indeed, be arguing that such valid contrasts as can be drawn between the two wars tend to favour the first rather than the second; and that most of the contrasts now commonly drawn are not valid at all.

Let us consider, first, Britain's motivation for war in 1914 and 1939. On the earlier occasion, the Liberal Cabinet's decision to intervene was taken only after long and anxious deliberation. At the beginning of the crisis opinion in the country was on the whole far from bellicose, and a strong element in the Cabinet was anti-war. A few were anti-war on principle, in the sense that they believed Britain should in no circumstances become embroiled in a continental struggle. Some, on the other hand, were convinced that Britain could not afford to allow France to stand alone against Germany in the West. This was the view of the Conservative opposition, including most emphatically the Conservative press.

Between the pro- and anti-war groups in the Cabinet there was an important group of doubters, in which the key figure was Lloyd George. Despite a reputation for pacifism deriving from his stand against the Boer War, and due to a misreading of his attitude at the time, Lloyd George was never, in fact, a pacifist. During the comparatively recent Agadir crisis, in 1911, he had taken a tough line against what he saw as unacceptable German pretensions. Instinctively he sympathised with France, on grounds of cultural and democratic solidarity, and he was also inclined to support her on grounds of strategic realism. On 27 July 1914 he defended the Entente to C.P. Scott, saying, 'You know I am much more pro-French than you are'.

Yet in the same conversation he insisted that there could be no question of Britain's 'taking part in any war in the first instance'. Only a fortnight before he had spoken in very bland and dove-like terms at the Mansion House, where his hawkish Agadir speech had been made three years earlier. He was reluctant to believe that the crisis over Serbia need involve Britain in war, and for several days he remained of that opinion, while not joining those of his colleagues who were out-and-out neutralists. His doubts were resolved by the German invasion of Belgium, by the spectacle of Belgian resistance, and by the evidence that the British people were profoundly stirred. Later, Frances Stevenson wrote that his mind was made up from the first, 'that he knew we would have to go in', but that the invasion of Belgium provided 'a heaven-sent excuse'. This may be too simple, as well as too cynical, an explanation. What is certain is that his decision to support intervention was a further powerful factor in unifying the country.

Obviously British mass opinion at the time was more emotional and less complicated than his. All the same I would not dismiss it as 'thoughtless patriotism', or even as mere patriotism, thoughtless or otherwise. There was, certainly, an underlying fear of Germany, both reflected and fostered by certain newspapers, particularly those controlled by Lord Northcliffe, and by a large literature on the subject of invasion.

The German threat to British naval supremacy had been causing apprehension at the popular level, and not without reason. Of course there was some jingoistic feeling, despite the considerable disenchantment with jingoism that had set in during the later stages of the Boer War. Yet the spirit of the British people in 1914 was not so far removed from that of Edith Cavell's famous words. Most of them were, to be sure, fervently patriotic, but their patriotism did not exclude a wider and vaguer, but none the less potent, idealism. Having experienced the mood of 1939, I have little doubt that that of 1914 was nobler and more generous. (That of 1940 was very different, though still not necessarily better than the 1914 spirit, as I will try to explain).

In some ways the British may have been too idealistic in their attitude to the First World War. That may be a more pertinent criticism than the opposite one. If they had been as down-to-earth as the French, to whom the war was essentially a struggle for survival, they might afterwards have avoided the calamitous mistakes that made a further war inevitable. When Dr Runcie said in his lecture that the First World War did not produce the religious revival that some were looking for, he was clearly right in the formal and orthodox sense. But in another sense it seems to me that the British were inspired in that war by a Christian, or at any rate a sub-Christian, mystique. The themes of blood-sacrifice and atonement were much in evidence, but with a political twist. Britain was thought to be fighting not just to preserve its own freedom and position in the world, but to save as well the whole human race from war itself. Those who died in the conflict were, therefore, seen as sacramental victims, purging the world of one of its worst evils.

All this was a far cry from the much-reviled balance of power, for which, however, there was and is quite a lot to be said. So long as power remains the basic element in politics, both internally and internationally – and there is no immediate prospect of its ceasing to be – it is surely better for it to be balanced, since trouble tends to begin when it gets out of balance. Of course civilised people need an inspiring cause when they go to war, but they also need to keep their feet on the ground. It is dangerous for them to have a cause so exalted that they altogether lose sight of mundane realities.

If in 1914 the British erred on the side of excessive idealism, in 1939 they erred the other way. There was little of knight-errantry about the spirit in which they entered the Second World War. This was true, at any rate, of the UK British, though the people of the Dominions (as the self-governing nations of the British Commonwealth were still called) showed the same spirit that they had shown in 1914, despite their harsh experiences in the first war, and despite the greater independence they had since acquired. It is worth remarking that it was only by virtue of the Dominions' participation, and of the less voluntary participation of India, that the second war could be described, at the outset, as a world war at all. But for them, it would have been an almost purely European contest until December 1941, and quite restricted even as such until Germany attacked Russia in the summer of that year. (France, of course, had overseas territories as well, but they were less important and anyway not self-governing.)

The fate of Poland in 1939 evoked, in Britain, none of the popular emotion that the fate of Belgium in 1914 had aroused. Poland was another far-off Slav country, like Czechoslovakia, which became the *casus belli* only because, when Hitler tore up the Munich Agreement and occupied Prague in March 1939, even the British government of the day began to see that he was unappeasable and so gave a 'guarantee' to Poland. Until then, no consideration of honour or decency had inhibited its attempts to appease him. The guarantee did not, of course, deter him in September 1939, but it did bring about a situation in which Britain most reluctantly declared war on the Third Reich. Nothing, however, was done to help Poland while she was being overrun. There was no diversionary attack in the West, and a period of 'phoney war' ensued.

During this period British feelings *were* stirred by the sight of a small nation holding a mighty neighbour at bay, but the mighty neighbour was not Germany, and the small nation in question would, in fact, before long be fighting on Germany's side. Sympathy with Finland was natural enough, but the British government's plan to intervene on behalf of Finland against the Soviet Union was, in the circumstances, sheer insanity, even though combined with a plan to deny Swedish iron ore to Germany, which was more relevant though scarcely more realistic. In any case, Finnish resistance ended in mid-March, and a month later the phoney war came to an end when Hitler invaded Denmark and Norway.

The resulting Norwegian campaign had the by no means predictable effect of bringing Churchill to supreme power, and was swiftly followed by the full-scale German onslaught in the West, the Dunkirk evacuation, the fall of France, and the isolation of Britain. The mood of the country at this moment was certainly far nobler than it had been the year before. In the summer of 1940 there was a heady spirit of defiance and an exciting sense of national unity. Instead of the cowardice of the 1930s there was, at last, heroism in the air. All the same, we have to realise that 1940 was a time when some of our worst national vices became, for the moment, virtues. Our morale then was largely compounded of self-righteousness, insularity, xenophobia and ignorance. We were sustained by the illusory belief that we had been let down by our allies and were better off without them.

In fact, it was we who had let the French down by our failure to give them the moral and political support they deserved after the First World War, and by our slowness to rearm when faced with a revived Germany bent on revenge. In the Norwegian campaign we behaved outrageously to the Norwegians, as is painfully clear from François Kersaudy's account of the campaign. At Dunkirk we behaved very badly to the French, and then added insult to injury by fabricating the idea that the BEF had escaped in spite of them, whereas in truth its escape was made possible by their dogged defence of the perimeter. Nicholas Harman describes this propagandist British version of events at Dunkirk as 'the necessary myth', because it contributed to British morale at a time of desperate crisis. But a myth it certainly was.

As for being better off without allies, this was pure self-delusion. Strictly, the United Kingdom was not alone in 1940, because the Dominions continued to give vital support, and because Roosevelt decided that it was in the USA's interest to back British resistance by all means short of war. Even so, there was no way that Britain could have defeated Germany if Hitler had not obligingly defeated himself by a succession of mistakes: above all, by declaring war on the United States four days after Pearl Harbor.

Francis Williams's projection of Britain's mood in 1940, though woven into the subsequent mythology, is in fact wildly misleading. The suggestion that Britain's resolve to fight on was inspired by a crusading vision of democratic revolution throughout Europe is the stuff of fantasy. The left-wing idealism expressed by Williams doubtless found some popular echo in relation to British domestic politics, where opinion was turning drastically against the Conservatives, and where the Labour landslide of 1945 was already in the making. But insofar as it related to foreigners, the idealism was not widely shared. This has to be stressed, because the presumption that Britain's role in the Second World War was morally superior owes much to the moral inferiority of the enemy. Beyond question Hitler's regime was far worse than the Kaiser's; as Dr Runcie says, 'A war which closed down Belsen and Buchenwald was worth fighting.'

Indeed it was – but surely that is rather beside the point. Britain did not go to war with Hitler because he was a horrible racist tyrant, or maintain the struggle against him in order to bring salvation to continental Europe. In the Second World War, as in the first, Germany was challenged not because its regime was odious internally, but because it was a menace externally. Insofar as the instinct of self-preservation was tinged with idealism, it was, I suggest, noticeably more so in the first war than in the second, though the degree of evil against which we were fighting was in reverse proportion.

In comparing the motivation for British involvement in the two world wars, I have strayed some distance into the second, because it seemed only fair to bring the spirit of 1940, as well as that of 1939, into the reckoning. Either way, I do not think that the spirit of 1914 suffers from the comparison. Now I must turn to the way the two wars were actually fought by Britain, saying no more about the period between September 1939 and the summer of 1940, concerning which the less said the better.

One most significant difference is that in the first war recruitment for the British armed forces was voluntary for the first year, and to some extent voluntary until mid-1916, whereas in the next war there was outright conscription from the start. One should not be *too* starry-eyed about the early part of the first war. Patriotism and a spontaneous eagerness to serve were certainly prevalent, but not universal. Within the voluntary system there was no lack of moral blackmail, and among those who did not volunteer for the forces enthusiasm for the war was not always manifest.

I was struck, for instance, by an incident recorded in a book of First World War letters that I was reading the other day (*My Own Darling: Letters from Montie to Kitty Carlisle*, edited and published by their son, Christopher Carlisle). In July 1915 Montie sails in *Aquitania* from Liverpool to Lemnos, with the 8th Northumberland Fusiliers, to take part in the Gallipoli campaign; and on 6 July he writes to his wife: 'Fancy, 80 of the stokers deserted before we sailed and a guard with fixed bayonets had to be placed on the remainder.' One looks in vain for any reference to this incident in the official histories. Neither Sir Archibald Hurd nor Sir Julian Corbett mentions it, and who knows how many other such incidents have gone unrecorded?

Yet, when every cautionary discount has been made, it remains true that the early part of the first war was different in kind from the rest of that war, and from the whole of the second, because until 1916 the British were participating essentially as volunteers. In his marvellous history of Britain in the First World War, *The Myriad Faces of War*, Trevor Wilson writes:

Nothing revealed the British people's commitment to this war better than the way in which so many of the country's young men volunteered for military service. There was no inevitability about this. It is quite possible for people to proclaim the justice of their country's involvement in a war and yet not intend themselves to participate, either by risking their lives or by paying higher taxes. From the first day Britain's endorsement of the war was not of this order. Doubtless scarcely any of those who rushed to the recruiting stations divined what sort of a conflict they were in for. This is no reason for presuming that, had they known, they would have held back.

Of course there was some change of mood in the last two years of the war, when military service was no longer voluntary, and when the initial optimism had been tempered by the mounting toll of casualties, with so little – until the last few months – to show for all the effort and suffering. But just as one should not exaggerate the rapture of the early years, so one should not exaggerate the gloom and disillusionment that followed. Throughout the war, and to the very end, the morale of British troops was remarkably high. Wilfred Owen, the most eloquent voice of the later period, carried on fighting despite his pacifism, and did not entirely lose what Julian Grenfell, in the early period, had called 'joy of battle'. Moreover, there was a nobility in Owen's disgust which was, perhaps, characteristic of the first war, and somehow rather missing from the second.

Much of the odium directed against the first war is concentrated on the generals – particularly Haig – and on the apparently unjustifiable human cost of their offensives. In Haig's case, it is indeed hard to justify the prolongation of the Somme fighting beyond mid-September 1916, or that of Third Ypres through October and into November 1917. Yet it should always be borne in mind, when judging the actions of those who held responsibility in the first war, whether soldiers or civilians, that they were engaged in warfare on a scale, and of a character, never previously known, and wrestling with problems for which there were absolutely no precedents. Their successors in the second war had their example to learn from.

It should also not be forgotten that the first war ended in a comprehensive military victory for the Entente Powers, to which the British Army made a decisive contribution. Moreover, the Central Powers were defeated in four and a quarter years, despite the virtual elimination of Russia as an effective ally after the Brusilov offensive in 1916, and despite the late and limited participation of the United States.

A young artillery officer, later an outstanding figure in the academic world, may be quoted as a witness of the final stages of the war on the Western Front. In his *Memories* Maurice Bowra describes the battle on 8 August 1918 when the Canadians and Anzacs, for whom his battery was providing a moving barrage, attacked the German line near Villers Bretonneux:

This was one of the few days in my military life when I felt the terrifying fascination of battle. The sinister silence before zero-hour, the sudden, simultaneous, deafening start of the barrage, the emergence of the tanks and their accompanying infantry, the struggle, always successful, to take well-held positions, the decisive advance forward, all contributed to a wild exhilaration in which we conducted our duties with fits of laughter and uproarious jokes.

No sign there of any war-weariness or cynicism.

When we turn to Britain's martial performance in the Second World War there can be no doubt that the great and good period was from June 1940 to February 1941 – the period of the Battle of Britain and overwhelming victories over the Italians in North and East Africa. Of these exploits the Battle of Britain was, of course, by far the most important, because it was a trial of strength with the main enemy, Germany, and because it averted the threat of an invasion which, if successful, would have resulted in Britain's total defeat and conquest. The air victory, or draw in Britain's favour, over south-east England in the summer and early autumn of 1940 was itself made possible by a temporary victory within the RAF before the war, of the advocates of fighters over the bomber-orientated orthodoxy deriving from Trenchard, which in the nick of time enabled the fighters that saved the country to be produced. It must also be said that Hitler threw away his chance of achieving control of the sky over Britain in 1940, when he switched his bombers from their deadly and potentially decisive attacks on airfields to indiscriminate raids on London and other cities. From this fatal mistake the authors of later British air strategy failed to draw the appropriate lesson.

If the Battle of Britain had been lost, it is hard to imagine how the country could have been saved. No doubt the invaders would have suffered heavy losses in the Channel, but so would the Royal Navy, without air cover. In all probability a sufficient number of Germans would have got ashore, with tanks and guns, and what would there then have been to stop them? The BEF had escaped from France, but left most of its equipment behind. 'Dad's Army' was good for national morale and social cohesion, but hardly for resisting the Wehrmacht. (Incidentally, I am in the curious position of being able to use the nickname 'Dad's Army' literally, because my father was at the time parliamentary under-secretary at the War Office, and the Home Guard was one of his responsibilities.)

Mention of him brings to mind an experience which may help to illustrate the pitiful state of our land defences as we awaited the threatened invasion. One weekend during the school summer holidays that year I was staying with my parents at the house of a friend of theirs, Lady Milner, on the border between Kent and Sussex. Also staying there was the great American broadcaster, Ed Murrow. On the Saturday my father inspected units on the south coast, taking Murrow (and me) with him. My most vivid recollection of this outing is of the scene at Dungeness, where a long expanse of beach was defended by a company of infantry, a few coils of barbed wire and a single 75 mm gun. Murrow pretended to regard these defences as formidable, which obviously pleased and heartened the company commander. In retrospect, one can only shudder at the thought of what would have happened at Dungeness and any number of other places if the Germans had arrived.

March 1941 until November 1942 was a time of almost unrelieved disaster for British arms, in mainland Greece, Crete, the Western Desert and the Far East. But it was, nevertheless, a time when the war was transformed by the enforced involvement of the Soviet Union and the United States, and when the tide of war turned, thanks very largely to the efforts of those two new allies. The turning-point in the West was the Russian stand at Stalingrad, and the cutting-off of a German army there. The turning-point in the Pacific was marked by the battles of the Coral Sea and Midway, in which American aircraft carriers, providentially absent from Pearl Harbor when it was attacked, more than held their own against the Japanese.

If there had been no British victory by the end of 1942 Churchill's continued leadership would have been in serious doubt, despite the prestige he had justly earned in 1940. But after a fortnight of hard pounding at El Alamein, Montgomery defeated Rommel by sheer weight of manpower and *matériel*. (The Eighth Army's numerical preponderance over Rommel's mixed force of Germans and Italians, and its superiority in equipment and air support, were quite overwhelming). Alamein was swiftly followed by the Anglo-American landings on the African shore at the other end of the Mediterranean, which in turn led, in 1943, to the invasions of Sicily and mainland Italy. In these operations, and for the rest of the war in the West, the Americans were predominant partners.

They did not, however, get their way with the British about the date for landing in north-west Europe. Like the Russians, the Americans did not regard Italy as a proper Second Front, and surely they were right. Italy was a *secondary* front, where moreover the Germans had the advantage of much shorter communications and a terrain that favoured defence. Fewer Germans were deployed there in combat than were present in the Balkans merely as a precaution against Allied landings, which suggests that the net diversion of German troops from the Eastern Front, as a result of the Allied campaign in Italy, may have been almost negligible. Yet, such was the reluctance of the British to undertake a cross-Channel invasion, it was delayed until the summer of 1944. Apart, therefore, from the brief campaign in 1940, it was only for the last year of the war that the British army was engaged with the main enemy on a main front.

This has to be remembered when the British casualty figures for the two world wars are invidiously contrasted. It is indeed true that in the first the total British figure of war dead was about a million, whereas in the second the comparable figure was between a third and half of that number. But this disparity is hardly surprising in view of the British army's much heavier involvement in the First World War. Another consideration, often overlooked, is that advances in medicine between the two wars enabled many wounded men who would have died in the first to survive in the second. Nevertheless the *scale* of losses in battle was not always or necessarily lower in the later war. According to one estimate, at Alamein the proportion of casualties among men actually engaged was as heavy as on the Somme. But Alamein was not only a much smaller battle, it also lasted a much shorter time. The relative economy of British soldiers' lives that was undeniably achieved in the second war was achieved, above all, by economy of fighting.

It is often said that Churchill, remembering the carnage of Gallipoli, the Somme and other First World War battles, was determined at all costs to avoid any repetition of it. This is not the whole truth, nor even the larger part of the truth. In some ways there was indeed more humanity in the second war than in the first: for instance, in the attitude to conscientious objectors, and in the treatment of those who broke down under the stress of battle. Moreover, Churchill certainly did want to avoid the squandering of British lives: so did Montgomery and other commanders with unpleasant memories of the Western Front. Yet this was not the principal reason – at any rate so far as Churchill was concerned – for hesitation about sending British troops across the Channel to grapple with the main German forces. The principal reason, sad to say, was that he had lost confidence in the fighting spirit of the British Army.

When, in February 1942, the Japanese were poised to attack Singapore, Churchill ordered the local commander, General Arthur Percival, to turn the city into a citadel and fight 'to the death', since Britain's 'whole fighting reputation' and 'the honour of the British Empire' were at stake. Nevertheless, Percival and the garrison of 100,000 surrendered in a week. Four months later, in Cyrenaica, 35,000 men surrendered at Tobruk after only 24 hours, whereas at about the same time a much smaller force of Fighting French held out for ten days at Bir Hacheim – an exploit that won Rommel's warm admiration. Faced with Singapore and Tobruk, Churchill was plunged into gloom. 'I cannot get over Singapore', he told his doctor, Lord Moran. And on another occasion, also to Moran, he said: 'I am ashamed. I cannot understand why Tobruk gave in. More than 30,000 of our men put up their hands. If they won't fight . . .'. He did not complete the sentence, but our imaginations can complete it for him.

In his deep anxiety about how British troops would perform against an insufficiently weakened Wehrmacht, he was susceptible to the siren voice of one who believed that the war could be won without a major struggle on land. Sir Charles Portal, Chief of Air Staff, had been Trenchard's favourite disciple and, like his master, was convinced of the war-winning capacity of bombing. He was the most dangerous sort of fanatic – the sort that appears reasonable. Portal managed to escape the odium in which 'Bomber' Harris was later held, because his manner was more artful and less abrasive. Yet Harris was his creature, appointed by him to carry out his policy. The policy was, quite simply, to defeat Germany by the terror bombing of German cities.

Churchill at first reacted to the idea with repugnance and scepticism. He did not at all like the thought of murdering women and children, and was anyway doubtful that it would work. But gradually Portal wore him down, and at length he agreed to a course of action which gravely blemished his own and the country's good name, without succeeding in its purpose. In February 1942 a directive was sent to Bomber Command that bombing should in future be focused 'on the morale of the enemy civil population', and in May the first thousand-bomber raid was carried out, against Cologne. Terror bombing remained the explicit prime activity of the RAF until 1944 when, with difficulty, a new priority was asserted, that of attacking road and rail communications in northern France in preparation for D-Day. During the long period of indiscriminate bombing hundreds of thousands of Germans were killed and many more mutilated, while whole cities were laid waste. Yet war production, skilfully redeployed, continued at a high level, and above all the morale of the people was not broken.

Nearly three centuries earlier Oliver Cromwell had set out to subdue Ireland by the wholesale massacre of civilians – a policy regarded as brutal even by the standards of his time. But at least it worked. The same policy revived by a British government in a supposedly more civilised age, and on a much larger scale, did not even have that justification.

Whatever the horrors of the First World War, it was a conflict between fighting men. In the second, for two years the British war machine was principally directed not against the armed forces of the enemy, but against unarmed civilians. Which was the nobler method of conducting a war? The question hardly needs to be asked.

Furthermore, a policy intended to spare British lives was, in fact, extremely wasteful of the lives of British airmen, who experienced quite as much fear as they inflicted, and who suffered very heavy losses. They should not be blamed for the beastly and dangerous work they were ordered to do. John Terraine makes an interesting comment on RAF casualties, particularly among bomber aircrew, in his history of the RAF in Europe during the Second World War (*The Right of the Line*):

> The aircrew total, 55,573, has a special significance; in the First World War the officer losses of the British Empire included 38,834 killed, and this slaughter of the nation's *élite* was widely regarded as the most tragic and damaging aspect of that war. It was to avoid such a thing ever happening again that Britain turned her back on a Continental policy, and looked to the Air Force rather than the Army for salvation. Yet . . . by and large RAF aircrew were exactly the same type of men as the officers of 1914–18; it is salutary to see how the pursuit of a 'cheaper' policy brought in its train only a much higher cost.

One statistic given by Terraine underlines the importance of defining 'British' in a broad, Commonwealth, sense when considering both world wars, and more especially the composition of the RAF in the second. Of RAF pilots in that war, 46 per cent came from the so-called white Dominions. Yet the combined populations of Canada, Australia, New Zealand and (white) South Africa amounted, at the time, to less than half that of the United Kingdom. Clearly, the Dominions' contribution to what Terraine sees as Britain's fighting *élite* in the Second World War was out of all proportion to their numbers.

Finally, what of the outcome of the two wars? In the first Britain's immediate *casus belli* was Belgium, and at the end of the war Belgium's freedom was fully restored. The same could hardly be said of Poland's in 1945. Poland and the whole of eastern Europe paid the price of the Anglo-American delay in invading the continent from the west, which was due, as we have seen, to British reluctance. In 1918 Britain emerged from the war not only independent and secure, but still a superpower. In 1945 she was independent, at any rate politically, and to that extent victorious; but in other respects she was a net loser, while superpower status was passing, as de Tocqueville long ago predicted, to Russia and America.

The First World War became, in a sense, more of a democratic crusade as time went on, mainly because Tsarist Russia fell out and the United States came in. The democratic doctrine of self-determination was the ideology of the victorious Allies in 1918, though of course their degree of commitment to it, and the ways they chose to interpret it, varied. The credentials of the Second World War as a democratic crusade were fatally flawed from the moment Stalin's Russia became a belligerent; and at the end of the war half of Europe merely exchanged one form of totalitarian dictatorship for another.

It might be thought that post-1945 would at least compare favourably with post-1918 in respect of the treatment of Germany. But does it, really? The war guilt clause of the Versailles Treaty, assigning guilt for the war to the entire German nation, was certainly an injustice and an absurdity. It was altogether better to confine guilt to the nation's leaders, more especially when they were Nazis, though the Nuremberg trials were hardly models of justice, granted Soviet representation on the tribunal. The economic provisions of Versailles were unrealistic rather than unjust, but Keynes's attack on them went much too far, challenging the whole moral basis of the treaty. In particular, he showed no understanding of France's need for reparations and security. His celebrated tract (*The Economic Consequences of the Peace*) was tendentious in argument and mischievous in effect. Nevertheless, it is true that Germany's economic treatment by the West was on the whole more enlightened after the second war.

Politically, the difference is very much the other way. After the first war the principle of self-determination was scrupulously applied to the defeated enemy. Germany's territory was left virtually intact; apart from Alsace-Lorraine, western Poland, Danzig, and (temporarily) the Saar, she remained the united nation that Bismarck had forged. In 1945 she was partitioned, and in addition lost nearly a quarter of her pre-1938 territory, including East Prussia. The severity of Germany's political treatment after 1945 was, of course, largely due to the Russians, who in 1918 had been the victims of a truly Carthaginian peace at Germany's hands. But the British have a substantial share of responsibility, through their opposition to a Second Front in 1943.

As for the greater durability of peace after the second war, this has resulted from two factors for which Britain can claim no specific credit: the end of American isolationism and the Cold War. Hot war has so far been avoided, not because the democratic revolution that Francis Williams looked for has occurred, but because – quite contrary to his desire – a balance of power has once again been established.

Did the Second World War promote a social revolution inside Britain? The victory of the Labour Party in 1945 was seen by many at the time as a revolutionary event, but hardly seems so in retrospect. One reason for it may have been that voters wanted to show their displeasure with the party which had been dominant throughout the interwar period and had got the country into another major war. A similar revulsion may help to explain the Conservative landslide in 1918 (for that was what the Coalition victory really was). The truth, surely, is that both world wars accelerated social change, but that neither caused a social revolution. The 1945 Labour government disappointed fewer hopes than the Lloyd George coalition, mainly because it was homogeneously committed to reform. Yet it is probably fair to say that the emancipation of women which resulted from the first war was more nearly revolutionary than any social change attributable to the second.

After the first war there was nobility in the British arrangements to commemorate the dead. The Imperial War Graves Commission did its work with sensitivity and imagination. (Much of the imagination was supplied by Kipling, who among other things devised the beautiful epitaph for the unidentifiable, 'A Soldier of the Great War, Known unto God' – his own son having disappeared without trace at the Battle of Loos.) The Unknown Warrior was another imaginative concept: a hero suitable for the age of the common man. And the Armistice Day cult – though in Britain between the wars it took the form, regrettably, of celebrating a once-for-all sacrifice, rather than of reminding people of the permanent need for sacrifice to avert danger – had nevertheless a beauty and dignity all its own.

After 1945 the process of commemoration was in no way refined or improved. On the contrary, a bad decision was taken to transfer the day of remembrance from 11 November to the nearest Sunday. The whole point of the two minutes' silence was that it normally interrupted the ordinary business of life *on a weekday*, so achieving a profoundly dramatic effect. To have it at 11 a.m. on a Sunday was to lose the effect and miss the point.

In conclusion, I must return to the contrast so persistently drawn between the two wars: that the second, unlike the first, was a genuine expression of popular feeling, and (as one might put it) of Rousseau's 'general will'. A.J.P. Taylor writes of the second war in his volume in the *Oxford History of England*: 'This was a people's war. . . . They themselves wanted to win.' The clear implication is that in the first the people were not similarly involved. Even if this were true, it would not necessarily mean that the second was nobler than its predecessor. In 1901 Winston Churchill had said with baleful prescience: 'Democracy is more vindictive than cabinets. The wars of peoples will be more terrible than the wars of kings.'

But in fact it is not true. Though Britain certainly had a more democratic franchise in 1939 than in 1914, the decision to go to war was no more democratic on the later occasion than on the earlier. The people had nothing whatever to do with the guarantee to Poland which provided the *casus belli*, and even Parliament, which was incidentally nearing the end of its statutory term, did no more than ratify a decision already taken by the government.

The British people were no less committed to the first war than to the second; in some ways, as I have tried to indicate, they were more so. Moreover, they felt the impact of war no less deeply. Even among the civilian population of the United Kingdom – which in one sense, admittedly, had a more direct involvement in the second, through exposure to bombing on a much larger scale – the toll of death and suffering caused by the Blitz is more than balanced by the heavier toll of bereavement afflicting the home front in the first war.

All in all I am convinced, therefore, that the motivation, conduct and achievement of Britain, whether as government or people, were nobler in the First World War than in the second, and that the conventional wisdom favouring the opposite view cries out to be re-examined. It is not only grossly unfair to the past but also, I believe, unhealthy for the present and misleading for the future.

SIX

FOR WANT OF CRITICS . . .
THE TRAGEDY OF GALLIPOLI

Robert O'Neill

26 April 1990

In Homage to the Participants

The Gallipoli campaign has been part of my consciousness since the age of five. I learned from witnessing my first Anzac Day ceremony, in my first year in primary school, some two months after the fall of Singapore, that it commemorated an event in Australian history like no other. In most of the forty-eight years since then I have attended commemorative services and absorbed both the Anzac legend and the Anzac facts which have been such dominant aspects of Australia's political and social history in the twentieth century.

Nobody who has taken part in one of the hundreds of dawn services that are held in Australia and New Zealand on 25 April each year is ever likely to forget their atmosphere of dedication. The faces of those taking part show a keen determination to remember and honour those who, in that same chilly darkness, began clambering over the sides of their transports into the small craft waiting to take them into their baptism of fire. The dawn services are a mark of respect for free men who willingly accepted huge risks in order to thwart what they saw as alien hegemonism, threatening Britain and therefore both Australia and New Zealand. The moral dilemma involved in invading a country remote from the theatre of war, which in the preceding months had done Britain little direct harm other than to defend itself against naval attack, has only recently found acknowledgement.

Anzac Day services and parades are expressions both of compassion for those who died and pride in the military reputation that they helped to found. The services also have a wider significance in recognising the birth of a sense of national pride that has kept 25 April for seventy-five years the most poignant day of the year for Australians and New Zealanders. The more radical of antipodean nationalists today repudiate the Gallipoli experience as an expression of national worth, seeing it rather as a piece of deplorable imperial subservience and bellicism. But to anyone with a sense of history and an understanding of how times change, Gallipoli will continue to be seen as an important verifier of the claims of Australia and New Zealand to be regarded as significant international actors. It is also a key source of the confidence which is essential if people are to feel that they are an independent nation.

The campaign cost the lives of 7,594 Australians and 2,431 New Zealanders. Another 18,500 Australians and 5,140 New Zealanders were wounded. For young countries of small populations these were terrible sacrifices of the coming generation. Few Australian or New Zealand families were without cause to grieve at personal loss. It is no wonder that Anzac Day became such a sacred act of remembrance in both countries

Of course it is a day to remember not only for Australians and New Zealanders. The regular attendance of the Austrian, German and Turkish ambassadors at the 11 a.m. service at the Australian War Memorial in Canberra showed that they well understood the significance of 25 April. After a service in the mid-1970s the newly arrived Austrian ambassador remarked to me that he found the seating arrangements notable. He had been placed, as was the custom, together with his German and Turkish colleagues, at one side of the seating for the diplomatic corps. He observed with a broad smile of satisfaction: 'In the course of a long diplomatic career I have had to attend many war commemoration services but as I looked at the three of us sitting here I thought this one is unique – it commemorates the only occasion on which we won.'

And so they did, and for very good reasons, not least of which were that they fought well and worked effectively together. In a campaign of extreme difficulty for all who took part, the Turkish infantryman distinguished himself not only by his bravery and sense of devotion to his comrades when under enormous pressure, but also by his humanity and evident regard for his enemy. Early fears about Turkish cruelty to prisoners and the wounded, and the use of dum-dum bullets, proved to be largely unfounded. Soon after the landings, Major Guy Dawnay, of General Sir Ian Hamilton's staff, wrote to his wife: '(The Turks) are treating our wounded splendidly! So believe no other stories you may hear.'[1]

The Turkish soldier, or Johnny Turk as his foes called him, was well served by his own leaders including the then Lieutenant Colonel Mustafa Kemal, better known to us as Atatürk, who at 10 a.m. on 25 April personally blocked that very promising Australian foray led by Captain Tulloch which reached 2,000 yards inland, across the shoulder of Battleship Hill and within sight of the straits. That thrust, made in the first six hours of the landing, penetrated twice as far as the deepest advance made on the Anzac front during the whole subsequent operation. It was to be the first of many that Kemal and his men were to contain.

The Turkish soldier was also fortunate in his German leaders and advisers, a band of some two hundred officers under the doughty Otto Liman von Sanders. By his own admission one of the oldest division commanders in the German Army, von Liman had not been intended for great heights in his own service when he was nominated on 15 June 1913 to lead the new German military mission to Turkey. In many ways he was a curious choice: perhaps it was the oriental flavour of his name which led to his selection. If so, someone had blundered because he was probably of Jewish descent. The 'Sanders' part of his name he assumed only with his ennobling, the granting of the right to use the prefix 'von' before his name. The Kaiser honoured him along with many others on the 25th anniversary of his ascent to the throne, a month after Liman's appointment in Turkey. Liman intended thereby to commemorate his wife, Amelia von Sanders, who had died in 1906. He is properly referred to as General von Liman. It is formally correct to call him, on first use of his name, General Liman von Sanders. The practice of many British historians of referring to him as General von Sanders, as if Liman was his given name, is wrong.

Perhaps in sending him to Constantinople the German General Staff was simply ridding itself of a tiresome senior officer without being too brutal to his self-esteem. A younger colleague, General Hans von Seeckt, who served as Chief of Staff in the Turkish General Headquarters in 1917–18, wrote of Liman's selection:

> The choice of the Chief of the Military Mission could scarcely have fallen more unfortunately. Found in Germany unsuitable for the command of an Army Corps, he was supposed to take over the rebuilding of the whole Turkish Army. One simply could not demonstrate indifference in worse terms: it was an admission that we had not understood the principle that, for the representation abroad of a strong nation, only the best would suffice. General von Liman was well enough known in the German Army to deter the best from serving under him. To him went the unsuspecting, the enthusiasts, the adventurers or those who were tempted by higher pay.[2]

Viewed in the light of Liman's performance in command of the Fifth Turkish Army, the formation defending the Dardanelles in 1915, these seem to be ungenerous comments. He made an early error in thinking that Besika Bay, on the southern shore, was the most likely place for a British landing. The forces he stationed on the peninsula were held too far back to frustrate a landing at its outset, but he wanted to keep them concentrated on the best axes for rapid movement. He was firmly of the opinion that an attempt to invade would be made and stirred up a whirlwind of controversy with War Minister Enver and those of his subordinates who in early 1915 discounted this possibility. Difficult, vain man that Liman undoubtedly was, he met the challenges of the campaign, and faced down his many armchair critics in Constantinople and Germany when enemy pressure was at its most intense.

He had his hour of glory in repelling the great offensive at Anzac and Suvla in August. Within hours of its launching he had deduced British aims precisely and marshalled his none too numerous forces quickly and at the right places. He ordered counterattacks rapidly and unerringly, going forward himself to observe that to be made at Suvla. Would that his rival, Hamilton, had emulated his action in dismissing the local commander, Feizi Pasha, for inactivity. Handing the sector over to Kemal, Liman had the satisfaction of seeing the 6,000 men that he could assemble for this one desperate thrust pour over the ridge of Tekke Tepe and strike the British infantry precisely at their most vulnerable phase, clambering up the steepest part of the slope, exhausted and confused. That success put paid to British hopes for a successful outcome to the campaign.

The great Suvla offensive was brought to nought at dawn on 9 August. Kemal, returning exhausted to the heights of the main ridge near Chunuk Bair late that evening, brought off a superb feat of front line leadership to remove the final threat to his position. Heartening his six remaining battalions that night he organised a counterattack to break the epic British and New Zealand drive for the crest. At 4.30 next morning he led the first assault line into battle, signalling direction with his whip. A few minutes later, when light had strengthened, that last band of Turkish reserves would have been swept off the forward slopes by naval gunfire. The New Zealand machine gunners took terrible toll of them as they advanced silently, with no fire support, holding their own fire until they were on their foes. Their determination and Kemal's leadership carried them through to success. The Turkish hold on the crest was thereafter never to be challenged.

We know the story well from our own side. It is well to think about it from that of the Turks if justice is to be done Kemal and his chief, von Liman. The old German may not have been one of his country's best officers but he had what it took when the chips were down. It is hard to believe that his qualities were not known to those who selected him for the position. For all his crustiness and obstinacy in dealing with Berlin and his ambassador in Constantinople, Liman served Turkey and Germany well as a senior commander and adviser in time of crisis. It is also only fair, however, to let the final word rest with Seeckt, who knew him well and showed by his own record that he also had what it took to exercise high command:

It should not be disavowed that in stubborn repulse of the stubborn attack he fulfilled what was required of him, but in holding fast just as stubbornly to preconceived ideas he let the real victory slip through his fingers. His incapacity not only to lead military masses but also to nurture them, and his pathological mistrust of any expert German assistance provided to him let the Turkish Army emerge from the Dardanelles campaign victorious but in ruins.[3]

It was not only the British survivors who were exhausted by the struggle for Gallipoli. We remember the Turks and their Austro-Hungarian and German allies today, the former fighting in defence of their own native soil against the aggression which nobody can tolerate if they value freedom. But thinking of them also reminds us of a great disparity in the historiography of the Gallipoli campaign. There are hundreds of volumes on the British and Anzac sides but only a handful covering the Turkish and German experience. With a few rare exceptions such as the memoirs of von Liman and General Kannengiesser, one of his subordinates, or the studies of Professor Ulrich Trumpener, they remain masked by the screen of a foreign language. If there is a task worth doing for those who want to keep alive the memory of this campaign it is surely to find ways of bringing the existing Turkish and German literature on the Gallipoli campaign to the reader of the new global language, English, and of commissioning new historical works by scholars of various nationalities which draw on Turkish and German sources.

Most importantly the British role in the campaign should be acknowledged, and by British I mean United Kingdom as distinct from imperial. It is easy to forget how vast Britain's role was. The national importance of the Gallipoli campaign to Australians and New Zealanders is such that there one is aware only of a sideshow down at Cape Helles. Perhaps the Anzac public relations machine has also done its work internationally all too well, so that the world is more aware of the Australian and New Zealand role than of the United Kingdom's own part. If the role of the United Kingdom does not always receive its due share of attention, that of the Royal Navy has even less justice done to it, severely underplayed by comparison with that accorded to the forces ashore, to the infantry perched high up on the cliffs and ridges, clinging on desperately despite a fierce enemy, crumbling soil, constant thirst, malnutrition, logistic shortages of all kinds and alternately roasting and freezing temperatures. But it was initially wholly a naval operation and, apart from occasional withdrawals, the Navy sustained and supported the Army throughout eight long months.

We should also remember the part played by the 29th Indian Brigade, particularly the 1st/6th Gurkhas on Chunuk Bair on 8 and 9 August.

As an Australian I am delighted that, through the auspices of the Gallipoli Memorial Lecture Trust, the United Kingdom is marking and keeping alive the memory of a campaign of rare significance, conceived, mounted and directed from this very city, in whose operations 119,696 men in British and Indian uniforms became casualties, including over 28,000 dead.

One hopes particularly in these days of European integration that there might be some counterpart to these commemorative efforts in France. The French part in the campaign was notable and bloody, if brief. It is understandable, however, that an operation which cost a mere 47,000 casualties, including 10,000 dead, in a war in which France lost 1.3 million in dead alone, will play only a small part in that nation's thinking on war and its impact. It is also appropriate particularly in the wake of recent relaxations in East–West tensions to recall the Russians who fell in the appalling winter campaign against Turkey in the Caucasus and those manning the cruiser *Askold*, a veteran of the Russo-Japanese War, which had daringly outrun the Japanese navy to escape from Port Arthur to Shanghai. They represented the great ally on the Eastern Front which stood to gain so much had the operation been successful. As General Hans Kannengiesser, who commanded a Turkish division on the peninsula, observed in his study of the campaign: 'Seldom have so many countries of the world, races, and nations sent their representatives to so small a place with the praiseworthy intention of killing one another.'[4]

In toto nearly one million men fought in the campaign, and the largest contingent of all was that of the Turks, some 500,000. According to official Turkish figures, 86,000 were killed and 165,000 wounded, but these almost certainly are a severe understatement. Of the Allied half million over 250,000 became casualties, including over 47,000 dead. Of the million men who fought at the Dardanelles, about one in seven died and a further one in three were casualties.

When one climbs the ridge of Chunuk Bair and surveys the tiny battlefields on the peninsula it is astounding to realise that so much intense activity was concentrated in such tiny areas. The British area at Helles was some three miles deep and two wide. The Anzac position was some two miles from north to south and much of it was half a mile or less in depth. One can walk the perimeter in a few hours. It is good to know that the Turkish government gave the seventy-fifth anniversary of the landings such prominent commemoration, and that ever since 1919, and particularly in recent years, it has been extremely cooperative with those who wish the battlefield to be marked more comprehensibly for visitors from home and abroad.

It is ironic that we should know the campaign by the name Gallipoli, which derives from the Greek for 'nice town'. As the Turks seem to have been content to adapt that name only slightly, to 'Gelibolu', they will doubtless forgive us, even if the Greeks think we choose strange words to describe a peculiarly horrible battlefield. The Turkish name for the campaign as a whole, Canakkale, corresponds to our reference to it as the Dardanelles. The Turks call that same waterway the Straits of Canakkale after the major fortress and administrative centre on the southern shore. To the Turkish defenders, Canakkale was central to their concerns, and this is why Liman worried so much about a landing at Besika Bay. If they held Canakkale they could supply the peninsula and keep the straits closed. If they lost it, their flank was turned.

The British invaders for their part focused their attention on the northern side because it was there that they imagined their road to Constantinople to begin. It is a moot point as to whether a greater Allied effort on the southern side would not have paid decisive dividends. The country was not easy and strong Turkish forces were concentrated in that sector, but they were led with nothing like the skill and ferocity of Kemal, and the initial French gains were impressive. But that possibility is simply one of the many 'ifs' of the campaign.

The Campaign's Significance for the Conduct of War

Infantry Combat

In thinking about its tactical impact one is inclined to wonder whether there is anything special to be said that could not be said about any of the opening campaigns of a major war. Troops on both sides were initially inexperienced and leaders had to learn to handle their responsibilities as they went. Soldiers had to learn that war is a twenty-four hours a day business, and come to terms with the fact that while on operations there is little real rest and there are no diversions except the boredom of inactivity. Aged and inadequate leaders chosen by the criteria of peacetime service had to be weeded out. They also had to learn prudence on the modern battlefield dominated by the machine gun. Will power, as General Fuller once observed in commenting upon French élan, does not make one bulletproof. All these things were learned smartly in the opening weeks, but they are so *sui generis* that they have to be learned anew in any war.

On Gallipoli there were the special arts of close-quarter trench warfare to be acquired, with front lines 20 yards apart and less, and the enemy in easy earshot or grenade and message tossing range. Senior commanders thought it a splendid idea for the front line troops to throw messages to the Turks promising good treatment if they surrendered. The troops themselves knew the idea was crazy but they complied. On one occasion, at Quinn's

Post, the reply came back squarely: 'You think there are no true Turks left. But there are Turks, and Turks' sons!'[5]

Communication also took place for other purposes. In November at Quinn's the Turks threw over a handsome cigarette case, inscribed in Turkish soldiers' French: 'Take, with pleasure. To our heroic enemy.'[6]

But the proximity of the trenches meant that life on both sides went on under constant threat of the bombs which could easily be tossed from one line to another and of the huge mines which patient sappers placed in tunnels beneath the feet of their enemies. Listening and counter-mining were the best defences against the latter. Men soon learned to fall on an incoming bomb with a full sandbag to smother its explosion, except those daredevils who caught and threw them back.

Both sides had to improvise, making devices such as periscopes so that they could fire without exposing heads above the parapet, and home-made bombs cased in ration tins to supplement the meagre supply of ordnance coming through from Alexandria or Constantinople. The life of a periscope soon became a matter of seconds as marksmanship improved to a phenomenal level, and the snipers who constantly covered the battlefield had to resort to the use of tiny, protected loopholes in sandbag fortifications built at night. Had mortars been widely available, they could have turned the course of the campaign, but at that point in the war Britain had only a handful of Japanese weapons, whose ammunition stock was soon exhausted, and the rather ineffective bomb thrower invented by Mr Garland of the Cairo arsenal.

The Turks throughout the campaign lacked proper mortars. At least they were able to build cover over their trenches for protection, a facility that their enemies were unable through lack of resources to emulate. Had the Turks been well supplied with either mortars or howitzers they could have driven the invaders out of their precarious holds in a short space of time. Such support did not become available, however, until Bulgaria entered the war. The failure of the British August offensives having helped King Ferdinand to see on which side of the bread the butter then lay, he threw his lot in with that of the Germans and Austrians and opened the rail link through Turkey. The timing of the British evacuation of the peninsula was particularly fortunate from this perspective.

Every war is replete with problems of transition in tactical methods, whose solutions sadly are dearly bought by those unfortunate enough to have to face them for the first time. In the case of the Gallipoli campaign, these problems were severe. Not only did men have to learn to cope with an intensity of automatic fire they had not faced before, the invaders also had to coordinate gunnery support from warships with which they lacked direct communication against targets they could not see. They had to fight on tiny, often steeply sloping and sometimes precipitous battlefields, overlooked by the enemy.

They had to live under appalling conditions of monotonous, vitamin deficient food, primitive sanitation made worse by the crowding of the positions, the stench reinforced by the odour of the corpses decaying in front of their trenches, plagued by dysentery, enteric fever and lice, and with only rudimentary treatment for the wounded until they could be moved to hospital ships. They received little mail and news, and as a result were prey to rumours sweeping the trenches, particularly to ones which lifted their hopes such as that an Italian army of 100,000 or a Russian of 50,000 was about to land. Perhaps the worst problem of all was that of ever present thirst. What none of the operation's originators ever thought of was that their army would be trapped for months on a desert shore, with its ultimate source of water, the heaviest commodity that men must have in bulk to survive, several hundred miles away in Egypt and Malta. Wells provided some supply but in summer they dried. Men in the high forward posts often received only one water bottle per day, which had to meet all needs. The Turks, by contrast, were well supplied with water from springs and wells, although they had to endure all the other hardships.

The Art of Command and Control

One problem of tactical operations that was not solved at the Dardanelles was that of command and control. Many will have seen Peter Weir's splendid film *Gallipoli*, and its horrifying demonstration of the consequences of a failure to synchronise watches. A fateful seven minutes elapsed between the cessation of the artillery fire on to the Turkish trenches at 4.23 a.m. on 7 August and the moment when the first line of the 8th Light Horse had to climb the walls of their trenches on the pegs they had hammered in for that purpose and spring out for the desperate 50-yard dash to the Turkish line. The Turks, badly battered by the barrage, had just enough time to recover their wits, take up fire positions, assemble relief personnel, organise the ammunition and take careful aim at the Australian trenches to cut down the assault that was so obviously about to be made. Those seven minutes were sufficient for them to make absolutely certain that a nearly impossible task was absolutely impossible.

This episode is one of those few in which the screen understates reality, for there were not three but four successive charges by the light-horse men in the following forty-five minutes. The last was triggered by a misunderstanding while the local commanders were debating whether or not the operation should be abandoned after the third line had been shot down. Nearly half of those who made up the four waves of attack were killed and another quarter were wounded. As Weir showed and Bean, the

Australian war historian, wrote, the last sight anyone had of Private Wilfred Harper was of him 'running forward like a schoolboy in a foot-race, with all the speed that he could compass'.[7] His elder brother Gresley, a Western Australian barrister, also a private, died in almost the same instant.

Coordination of fire support for the infantry was a major problem throughout the campaign. Not much artillery could be landed and it had to be sited near the beaches, hundreds of feet below the front trenches, facing the gunners with formidable crest clearance problems. For telling bombardments, naval gunfire was also needed, but ship to shore communications for target identification and correction of the fall of shot were meagre. The flatness of the trajectories of the naval guns made observation all the more vital when operations were undertaken close to the ridgetops. It is still not certain what caused the disaster which befell Major Allanson and his mixed force of Gurkhas, Warwicks and South Lancashires immediately after they had driven the Turks off the crest of Chunuk Bair on 9 August and could gaze down on the straits. But it is certain that they were shelled from their own side and as a result had to cease their pursuit of the Turks down the far slope of the hill. The Turks were then able, with a great effort, to counter-attack successfully. Whether the shells came, as Allanson thought, from one of the ships or, as Bean and Rhodes James are inclined to think, from a shore battery, is immaterial to the point that the command and control system was hopelessly inadequate for operations of such complexity. These problems were never really rectified on Gallipoli but they set soldiers thinking about them, both to improve on the existing radio and telephone systems and to design better procedures for the preparation of orders and the control of fire support by forward observers. Thirty years later operations of comparable complexity to the assault on Chunuk Bair were being undertaken in the Mediterranean and the Pacific with high confidence.

The Technique of Amphibious Operations

Perhaps the most important tactical lessons to come from the Gallipoli campaign were those relating to amphibious warfare. This extremely complex art, often shown to be sadly deficient in earlier British operations such as those at Constantinople itself in 1807 and Walcheren in 1809, can hardly be regarded as having been mastered by Britain and her Allies in 1915. The landings were marred by serious errors in navigation. The landing craft themselves were poorly suited for the task, being capable only of loading men, or what a man could lift, over their sides. It was difficult for troops to climb into their landing craft. Ships carrying supplies had to be unloaded into lighters. Piers had to be built before supplies could be brought ashore in any quantity. Command and control techniques were lamentable for coping with the problems of two services, army and navy, working together. There was no real understanding of how to cope with the most vulnerable phase of a landing – the moment when the troops hit the beach and have to be reorganised for the assault inland. The result was chaos and confusion among those who raced across the sand into the cover of scrub or cliffs and death for those who delayed while looking for the others of their section or platoon. The above mentioned problems of fire-control were a further complication for the landings.

The challenge of offensive amphibious operations was taken up by the United States Marine Corps immediately after the First World War. As early as 1913, Major Ellis had suggested that the future of the Marine Corps would lie not in base defence as in the 1880s and '90s but in the amphibious attack role, seizing Japanese bases across the Pacific in the event of a major US–Japanese war. This idea was taken up with a will and developed by General Lejeune, the Marine Corps Commanding General, in the early 1920s. The defensive Advanced Base Force became the offensive Expeditionary Force. Landing exercises were conducted and years of doctrinal development followed. Until the development of specialised landing craft with bow ramps or doors, the whole enterprise remained essentially one of theory.

By great good fortune this whole process came to fruition in 1941 with the successful testing of the Higgins bow ramp landing craft, the development of a tank lighter derived from the Higgins craft and the production of the first 200 Amtracs, or amphibious tractors, tracked vehicles which could swim to the beach and then drive on inland without pause. It would be interesting to know how closely the US Marine Corps studied and benefited from the Gallipoli operations. The official history of the Corps has little to say on the subject, but it is difficult to believe that the biggest amphibious operation to that date was not the subject of close analysis by American specialists, and also by the Japanese, who were developing their amphibious capabilities in the 1920s and '30s.

Sadly Britain did little in the interwar years to build on the experience so dearly bought by her own forces in 1915, but the outbreak of the Second World War transformed that situation. After the evacuation from Dunkirk, Churchill's mind turned to the problems of landing a force to liberate the European continent: his Dardanelles experience stood him in good stead. Combined Operations Command was established in 1940 and Churchill pressed for the development of the ships and landing craft needed to put a huge army back into a strongly defended Europe. There soon followed the development of the Landing Ship Tank, or LST (some of whose passengers were to claim that these initials stood for large, slow target); the smaller

LCT; and the assault and mechanised landing craft. Without amphibious operations the Second World War could not have been won, and without the experience of thousands of British naval and army personnel in the Dardanelles landings, that capacity would not have been raised as swiftly and surely.

Problems of Theatre Command

At the level of theatre command there is much that the Gallipoli campaign can teach, but it is almost entirely of a negative nature. One thing in favour of the British-dominated force command structure was the organic politico-military nature of the Empire from which most of the force came. Apart from the French, many of whom were at the Dardanelles for only a short period, and the Russians, whose direct contribution was marginal, the forces assembled for the operation, although nationally and geographically diverse, were all British or British-derived. In the light of the French refusal to stay ashore at Kum Kale and consolidate their unexpected success in the first two days of the operation, this composition was clearly fortunate. What other bond could have induced the Australian or New Zealand governments and people to sustain their total commitment to British authority throughout a long campaign in which so much went amiss?

The antipodean contingents had been raised and trained by British officers, and had continued their development during and after the South African War under close British tutelage. They were immature in that they had not yet thrown up a cohort of senior commanders of their own and therefore they were willing to accept British leadership in the field. The Australians had their own division commander but at the level of Anzac Corps Headquarters and higher, the command structure was entirely British. The British authorities had the good sense not to try too hard to break up the Australian and New Zealand national contingents, thereby preserving a sense of identity which helped maintain political support for the imperial war effort in the Dominions.

The imperial system was not without its frictions but earlier experience of working together served to lubricate the mechanism and keep it from seizure even in times of great stress. British officers such as Birdwood and Sinclair-MacLagan had already acquired useful knowledge of independent-minded colonial troops and their sometimes touchy political masters during the South African War and since. The colonials, for their part, had also enjoyed similar opportunities for studying the peculiarities of their British superiors. The putting together of so diverse a force after the age of imperial devolution would have been a much more complex affair. The last conflict in which such an arrangement was used, the Malayan Emergency, is now thirty years behind us. The politics of any such combined operations undertaken in future will make the Dardanelles command structure seem the utmost in simplicity.

It is not relevant to my theme to consider *ad hominem* issues such as the suitability of particular individuals for the posts they held during the campaign. There is much to be argued on that score about most generals and admirals involved, but much has already been said and written on it and it would be poor use of my time to add to it. What is of particular relevance to my theme are the arrangements, or lack of them, made by the British government for overall theatre command. They reflected the fundamental weakness of the whole British command structure at that time, namely the total separation of the Army from the Royal Navy, each under its own powerful political head, in a system where overall command could be exercised only at Cabinet level. It is difficult to believe that in 1915 the formation of a proper Ministry of Defence was still some thirty years away. Hence it is not surprising that such a system proved unable to conceive of the need for a joint force command, with one man in charge of all force elements, army and naval, in the theatre of operations.

The result was frequent chaos and confusion, as the Navy withdrew its ships for its own good reasons such as danger of enemy submarine attack, while the ground forces had to live with the consequences. Given General Hamilton's total dependence on the Navy for mobility and communications, this situation was potentially disastrous. At the height of the Suvla crisis in August, when Hamilton finally suspected that things were going badly and his presence was urgently required on the scene, he was held up for six hours because of boiler trouble in the destroyer assigned for his use. A call to Admiral de Robeck, the Fleet Commander, or his Chief of Staff, might have yielded another ship immediately, but both services were confined in their habitual straitjackets and the necessary contact was not made until late in the day. A joint staff could have solved such a problem in a trice.

At the key conference of senior naval officers held on 9 May in *Queen Elizabeth* to consider resumption of the naval attack on the straits, not a single soldier was present. Had de Robeck been of a more daring disposition and taken the fleet into the straits, the Army could have been left literally high and dry while their supporting warships were placed at great risk. In the worst case the Army could have been virtually marooned on the peninsula. As events turned out, the ensuing crisis of relations between Churchill and Fisher killed the idea of a further naval offensive, but the fate of the army could have been prejudiced without its having had any effective voice in the matter.

When Churchill gave reluctant assent to the Navy's call to withdraw the spanking new super-Dreadnought *Queen Elizabeth* from the theatre for her own protection, Kitchener was simply informed that the Army's most powerful source of fire support was departing. He raged at Fisher alleging treachery and Fisher raged back but *Queen Elizabeth* went. When the German submarine U 21 appeared off the peninsula and sank *Triumph* on 25 May, de Robeck withdrew all larger ships from the support of the operations ashore. Army morale plummeted and the Turks were jubilant. The departure of the battleships deprived the army of its badly needed long-range fire support. The Turkish batteries on the south side of the straits were then left unmolested and brought their fire to bear more heavily on the troops on Cape Helles.

The only place at which such conflicts of interest between the services could be resolved, the Cabinet, was by this stage in turmoil following the fall of the Liberal government and its replacement by a coalition. Interservice disputes at the Dardanelles were simply overwhelmed by higher events and those at the front were the principal victims of an appallingly defective system.

The peculiar nature of the First World War enabled Britain to get away with its antiquated military command structure but the lessons of 1915 were not lost on Churchill in 1940. When faced with the overall responsibility for leading the nation in war he did not, like Asquith, sit idly in Cabinet meetings writing letters to a lady love. He took command in a very direct way as both Prime Minister and Minister for Defence, and he presided over the Chiefs of Staff Committee with great assiduity. It required yet further experience before the theatre command system finally evolved in the later stages of the Second World War, but again the Dardanelles played a useful role in educating Churchill and some of his later military subordinates in the need for proper joint service command arrangements at both chiefs of staff and theatre levels.

The Conduct of War at Cabinet Level

The organisation of the British Cabinet for the conduct of war in 1914–15 was so defective that virtually all one can say is 'Don't ever do it like that again!' Asquith, although a notable Prime Minister in peace, was most unsuited for the role of supreme national commander in war. He was fortunate in having two strong subordinates to conduct the land and sea operations, but in the face of their strength, particularly that of Churchill, he came close to abdication of control. Small wonder that there were problems of inter-service friction. The Cabinet supporting staff were inadequate for the task. Hankey did his best to transform his peacetime role as Secretary of the Committee of Imperial Defence into that of Secretary to a War Cabinet, but he lacked skilled assistants and the government had no idea of how to conduct a global war when the stakes were limitless and the nation's resources were at full stretch.

By early November 1914 it was clear that the traditional Cabinet system was in difficulty in conducting a major war. Churchill's order to bombard the Turkish forts at the entrance to the Dardanelles was given without Cabinet discussion, yet it was a major act of policy which carried consequences rightly called by Hankey 'far-reaching and unfortunate'.[8] It confirmed rather than challenged German influence in Constantinople, and it put the Turks on notice to improve the defences of the straits. Kitchener's raising of his new army was a far-sighted move, but he took it on his own responsibility, and soon caused trouble because he was recruiting men totally necessary to defence production and the war economy.

Then followed the War Council, bringing in Balfour from the opposition and Fisher and General Wolfe-Murray as service experts. It had obvious point, if obscure constitutional status, but in four months it expanded from eight to thirteen members, losing cohesion and control. And for the crucial period between 19 March and 14 May, an interval of eight weeks, it did not meet at all, believing that its work was done. But Hankey has made the stunning revelation that: 'After the failure of the naval attack on the Narrows on March 18th the naval and military officers in command at the Dardanelles soon decided that a landing on the Gallipoli Peninsula was more likely to succeed. The War Council was not summoned again to consider their recommendations.'[9]

The key decisions regarding the escalation of the attack to the level of a major amphibious operation were taken piecemeal by three men, Churchill, Kitchener and Asquith, who failed properly to examine the real difficulty of what they were attempting and the implications of meeting stout resistance. Hankey could see that matters were being handled badly. His diary entry for 19 March shows his concern: 'Wrote a memo to Prime Minister imploring him to appoint naval and military technical committee to plan our military attack on Dardanelles in great detail so as to avoid repetition of naval fiasco, which is largely due to inadequate staff preparation.'[10]

He was barking at the moon. Asquith continued to permit Churchill and Kitchener to enmire themselves, their nation, the Empire and their allies in a swamp which was to claim the lives of 150,000 men, inflict colossal hardship on a further 850,000, expend untold amounts of money and resources, inflict misery on the thousands of families of the men who died and blight the lives of all those who had to tend the physically and psychologically maimed survivors over the next generation.

The political foundations of the operation were so weak that Fisher's resignation in mid-May pulled down the government and compelled Asquith to form a coalition. The War Council was replaced by the Dardanelles Committee of eleven senior ministers, to whom a twelfth, the dissident Carson, was added in August. It proved impossible, however, to restrict such a high level body to the conduct of the Dardanelles campaign alone and it evolved, with Hankey's guidance, through the summer of 1915 into a full War Committee, finally taking that name in November. Then with the advent of the Lloyd George government in December 1916 a proper War Cabinet was formed. It had been a long learning period, but much had been learned. Again it was fortunate that Churchill, who had held high office for much of this time, was able to bring the benefit of this experience to the conduct of war twenty-five years later.

I shall dwell no further on the myriad lessons there are to be derived from the Dardanelles for the conduct of war at the highest level. The system available at the outbreak of the war was ludicrously incapable of conducting a total war on a global basis. Unfortunately it took a very long time for men steeped in and dedicated to the Cabinet system of government to find ways of making it an efficient means of directing a national and imperial war effort.

At least since the Dardanelles the need for rigorous staff work and extensive debate has been recognised. As Churchill and some of his successors have shown, the outcome of debate may well be that the Prime Minister's mind is unchanged. So be it: leaders must be able to lead strongly when their country is in peril. But all leaders who have read anything about the Dardanelles will remember three sanctions that a democratic system can readily apply to those whose policies yield disaster: loss of office through reconstruction of the government; loss of power to govern; and the long trial by ordeal which commences when a commission of investigation is established. But they are inevitably damaging sanctions to have to apply and a wise leader sees to it that he does not incur that risk too closely.

Conclusion

Churchill was culpable in several ways. He countenanced and played a dominant role in a slipshod decision-making process. He manipulated the words of his subordinates such as the unfortunate Admiral Carden in order to get his way with Asquith and Kitchener. He bulldozed everyone from the Prime Minister and Kitchener through to Carden and de Robeck to ensure that his wishes were translated into action. Yet he did the nation and the Empire a service in hatching a brilliant alternative strategy. I do not mean that it was the right strategy, but it showed that a creative and subtle mind was at work to steer Britain and the Empire through to victory without driving the whole effort into the abattoir of the Western Front. Abortive though the Dardanelles offensive proved, it was none the less the right sort of alternative to look for. The ultimate cause of the tragedy was the lack of tough-minded, confident, well-informed people at Cabinet level who could criticise Churchill's ideas as he formed them. For want of critics one of Britain's best strategic minds led the Empire to disaster.

Notes

1. Dawnay Papers, Imperial War Museum, cited in Kevin Fewster, Vecihi Basarin and Hatice Hürmüz Basarin, *A Turkish View of Gallipoli-Canakkale*, Hodja, Melbourne, 1985, p. 73.
2. Hans von Seeckt, 'Gründe des Zusammenbruchs der Türkei Herbst 1918', Bundesarchiv/Militärarchiv file N 247/202c, cited in Jehuda L. Wallach, *Anatomie einer Militärhilfe: Die Preussich-deutschen Militärmissionen in der Türkei 1835–1919*, Droste, Düsseldorf, 1976, p. 137.
3. Seekt, *ibid.*, cited in Wallach, *op. cit.*, p. 191.
4. Cited in John North, *Gallipoli the Fading Vision*, Faber and Faber, London, 1936, p. 21.
5. C.E.W. Bean, *Official History of Australia in the War of 1914–1918*, Vol. 2, *The Story of Anzac*, Angus and Robertson, Sydney, 1944, p. 162.
6. Bean, *op. cit.*, photograph facing p. 899.
7. C.E.W. Bean, *The Story of Anzac*, p. 618.
8. Lord Hankey, *The Supreme Command 1914–1918*, George Allen and Unwin, London, 1961, Vol. 1, p. 223.
9. Hankey, *op. cit.*, p. 299.
10. Hankey, *op. cit.*, p. 293.

SEVEN

... WHEN TWO STRONG MEN STAND FACE TO FACE, THOUGH THEY COME FROM THE ENDS OF THE EARTH!

Osman Olcay

24 April 1991

What is being commemorated today after three-quarters of a century is a saga depicting human heroism and folly both at their culminating peak and their abysmal depth. The heroism consisted not only in the dauntless courage displayed under fire but, even more, in the unbelievable endurance of the misery inflicted by the elements among the filth, famine, thirst and fatigue matched only perhaps by the circumstances of the cramped trench warfare on the Western Front.

The folly can now be proved to have been inevitable in view of the basic errors of knowledge, information and therefore of judgement then prevailing, especially on the Allied side. The enemy – that is the Turk – was not only underestimated by the then British government and public, as far as its potential military capabilities were concerned, but it was also the object of disdain and contempt, if not of racial hatred on the part of some misguided and prejudiced politicians then holding power. Gone were the days of comradeship of the Crimea, and of Florence Nightingale, or Disraeli for that matter. Byron was back in spirit, inspiring the Hellenophiles of Whitehall to embark on an operation which would indirectly lead to the restoration of the Byzantine Empire. I will have more to say on this aspect of the Dardanelles episode of the First World War later.

So much has been said and written on the details of so many errors committed by statesmen, and more especially by commanders in the field or on the seas, with reference to the strategic or tactical conceptual approach or execution of military operations relating to this campaign that I will try to confine myself to broader issues.

The aim of opening this new front was in fact set so high, that perhaps if it had been attained – despite what all the classical studies of the campaign agree upon, including some Turkish sources – I cannot help wondering how much bloodier and more utterly destructive results it might have produced. Consider the possibility of actual fighting in and around Istanbul with the participation of the Balkan troops in the kill. Imagine Tsarist Russia fully engaged in destroying eastern Turkey and thus ultimately forced to confront the Arab territories of the Ottoman Empire, which were also jealously coveted by Britain and France. I am not entirely convinced that with these possibilities the First World War would have been much shortened or Russia saved from revolution.

Furthermore, all these considerations omit the amply proven fact that Russia had made it clear that she would not tolerate any Greek implantation in 'Constantinople', meaning to say that the straits and the See of the Orthodox Church were to be her *chasse gardée*. There is on the subject a fascinating study by a Turkish scholar, Professor Tuncoku of the Middle East Technical University in Ankara, starting with the involvement in the Gallipoli naval scene of the Russian battle cruiser, the *Askold*, all the way from the Pacific Ocean.

Let us return to the actions whose commemoration takes place annually and in which Turkish representatives all over the British and Anzac world have by a sort of tradition participated regularly. In fact, viewed from our part of the map, the real cause for celebration, logically, should be the withdrawal, after some nine months of insane warfare, of the greatest invading force which had ever set foot on Turkish soil to that date. The anniversary would then have taken place on 9 January.

But at home we Turks commemorate 18 March, when our centuries-old castles, with their outdated cannons along the Strait of Dardanelles, proved heroically their impregnability, and when our almost non-existent fleet and few minelayers practically paralysed, maimed or destroyed the largest Anglo-French naval force ever assembled, trying to force their passage to the Marmara on that date in 1915. On that fateful day each obsolete Turkish gun, each trawler, the only active yet obsolete submarine, seem to have acted as though inspired by the same spirit as the gallant British sailors at Trafalgar: 'each and every man did their duty.' Thus, whatever the subsequent attempts to re-enact the same scenario – which, by the way, might have succeeded at a second or a third try, had the worsening relations between Churchill, Kitchener and Fisher permitted its materialisation – Istanbul's destiny was to be spared from destruction, but not alas ultimately from enemy occupation for the first time in its 500 years as the capital of the longest living Empire in Europe, as a result of the defeat of the Central Coalition. Turkey had joined it half-heartedly, less by choice or enthusiasm for the German cause, generally speaking, than as a consequence of yet another of the errors – if not sins – committed by the British government to which I alluded a moment ago. Barbara Tuchman has this to say on this subject: 'While they – the Turks – were hesitating, England helpfully gave them a push by seizing two Turkish battleships then being built under contract in British yards . . . [which] had cost Turkey [an] immense sum . . . [which] was raised by popular subscription . . . every Anatolian peasant [having] supplied his penny.' She goes on to say 'Under the cumulative effect of the "Sick Man" and "Wrong Horse" concepts, England had come to regard the entire Ottoman Empire as of less account than two extra warships.'

We can ponder upon the unique circumstances that led the youth of several nations, who had no immediately visible interest to defend, no hatred of the other side, no historically justifiable quarrel to settle, no threat to their existence, homes, wealth, life, honour or values, to disembark in massive formations on the shores of a country they wouldn't be able to pick out on a map. Come to think of it, many – almost all the Anzacs – were volunteers!

The best way to repay those heroes on both sides for the supreme sacrifice of their youth would have been, for the successive generations which followed them, to have erected on the ruins of their generous lives the foundations of a world finally at peace with itself and the Brotherhood of Mankind. Having served, alas, too long as a diplomat by profession, having also lived through a stormy period at the United Nations, I do not have many illusions left. And yet . . . I cannot resign myself to the conclusion that all sacrifices were in vain and that nothing except, perhaps, some war experience to be used for more efficient or economic ways of destroying future enemies, has emerged from this blood-stained peninsula for the benefit of humanity.

One thing seems sure, though it may perhaps not be assigned entirely to the Dardanelles experience: there is greater care nowadays not to dismiss lightly any people, any race, any national or religious group on the basis of these differences. I choose my words with a purpose when I say 'dismiss lightly'. Nationalism at its worst, racial hatred in the most brutal form, pathological nostalgia for Hitlerism, wars which threaten our existence even today, have not been eliminated. But we are more aware today than at any time in history of the unity of men and the uniqueness of our world not only as the abode of mankind but of all forms of life. Somehow, it seems to me, we owe this awareness to the awakening on the shores of the Gallipoli peninsula, when the Mehmetcik – the Johnny Turks – ran across the Johnnies and Tommies and the two sides, though very dimly as if it were through a misty curtain, realised that they had nothing more to fear from the men facing them than what a man may have to fear from his own behaviour. The mutual suspicions based on ignorance wilfully nurtured through war propaganda media, the usual terminology of vilification: 'godless', 'less than human', 'barbarian' and sequels of horror stories relating to mistreatment of prisoners or wounded soon faded away. It was perhaps easier for the Anzacs to adapt their vision to reality than for the British, too long influenced by Gladstonian or Asquithian thinking and the utterances of Mr Lloyd George. Churchill of course was not blameless, but he already had, and has since displayed in what was to be a long and legendary public life, so many redeeming virtues that his Turcophobia, which he later abjured graciously anyway, has now been forgotten and long forgiven in Turkey.

Page after page of Alan Moorehead's classic book on *Gallipoli* is devoted to the description of scenes we would nowadays be tempted to consider surrealistic and which, I believe, are unique in the annals of warfare; men helping each other, in the middle of opposite trenches full of utterly exhausted and nervous sharpshooters, to carry wounded and bury dead while exchanging gifts, jokes and compassionate greetings, even good wishes and calling cards with inscriptions such as 'Profession – student in Poetry' before returning to their respective sides to continue their murderous daily business.

But, besides this very humane aspect of the war scene, one cannot but be disturbed by another peculiarity of the battleground: it was totally devoid of any form of civilian life and activity as though the whole of the peninsula was a kind of monstrous chessboard where war gods were matching their wit and willpower. No inhabitants were to be seen, not even behind the Turkish lines. This odd situation was in marked contrast to what happened on any other front in northern or eastern France, the Low Countries, Central Europe, or Mesopotamia or eastern Turkey for that matter. As a result of that, the troops remained engaged in a kind of titanic wrestling hold which was to last, day-in day-out, until the end. The invaders never were to see beyond the horizon visible to them from the heights they managed to reach on the first days. It was the lack of preparation – no proper maps were available – the wrong landing spots, it was the unexpected, almost unfair roughness of the terrain. On top of it all there was another factor, generously recognised by most if not all who have studied the campaign: Mustafa Kemal.

Here, I would like to explain the title of my lecture: the traditional quotes from Kipling's 'Ballad of East and West' are those which I am inclined to consider as the wrong or negative verses, reflecting the imperial mood of its author: 'Oh! East is East and West is West, and never the twain shall meet/Till Earth and Sky stand presently at God's great Judgement Seat.'

'But' – goes on the poem – 'But, there is neither East nor West, Border, nor Breed, nor Birth/When two strong men stand face to face, though they come from the ends of the earth!'

Now valorous, chivalrous, noble and intrepid young men by their thousands were massed on the inhospitable shores of a bleak promontory jutting out between the Aegean and Marmara seas, facing one another in two camps: one side ready to shed their blood and lives to ensure the vindication of a master strategy born of the genius of one great Englishman, while on the opposing side a yet unknown man of genius, who would thereafter be seen to assume the destiny of his people until his death less than a quarter of a century later, was bent on defeating that strategy to save his country.

Winston Churchill little suspected that this young officer who, from the moment the invasion started, was to take on all the vital responsibilities for the campaign on the Turkish side – little could he have suspected that, by some strange historical hazard, Mustafa Kemal would be his Nemesis. These two giants were to become more and more aware of each other's existence along the course of their lives.

They were doomed to influence each other's destiny but were never meant to meet face to face. Mustafa Kemal, still a lieutenant-colonel, was indirectly responsible for the failure of Churchill's grand strategy, causing him to resign from government and volunteer for action on the Western Front with the rank of, coincidentally, lieutenant-colonel. Ultimately, after many ups and downs in politics, whose fascinating details do not belong here, Churchill was to reap many of the fruits of his hard-earned experiences of the Dardanelles and use them on a much grander and even more dramatic scale in the defence of Britain's home soil some decades later.

For Mustafa Kemal, the younger of the two, whose star was to rise steadily thereafter, Gallipoli was the beginning of an unending and ever increasing series of triumphal victories both in the military and later the political arena, culminating in his recognition by friend and foe alike as the Man of Destiny who almost single-handedly raised his country from the ranks of backwardness and hopeless destitution to that of a forward and upward-looking young and modern state, respected by the community of civilised states and whose alliance and friendship were appreciated by many, including Churchill himself. When Kemal died at the age of fifty-seven he was universally mourned as a war hero, a statesman, a national builder and a genius whose versatility was an example and a source of inspiration all over the world, especially in the East.

Mustafa Kemal had never visited England. Churchill, while older than Kemal, outlived him for many decades of war and peace in Europe and reached the same worldwide status almost immediately after Kemal's death, less than a year before the start of the Second World War. He did not set foot on Turkish soil except for a few brief hours in the first months of 1943 to meet the most famous Turkish statesman after Atatürk (as by then Mustafa Kemal had come to be known), President Ismet Inönü, at Adana to discuss the modalities of a possible military operation to be initiated by or through Turkey – which did not occur – in the Second World War.

In all fairness, I have to mention that, immediately after the end of the First World War, when the Allies were occupying Turkey and contemplating carving out a large part of its territory as a gift to Venizelos' Greece while Mustafa Kemal – the rebel – was branded as a common bandit, it was Churchill's voice which was heard, as a wise statesman, counselling respect and attention to the national hero of the Turks.

Pursuing my attempt to draw attention to what I perceive to be a constant parallel between Churchill's and Atatürk's destinies, let me recall two commands, or two appeals, launched with twenty-five years' distance in time. The first at the Dardanelles at Ari Burnu by the young Turkish staff officer to a group of soldiers, not from his own unit, whom he caught hastily running away from the invading troops. The brief exchange between the officer and these men has epic beauty: 'Stop. why are you running away?' – 'Sir, the enemy.' – 'One doesn't run away, but fights!' – 'We have no ammunition left.' – 'You still have your bayonets. Fix them and lie down.' 'And that', reported later the young Mustafa Kemal, 'is the split second in time that saved the whole defensive front from collapsing.' The date was 25 April. The enemy was forced to lie down when the 57th Regiment came to dislodge them. Incidentally this same 57th Regiment is known to have lost each and every man in battle. The order they had received from Mustafa Kemal was crystal clear: 'I don't order you only to advance, but to die. By the time we are all dead fresh troops and new commanders may replace us!'

Do you not see the same element of determination, the same spirit in Churchill's magnificently defiant speech: 'We shall fight them on the beaches . . .'?

In fact, what is even more significant than the spirit and style, of which the examples are many, is the fact that both men were confronted with a situation which was unique in the long and eventful military history of their respective countries: they were defending their homeland and not some far-away territorial possession of their respective empires. Turkey was to draw the obvious conclusion in less than a decade. It of course took longer for England to dispose of an overseas empire composed of innumerable pieces of land dispersed throughout the surface of the earth.

There was again less adventurism in Mustafa Kemal than in Churchill. Enver Pasha, the then youthful Deputy Commander-in-Chief of the Ottoman Armed Forces (one should bear in mind that the Commander-in-Chief was by definition the Sultan. It would also be useful for a full comprehension of the situation to remember that Enver was the Sultan's son-in-law), was in that respect more Churchillian, of the Churchill brand of the Boer War or of Omdurman, accustomed to consider the world as a chessboard for imperial players. (Enver, the most daring of the Young Turks, who made and unmade governments in his short politico-military career, died sword in hand charging single-handedly on horseback a horde of Armeno–Russian cavalry somewhere in Central Asia, some nine years later.)

Mustafa Kemal's star took longer to rise but, once risen, neither fell nor dimmed until his death. One of his characteristics was his dislike of foreign interference, which was, alas, the dominating factor which led, after centuries of neglect and dereliction, to the dismal downfall of the Empire. He had difficulty enough in bearing with Enver, his contemporary (who, in the course of one year, had risen from lieutenant-colonel to the rank of general and supreme commander), let alone in accepting meekly the role of some kind of subordinate to German officers. Furthermore he, from the start, did not believe in a German victory.

Once the campaign was over in Gallipoli, Churchill was back on active military duty; Mustafa Kemal had the ungrateful task of trying to supervise the orderly withdrawal of Ottoman armies from the deserts and morasses of Mesopotamia, to regroup all the remnants of the armed forces within Turkey to defend the homeland and obtain a fair treaty arrangement when the senseless conflict ended.

It was not to be. Turkey was occupied through the ambiguous terms of an Armistice arrangement and not by force of arms. In addition, she was dismembered and portions of her vital parts distributed with profligacy to her arch-enemies who joyfully joined the quarry. That was still the work of the anti-Turkish-by-tradition or pro-Hellenic segment of the establishment in power. Friends of the able and subtle Cretan statesman Venizelos, or of the gun merchant Sir Basil Zaharoff, one of the richest men in England, among whom Mr Lloyd George was still – if not for long – the most prominent representative, were adamantly engaged in disposing of Turkey. Churchill himself was not yet won over to be at least fair to our side. There was yet another Dardanelles episode to come.

After a long and bitter war, with many bloody battles ending finally in total victory, involving the surrender of the entire command of the Greek forces, followed by untold massacres of the civilian population committed in western Turkey by the retreating armies of the invading Greek forces, Mustafa Kemal's final goal of recuperating to the last square inch the national territory he had vowed to liberate was about to be accomplished when Turkish forces once again were met and stopped on the shores of the Dardanelles by British armies of occupation. It took all the statesmanship, soldierly discipline, and probably the bitter experience of the Gallipoli campaign on both sides, to achieve a peaceful solution of this last conflict.

Thereupon, day by day, patiently, with yet further unsavoury manifestations of mutual mistrust, the relations between the two main antagonists at Gallipoli started warming up until Turkey and the United Kingdom became members of many of the same western organisations.

I shall now look on an entirely different facet: the wider and remoter aspects of the Dardanelles saga. We all know, and this is one of the most dwelt-on sides of this campaign, that it was the cradle of nationhood and statehood of Australia and New Zealand, countries which not only came of age, but discovered unsuspected virtues and qualities in themselves which made them stand as different from the stock they originally came from.

What is less known, because the western media – in the widest sense of this term – either had no interest or, more likely, considered it inconvenient to diffuse, are the facts about the fascination the episode of Gallipoli created in India, especially among the Muslim population of the subcontinent. I recently came across the story of some daring young Muslim Indian students of the University of Aligarh who, despite strict control, managed to make the journey to Turkey during the Balkan Wars to help defend the integrity of the Ottoman Empire. But what, to me, is even more fascinating, is that some of them are known to have remained long enough there, to serve as voluntary medical aides in a military hospital established in Canakkale at the Marmara entrance of the straits throughout the duration of the Gallipoli campaign. The principal medical officer in charge of the hospital was no less famous a person than Dr Tevfik Rüstü Aras, Foreign Minister of Atatürk for decades, a well-known international diplomatic figure whose last official position was that of Ambassador to the Court of St James at the outset of the Second World War.

As to the reluctance of Hindus to embark on a war against Turkey, one has only to read most interesting passages from the fascinating book composed of letters addressed by Pandit Nehru to his daughter, the future Prime Minister of India, the late Mrs Gandhi. Nevertheless, units and formations of the Indian Army fought with distinction at Gallipoli and still more in Mesopotamia.

So much has been said about Gallipoli. So many ideas, theories, expressions of wisdom emerged from the tragedy enacted there. The more I think of it, the more I recognise common traces of inspiration derived directly from the blood-soaked trenches and fields of the peninsula, both in the Turkish War for Independence and in the Battle of Britain. Canakkale – as we traditionally call this battlefront – was the inspiration for our victorious battles of Sakarya and Kocatepe in the early 1920s which culminated in the sweeping pursuit of the enemy to the shores of the Aegean at Izmir in September 1922. It was Turks defending to the death the last surviving piece of what for them was and is today Turkey, and not some imperial conquest.

I believe I am not mistaken in drawing the same conclusion for the Battle of Britain. Neither Napoleon nor the Invincible Armada nor any other

European coalition had come so near to invading the sacred soil of Britain as Hitler did. Churchill, who had faced the indomitable resolution of those defending tooth and nail their hearth, home, honour and all cherished values at Gallipoli, rose in splendid prose to offer only 'blood, tears and sweat' to be shed in defence of the same values for his people when the time came for reckoning, and he had the entire country backing him enthusiastically and all the Free World – as it was then called – in admiration.

When Atatürk visited the last battlefield he trod upon in his lifetime as a soldier, his eyes were filled with the same horror as Churchill returning from the ruins of what had been Coventry, or visiting nightly the devastated areas of Blitz-struck London.

Allow me to say, in favour of the First World War, remembering the conclusion of the lecture by John Grigg (see pp. 63–4), about the greater nobility of that war, that though Turkey suffered immensely in its flesh, through massacres, occupation, depredations, treason and famine, especially as a result of the Greek atrocities committed during the ultimate retreat from Anatolia, she did not have the means in 1922, as neither had any of the victors of 1918, to inflict a Dresden or Hamburg or Berlin type of nightmarish revenge as applied by Churchill to the authors of the devastation of Britain in the Second World War.

But reason, humanity, a forward-looking perspective in international law and morality have to prevail.

'Damn the Dardanelles – they'll be our graves!' exclaimed Lord Fisher. Today I believe I can hopefully say: 'Hail the Dardanelles! They will always be a reminder of the cradle where took place the national awakening of so many amongst us. They shall also be forever the symbol of all those human follies, temptations and errors we should eternally beware of.' It is to be hoped that it will remind us that on the eve of the twenty-first century, East and West as well as North and South have no other hope for preserving life on this planet of ours than getting together and collaborating to achieve that loftiest of all goals: Peace on Earth. A step towards that goal can be discerned in the inscription enshrined on the memorial above Anzac Cove in Turkey and at the Atatürk Memorial Garden in Australia. It reads:

> Heroes that shed their blood and lost their lives. . . . You are now lying in the soil of a friendly country. Therefore rest in peace. There is no difference between the Johnnies and Mehmets to us where they lie side by side here in this country of ours. You, the mothers, who sent their sons from far-away countries, wipe away your tears; your sons are now lying in our bosom and are in peace. After having lost their lives on this land, they have become our sons as well.

EIGHT

THE HUMAN STORY

Nigel Bagnall

30 April 1992

As a young officer, I had been deeply moved by an account of a heroic but forlorn charge by the Australian Light Horse. Feeling that their sacrifice should not be forgotten, I wrote an article myself. It had little literary merit but the sentiment I was trying to express was sincere. And so it is now; I have nothing profound to say about Gallipoli, no new lessons to draw and no fresh revelations to disclose. Instead I want to talk about some of those who fought and died there, to say something about their origins, their character and the manner of their death, and then finally to draw some tentative conclusions about their sacrifice.

I hope that the Revd Henry Hall would approve of my intention even if he could not applaud my words. So let me begin by saying something about his old division, the 29th, with which he went to war and of which he felt so justifiably proud.

With the exception of a single Scottish Territorial Army battalion, the 29th Division was formed from regular English, southern Irish, Scottish and Welsh infantry regiments. At the outbreak of war, two of the battalions were already in the United Kingdom but the others were withdrawn from garrison duties overseas: six from various parts of India, two from Burma, one from China and another from Mauritius. The artillery was all regular but the engineer, pioneer, medical and signal units belonged to the Territorial Army, while individual British volunteers had come from all parts of the Empire: New Zealand, Canada, South Africa, Ceylon, Africa and Newfoundland.

When the troops poured in they were billeted throughout the heart of England; in Leamington, Warwick, Banbury, Rugby and Stratford-on-Avon. Here they were made warmly welcome by people who had previously had little encounter with what was largely an overseas army. Padre Creighton provides us with an insight into this new-found relationship, and gives his first impressions of the officers and men to whom he was to become so attached:

I went to a concert in St George's Hall. The Lancashire Fusiliers band was playing noisy but cheery music. They are to play at church on Sunday. A very nice, rather talkative corporal accosted me in a shop afterwards and asked if I was to be their chaplain. He gave me lots of useful information. He said the men were not at all religious, and I would have a lot of disappointments, but would find them very civil. They did not like going to church. They had a splendid chaplain in India – a real soldier's chaplain, quite unlike the English ones. He seemed quite prepared to instruct me, and very pleased that I was prepared to let him.

The Padre then goes on to compare the regulars of the 29th Division with the volunteers of Kitchener's Army with whom he had previously been serving.

Regulars are very different. They seem extremely smart and seasoned and have an air that there is nothing they don't know about soldiering. It makes so much difference feeling that they are absolutely ready for the front. I found people friendly before, but nothing could exceed the friendliness here, there is nothing they are not prepared to do. The men seem to be very well behaved, but of course in a town of this size [it was Nuneaton] there must be much that is wrong. I can only say how thankful I am that I do not come to them utterly green.

The good Padre's concern was, as we shall see, about girls. 'After breakfast', he writes, 'a motor car came for me and took me to the Stoddingford Church where the Royal Fusiliers were parading at ten o'clock. The band provided the music and also the choir. The vicar took the service and I had asked that no ladies should be present. However I saw some girls in the gallery with the soldiers. Fortunately they were ejected before my sermon.' Free from embarrassment, he then went on to appeal to the men not to take advantage of a lot of over-excited girls. The problem has a ring of timelessness, as does the gossip Padre Creighton next encountered:

Mrs M told me she has heard stories of soldiers leaving their billets at late hours to meet the girls in back streets, so I decided to investigate a little on my own. At 10.30 p.m. I went for an hour's walk along a path by the canal. It was a lovely moonlight night but I saw no one there, and only found a few soldiers behaving quite orderly in the streets, in one or two cases with girls, but quite openly. I find they are allowed out until midnight. One of the other vicars has told me that he has been out three nights, but saw nothing. I am very glad, the men who are so easy to get on with and always cheery and laughing, seem to be behaving very well.

On board the troopship taking them to Egypt, Padre Creighton continues in the same theme before turning his attention to the officers.

> The men have been writing reams of sentimental letters to the Nuneaton girls. Though they grumble a little, they take everything for granted as it comes along, longing only to be back with Susy or May.
>
> The Colonel [who is not named but must have been Lt Colonel Ormond of the Lancashire Fusiliers] is a most charming and interesting man, and his whole regiment thinks very highly of him. The tone amongst the officers seems very high, and they strike me as a nice, clean living, straightforward, moderate lot of men. They all work hard at their jobs and have a strong sense of responsibility. Many of them, however, spend much of the day mildly gambling at poker. I tell them quite plainly that I think it would be a lot better if they neither gambled nor drank. Though they are such good, nice fellows and easy to get on with, none of them agree.

The Padre was, however, apparently infected by at least one of these peccadillos since later in the campaign George Davidson, a Medical Officer, tells us that: 'Padre Creighton is to-day offering five pounds to a shilling that it will be Christmas before we take Achi Baba.' Achi Baba was a prominent hill feature dominating the southern end of the peninsula which remained in Turkish hands throughout the campaign.

But I am running ahead of events and we must return to 25 April 1915, when a perfect Aegean spring broke on a still Sunday morning. The whole Helles region was lifeless; not a sound was to be heard until the naval bombardment started with a thunderous roar at 5 a.m. The troops were then transferred from the warships and transports to lighters, and from there again to boats which were rowed ashore by sailors. Let Captain Clayton of the Lancashire Fusiliers, who was killed a month later, take up the story:

> We thought nothing could survive the ship's guns, but they bombarded too far inland and the trenches overlooking the landing beaches were not touched, so the rifle and machine gun fire poured into us as we got out of the boats and made for the sandy shore. There was tremendously strong wire where my boat landed. I got my wire cutters out but could not make the slightest impression. The front of the wire was now a thick mess of men, the majority of whom never moved again. The noise was ghastly and the sights horrible. I eventually crawled through the wire until reaching a small mound which gave us protection, where we lay gasping for breath until fixing our bayonets and clambering up the cliffs.

When we started the enemy withdrew, but on reaching the top they were ready again and poured shot into us. However we pushed on along the open ground and had an awful time, the place was strewn with bodies.

I could continue to recount the horrors they experienced indefinitely, but I am sure the men of the 29th Division would wish to be remembered in other ways; for their gallantry in winning twelve VCs; for their spirit which was to endure unbroken throughout the campaign; for their high reputation even among the Anzacs who, as the doctor diarist records, 'many and many a time I have heard wax eloquent over the division's doings, and this from fighters no troops in the world can surpass, or perhaps equal, but they have always declared that they could not have done what the 29th did'.

Finally, those who fell with the division and untold others would wish to be remembered for their cheerfulness and sense of humour, epitomised by another quote from George Davidson. Two bodies of troops were passing in the darkness when a sergeant called out: 'Are you the West Riding?' – referring to an engineer field company – only to receive the reply, 'No, we are just the poor bloody Monmouths walking'.

Now let us turn to the Anzacs, the Australians and New Zealanders who, though outnumbered ten times over by the other Empire troops, earned themselves a distinctive legend which has passed into history. The Anzac Corps consisted of two divisions, one of three brigades which were all Australian and the other of two brigades, one Australian and one New Zealand. But it should not be thought that the Dominion troops shared a common identity. The New Zealanders were less boisterous and self-assertive than the Australians; they were more inclined to conceal their feelings and accept the restraints of authority – differences in temperament which were reflected in their attitude towards combat. Though of equal courage and fighting prowess, whereas the Australians were initially strangely negligent in the defence but unmatchable in the attack, the New Zealanders were generally steadier when on the defensive and less reckless in the assault.

In many ways the New Zealanders felt closer to the English than to their Australian neighbours who tended to overshadow them. I say 'English' intentionally, since it was only as a result of the Gallipoli campaign that the Australians and New Zealanders found their national identity. Until then they had tended to regard themselves as British citizens living abroad. As the Australian diarist E.F. Hanman records: 'Deep down in our hearts we knew that England, dear old England – Home – needed us and was hailing us now as her sons.' In a similar vein the New Zealand historian,

Christopher Pugsley, wrote: 'The causes of the conflict were not entirely clear but that did not matter. Britain had declared war on our behalf, and that was enough. We did not even consciously go to war as New Zealanders. Nothing in our experience had forced us to consider our relationship to the land in which we lived.'

So, inspired by patriotism, the Anzacs flocked to the colours, never doubting that the British Empire would emerge victorious but fearful that the contest would end before they could play their part. In New Zealand, for Spencer Westmacott part-time soldiering had been the only relaxation from the back-breaking task of clearing his land of scrub. Now, with the outbreak of war, he was at last going to have the chance to see some active service. Rising early he milked his cow for the last time, breakfasted, tidied up and changed out of dungarees into uniform. Then mounting his horse, but feeling rather foolish, he drove his cow before him to Mrs Morton for safe keeping before riding on alone.

In Australia the picture was much the same. Labourers laid aside their tools, lawyers quitted their desks, cattle station owners saddled up and led their men to the recruiting centres where the volunteers were assembling. Here, as Hanman relates, their enthusiasm was tempered by mystification. 'What are these chaps with such smart uniforms, such a magnificent martial bearing and such pretty little bits of red and gold spotted on their hats, shoulders and sleeves? Surely they are Captains: but no, by their voice and pompous manner, they must surely be no less than Generals! But wait, worried recruit, when you have been in the army one short week, you will know, only too well, that they are the Sergeant-Majors of the Instructional Staff'!

Their preliminary training completed, the Anzacs embarked and set sail for an unknown destination, generally thought to be England from where they would move to the Western Front. The only breaks from the monotony of shipboard routine were the meals though, judging by the account of one private soldier's exchange with the Orderly Officer, these can have provided but little solace.

Orderly Officer: Any complaints, men?
Private: Yessir, taste this, Sir.
Officer: H'm, rather thin and greasy, otherwise not bad soup.
Private: That's what we thought, Sir, but the cook says it's tea.

Eventually the long sea voyage ended but, with Turkey's entry into the war, the Anzacs found themselves disembarking not in England but in Egypt. Here they occupied tented camps pitched around Heliopolis and began a period of intensive training; slogging route marches and endless night exercises. But it was not all work; there were also excursions into Cairo where, with money in their pockets, the boisterous Anzacs set out to see what the city had to offer. There is no need to dwell on the details, but had Padre Creighton taken to the streets of Cairo as he did in Nuneaton, he would have been severely shaken, as were many others, though for different reasons. After one particularly hectic night, when the Australians went on the rampage in the more seedy quarter of the city, photographs taken the next morning show what looks like a Second World War town after a heavy blitz.

But whatever those who had suffered during this tumult thought, when the Australians marched through Heliopolis to embark for Gallipoli, they were given a rousing sending off. As Hanman relates:

> The wide deserted streets rang with the heavy tramp of our approach, we knew every shop by heart, the nature of their wares. Here was the chap we called Moses with his special prices for soldiers, special prices they were too – double those of anybody else!
>
> Now we are singing, the noise was terrific, quite sufficient to raise the dead, let alone the slumbering town. Suddenly the house tops are crowded with Europeans in night attire, cries of Vive L'Angleterre, Bon Voyage, Vive L'Australie fill the air, fluttering handkerchiefs and flowers are snatched by eager fingers and hidden in the pockets of khaki tunics. But the majority of these little symbols of hope, of love, of patriotism now lie buried with their owners.

But though many of the Anzacs were to die, they did not fall in their shoals on landing as had the 29th Divison, nor did their exhilaration fade as their picket boats grounded on the shelving shoreline. Through a navigational error, instead of being put ashore on an open beach, not improbably wired and covered by machine guns as at Helles, they were deposited at the foot of a steep escarpment which was only lightly held.

But, in scrambling up the successive ridges and among meandering gullies, units became disorientated and mixed, while the Turks were given time to rush reinforcements to the threatened area. Successive scrub-covered ridges had to be cleared against increasing resistance; and as the weight of fire grew, so the Australians' ranks were thinned, the impetus of their attack slowed and then faltered. With the assaulting battalions reduced to little more than handfuls of exhausted and often leaderless men, all they could do was to hang on desperately against the Turkish counter-attacks.

So both sides dug in with the Anzacs on the lower slopes, cramped and exposed but at least supported by naval gunfire. The stagnation of trench warfare set in at Gallipoli as it had done in France. An extract from

Christopher Pugsley's account of the fighting at Quinn's Post, a key forward position in the firing line, gives the flavour:

> As the Turkish line was only a fifteen second dash away, the front and support trenches on and immediately below the crest were always crowded to repel an attack. Casualties were heavy, there were mangled bodies of our own men and the Turks everywhere and the stench was nearly unbearable. The heat was intense and the flies swarmed in their millions, you couldn't drink your tea or eat your stew without them flying in and out of your mouth.
>
> With the shortage of water it was impossible to keep clean and sickness was rampant, clothing was infested with lice and only a lighted candle could sizzle them out from the seams.

But with the arrival of Colonel Malone, a typical old New Zealand pioneer with an almost incredible tenacity of purpose and willpower, things were to change. His first step was to order the domination of no man's land by snipers, to be selected from men who had spent their lives hunting in the bush. Trenches were then deepened and covered, the area cleaned and sanitation measures strictly enforced. The fighting would still flare up with vicious raids and counter-raids but, with the New Zealand snipers' ability to dominate the immediate area, supply columns could get through unscathed and casualties could be evacuated without having to wait for the cover of darkness.

But even Malone could do nothing about the food which, though abundant, was distastefully monotonous. The bully beef was salty and stringy, the cheese smelt and ran like yellow lava in the heat, while the biscuits were an epic in themselves, great 4-inch square slabs as hard as rocks. Down on the beaches tins of them were used by the Australian Army Service Corps as miniature fortresses to protect themselves from the constant shrapnel.

With this picture it is nearly time to leave the Anzacs, so let me end by quoting a wounded Australian's account of his arrival at London in a hospital train. Maybe it is a bit sentimental but it provides an insight into the character of the Australian soldier and gets behind his rough profanity which, as their medical officer Joseph Beeston describes, 'oozes from him like music from a barrel organ'. Percival writes:

> At a railway station not far from Plymouth I was put in a Red Cross train for London. Directly the train pulled up at the station an old woman, dressed in very poor clothes of deep mourning, came down the length of the train doling out pitifully small quantities of cigarettes and sweets.

By the time she had got as far as our carriage her little stock of gifts was exhausted. But she came up to me and said: 'My boys, it was all I had, I am so sorry I could not bring more.'

The tears stood in her eyes as she told how three of her sons had been killed in France; and that just about started me – aye, and a good few others near by – gulping down lumps in our throats. I saw some of our chaps surreptitiously wiping away tears which would not hold back, try as we might. She was such a little shabby, poor and loving old woman and she gave us all she had.

Here I must leave the Anzacs to say something about the Gurkhas because, providing a brigade, they formed the single largest national contingent from the Indian Army which fought at Gallipoli. The system of recruiting for the Gurkhas was that each battalion sent recruiters to their regimental areas in Nepal, often three weeks' march into the hills where there were no roads and where, during the rainy season, most of the rivers became impassable. The recruits were mainly shepherds or cultivators of small holdings, intensely tribal in their outlook but loyal, brave, truthful and self-reliant with a delightful sense of humour. Though inclined to be hasty tempered, a Gurkha's anger goes as quickly as it comes and he seldom bears a grudge.

Like the Anzacs, following Turkey's entry into the war the Indian Army contingent was disembarked in Egypt but here the similarity ends. There was no further training or relaxation for the regular troops, who were deployed in defence of the Suez Canal until embarking for Gallipoli.

The original plan had been for a brigade of Gurkhas to join the weaker of the two Anzac divisions, but in the event the first Gurkha battalion was disembarked at the end of April across the hard-won Helles beaches, with two more following some six weeks later to form an all-Gurkha brigade attached to the British 29th Division, whose memory is commemorated in Eltham church. It is appropriate that we should remember the Gurkhas, as well as the Sikhs and Punjabis before them, who fell fighting with the 29th Division.

Though the Gurkhas participated in some bitter fighting while at Helles, their greatest ordeal was endured at Anzac, where they were disembarked in August to take part in a break-out that came within a hair's breadth of success. The 6th Gurkhas, under the command of Major Allanson, had fought their way to the top of the great Chunuk Bair feature. From here could be seen the straits, and to the south the winding road that led to Achi Baba – the hill Padre Creighton had been prepared to bet could not be captured before Christmas.

But the opportunity was missed. Not only were the Gurkhas not supported but, being mistaken for Turks, they were bombarded from the sea and in the resulting confusion Chunuk Bair was lost. Below the crest, however, as the wounded Cecil Allanson later wrote: 'Every man remained glued to his trenches, with rifles almost red hot; how I admired them and how I blessed them. It all wanted courage, after four nights without sleep, only two days meagre rations and one water bottle.'

We must now leave the Gurkhas but, before doing so, let me quote the words of Professor Turner in the preface to his Dictionary of the Gurkha language:

As I write these last words, my thoughts return to you who were my comrades, the stubborn and indomitable peasants of Nepal. Once more I hear the laughter with which you greeted every hardship. Once more I see you in your bivouacs or about your fires, on forced marches or in the trenches, now shivering with wet and cold, now scorched by a pitiless and burning sun. Uncomplaining you endure hunger and thirst and wounds: and at the last your unwavering lines disappear into the smoke and wrath of battle. Bravest of the brave, most generous, never had a country more faithful friends than you.

Professor Turner has said it all, so now let us turn to the French whose relatively small expeditionary corps of two divisions was, like the Anzacs, to play a vital role from the outset. The initial task given to the French was to mount a diversionary attack on the Asiatic coast at Kum Kale, which lay across the straits opposite the peninsula's southern tip. Once the task, which was allotted to the 6th Colonial Brigade, had been completed, the brigade was to re-embark and join the French main force on the British right flank.

Doctors appear to have been diligent diarists, and it is once again a medical officer who gives us an informal account of his experiences. Serving with the 6th Colonial Brigade, his uncensored letters to his English wife were published under the pseudonym of Joe, though why he chose to write anonymously is not clear. It cannot have concealed his identity from the authorities at the time, while it masks him in obscurity today. So Joe he must remain:

The 6th Colonial Brigade was composed of one battalion of white troops and two of blacks. The greater part of the Europeans consisted of a fine body of young recruits from Lyons, though I fear there are a number of young soldiers who have little power of resistance to illness. As for the Senegalese, they have already been at the front in France and include a large number of veterans who had proved their worth in Morocco, then at Flanders, Ypres and Dixmude. They have come from the garrisons of

Nice and Mentone where, during the most severe period of the winter, we were obliged to keep our black troops in reserve. The officers, who are for the most part colonials, are worthy of such soldiers.

After embarking at Marseille, Joe gives an account of conditions on board which have little in common with those experienced by the Anzacs. 'I have a splendid cabin de luxe', he writes, 'bathroom, table in the middle and we take our meals with the ship's captain. It would be possible to live on board comfortably for months. On shore I have meals with the Colonel and his aide-de-camp. We have an excellent cook and the three of us receive rations for eight men.' It all sounds very French, though below deck things had been rather different. 'The stables smell strongly', he writes, 'and we cannot even open the portholes because the horses put their heads through them.' Unfortunately and rather surprisingly, the doctor makes no mention of the men, so we have no idea whether they fared better than the Anzacs or, for that matter, the French horses.

After crossing the Mediterranean to the North African ports of Tunis and Bizerte, where further troops from Algeria and Tunisia were embarked, the convoy set sail for Alexandria. Here the French were feted, showered with presents and received with spontaneous generosity. Perhaps not very tactfully and certainly with little modesty, Joe writes to tell his wife that 'Yesterday I had dinner in the town where there are no lack of pretty women. I must confess that, in this country which arouses memories of Cleopatra, women have great charm and fascination. I think I am one of the officers most in request.'

From Alexandria the French were moved to Lemnos and Skyros, two of the islands lying off the peninsula which provided forward bases. Here the troops began to realise what a desperate struggle lay ahead. As Henri Feuille, a Territorial artillery captain, records: 'Unfortunately the blow we are about to deliver, however powerful it may be, is going to come too late. In the opinion of all the sailors who have taken part in the earlier operations – when the British and French navies tried to force the straits unaided – we are going to find ourselves in considerable difficulties. Under German direction the Turks have strongly fortified the peninsula, and what would have been a relatively simple operation two months ago, is now going to be an extremely perilous one.' They proved to be painfully prophetic words.

Though the French, like the Anzacs, did not suffer heavily on first putting ashore on the Asiatic coast, after fighting their way inland resistance stiffened and they were subjected to repeated counter-attacks. In the savage fighting that followed, the French slowly gained the upper hand and the Turkish defences started to crumble. But though some of the junior commanders wanted to exploit their success, the landing of the 6th Colonial Brigade was only intended to be a diversion, so after losing about a quarter of its strength in two days' fighting it was withdrawn.

As the history of the British 29th Division records; 'The 27th April brought a welcome change. The Turks began to retire and the French to arrive. They had accomplished the work of distracting the enemy from the peninsula by the brilliant landing in force at Kum Kale, and had successfully evacuated their Asiatic lodgement when their task was completed.'

Though their numbers were greatly reduced following the decision to send troops to Salonika, the French continued to fight on grimly until the Allies abandoned Helles in early January 1916. Like their British Allies the French withdrew without losing a single man or any of their equipment, horses or mules. Whatever the mistakes and muddle of the landings, that the evacuation was conducted with such skill and daring reflected the greatest credit on the planners, the troops themselves and the Royal Navy.

The final national contingent about which I want to talk is that of the Turks. Unfortunately I have been unable to trace any Turkish source which provides the sort of informal insight I have been giving for the other nations. I have had to draw on very sketchy German and Allied material, so what I have to say will be regrettably brief. I will start by quoting Hans Kannengiesser, who was one of the most influential of the 500 Germans serving with the Turks at Gallipoli.

'The Turkish soldier', he writes, 'of whom the large majority are Anatolian, is poorly educated but brave and trustworthy. Content with very little, it never enters his head to dispute the authority of those above him; it was the will of Allah that he should follow his leader without question. He is deeply religious and believes that his life is only a prelude to a yet better one.' Kannengiesser has a lot to say about the problems he encountered in dealing with the Turks, but it is not my purpose to raise such matters, so let me give the views of two Australians. The first is that of Colonel Joseph Beeston, whom we have already met.

'One cannot conclude these reminiscences', writes Beeston, 'without paying tribute to Abdul as a fighting man. All I know about him is in his favour. We have heard all about his atrocities and his perfidy, but the men we met fought fairly and squarely. At the beginning of the campaign it was commonly reported that the Turks mutilated our wounded. Now I believe that to be an unmitigated lie, probably started by men who had never set foot on the peninsula.' Beeston goes on to give two examples of when Turks behaved with exemplary honour. The first was when the Australians had tried to conduct a further landing to enlarge the Anzac bridgehead, but were forced to retire and leave their wounded. But Turks signalled to take them off and then never fired or abused the white flag. The second instance occurred when an Australian field ambulance was deployed under a hill and a howitzer battery took up a position just in front of them. The Turks sent word that either the field ambulance or the battery of guns must move, otherwise they would have to open fire indiscriminately.

When it comes to courage, Private Cashman of the Australian infantry tells how a Turkish officer tried to rush a machine gun post while the gun was temporarily out of action. Twice he led a small party across the narrow stretch on no man's land near Quinn's Post. Twice all his men were killed and he miraculously escaped. Yet against all expectation he came on again for a third time, firing a revolver in one hand and wielding a sword in the other. Though wounded he managed to reach the Australian post where he was finally killed. Cashman concludes his account of the incident with the simple words: 'This was the bravest act I saw at the front.'

Here we must leave the Turk, a courageous and honourable foe who defended his homeland with stubborn devotion and unshakeable loyalty to his leaders. But I must make an important point because it is fundamental to the conclusions I will be drawing. It was the Turkish leaders who brought their country into the war. Impressed by the military might of the Central Powers and convinced of their ultimate victory over the largely unprepared western Allies, they saw an opportunity for aggrandisement at the expense of their age old enemy, Russia. It was the appeal for help on the part of the Russians that led to the British and French endeavour to seize Constantinople by forcing the Dardanelles straits and, when this failed, to the landings on the Gallipoli peninsula.

What are the conclusions to be drawn from all this?

I have given some illustrations of how the campaign was seen by patriotic, gallant and often simple men on both sides. From our perspective 77 years later, what was it all about and was their sacrifice worthwhile? For sacrifices there were, many of them and on both sides.

For the Turks the answer is relatively clear. They successfully repelled a foreign invader; and we can now see that, for Turkey as much as for Australia or New Zealand, the foundations of a modern nation were laid at Gallipoli.

For the Allies it is more complex. In their immediate military objectives, they failed; and in proportion to population the burden of sacrifice fell most heavily on Australia and New Zealand, whose soldiers nevertheless displayed a gallantry, an endurance and a model of military excellence, that has become a byword in history. Indeed the Allies did enough to suggest that with better preparation and leadership the Turks could be defeated, as was later shown in Allenby's campaigns in Palestine. And some of the lessons of

Gallipoli were no doubt applied in the Second World War – both in its higher strategic direction and in the planning of successful amphibious operations.

But there is a more fundamental point. The twentieth century has seen a marked change in attitudes towards war, at any rate in those nations which have a coherent public memory of one or both the world wars. At the beginning of the century war could be seriously acclaimed as a noble manifestation of human activity or even, as Nietzsche put it, 'Nature's pruning-hook'. Several of the belligerents in 1914 appear to have been almost eager to go to war, whether for territorial and economic expansion, through frustration at political or diplomatic impotence, or from feelings of political obligation. We are familiar with photographs of straw-hatted young men cheering in city streets, including one in which the youthful Hitler has been spotted in a crowd in Munich.

It is very different today. War is regarded unreservedly as an evil, and the first object of most defence policies is to prevent it by making clear that in certain circumstances its horrors will be unleashed. We call this deterrence. Its evolution has been gradual. The slaughter of the First World War, at Gallipoli as much as on other fronts, prompted the first shift; and the memory of it inhibited Britain and France from taking timely measures to resist Hitler. Consequently Hitler himself was not deterred. Nevertheless the much greater casualties of the Second World War, with the demonstration of the power of nuclear weapons, compelled a still more fundamental rethinking after 1945. In one manifestation of this, the democracies of North America and Western Europe resolved to make clear to the Soviet Union that, should it contemplate aggression, it must reckon that they would respond to an attack with all the means at their disposal. Had they not so resolved we might, instead of being able to rejoice at the new-found freedom of the peoples of Eastern Europe, have joined them in their bondage: at the very least, the East/West military confrontation fostered a climate of caution in the conduct of international affairs.

Elsewhere, it is true, there have been many wars; and neither General Galtieri nor Saddam Hussein was deterred from taking action which brought military defeat by stronger opponents. But this only re-emphasises an important truth, that military strength means little unless accompanied by positive diplomacy and clear political signals. We can rejoice that the horror and futility of war are more clearly understood – and Gallipoli contributed to this – but if we are to use this understanding for the prevention of conflict in an uncertain world we must remain prepared to shoulder the burden of defence and to demonstrate a determination to uphold international law and order.

NINE

TURKEY AND BRITAIN: A PARADOX

J. Enoch Powell

28 April 1993

I cannot claim any very direct personal connection with Gallipoli but like so many of my fellow citizens I can catch the hem of its garment. The 9th Battalion of my regiment, the Royal Warwickshire Regiment, including the late Field Marshal Slim, then a subaltern, landed on V Beach to join the immortal 29th Division and later took part in August 1915 in the attack from Anzac Cove. My wife's father was invalided to Cairo from Gallipoli after serving there when a subaltern in the Royal West Kent Regiment. And she still possesses the list of the kit which he was required to take with him to Gallipoli and his Service Sheet which records his involvement.

I want, however, to take a perspective wider than the actual engagement. The commemoration of the Gallipoli Campaign is an inducement to muse upon a paradox.

The United Kingdom has historically been preoccupied with the Ottoman Empire and with Turkey. That this should have been so was far from natural. One must fight shy of the temptation to talk or think about such things as the national characteristics of the two peoples, the Turks and the British. It is, I agree, remarkable that so staggering a disaster inflicted upon British arms neither created at the time nor left behind it a rooted hostility such as our more successful encounters with other opponents have left behind. The ideas of 'liking, trust, friendship, admiration' have no place in the vocabulary of international affairs. Some nations strike us more agreeably than do others. That may tell us something about them and us; but a world where the behaviour of nations is not governed by the perceived requirements of self-interest and self-preservation is a sugar-puff confection, not a picture of real life.

After Ottoman power swept across the Balkans and consolidated its hold on that region – if an anchor date is obligatory, the second Battle of Kosovo in 1448 is perhaps as good as any – it would not be difficult to understand why the destiny and the strength of the Turkish Empire should preoccupy the rulers of Austria and of the countries of eastern Europe for generations upon end.

Almost as easy to understand is why the France of Louis XIV, obsessed with dominating Western Europe and with maintaining a balance of power between its rivals, would be gratified by the successes of the Ottoman sultan and fortified by his alliance. Did Louis XIV's pastrycook not keep him from forgetting the usefulness of the crescent whenever he served him at breakfast with the delectable croissant?

Austria, Germany, France – yes; but how explain why England, an insular and remote state, impregnable out here in the eastern Atlantic, followed like a lodestone the policy – I quote words attributed to the Younger Pitt – 'of preserving the integrity of the Ottoman Empire'? How came the safety and welfare of the Sultan in far-away Istanbul and of his dominions across the Mediterranean to be so earnestly and so persistently a pressing concern to this 'sceptred isle'? There *is* a paradox here; and the unravelling of it has lessons perhaps for the future as important as the light it sheds upon the past.

A treaty of peace between the Ottoman Empire and Austria, Poland and Venice, with whom Turkey had been at war, was signed in 1699 at Karlowitz, then in Hungary, now in Croatia – a place equally famous (so I am informed) for its slivovitz. Venice was there naturally as an Aegean power and thus a near neighbour of Turkey; but linked on that occasion with Venice in promoting peace were the English (they had not yet become 'the British'). Why were they there? Not surely to waste their time nor as busybodies; but the conjuncture is instructive.

By the end of the seventeenth century England had brought to the coalition against France, led by Holland, the asset of a powerful navy and the wealth of a commerce which had signally surpassed the fleets and the economic success of the Netherlands. England had become – rather say, she was in course of becoming – a great power, and not just a great power on the adjacent continent but a world power and in particular a power in the East. Far-sighted observers who noted the new English factory established at Calcutta under the walls of Fort William in 1687, twelve years before that treaty at Karlowitz, might have predicted that in India England was destined to outlast not only the Dutch but the Portuguese and the French. It was the possession and the government of India that were to make England a world power. They it was that enabled a small Atlantic island to play a dominant role in the eastern hemisphere, a role extending westwards to the Persian Gulf and the Middle East and eastwards to Singapore and China.

Barely a hundred years passed after the founding of Calcutta before Napoleon Bonaparte landed in Egypt to follow what he thought was the shortest route to overthrow Britain. It was not the British alone but others observing them and dealing with them over whom the British Empire in India cast a mesmeric spell. Consider then how powerful must have been the mental effect of it upon the inhabitants of this island itself. Before Disraeli converted his 'faery queen' into the Empress of India, they had learned to think of their state as one encompassing not only the British Isles but the India which gave it its strength and greatness. A diminutive archipelago in the eastern Atlantic interdependent with a huge territory thousands of miles away – how should not the physical communication between these strangely assorted Siamese twins be literally a matter of life and death? What Napoleon thought the British thought and others also.

Thus the maintenance and safety of Britain's connection with India became the arbitrament of British foreign policy, defence policy, all sorts of policy. The organisation of the Army, the design of the ships of the Royal Navy, the alliances, enmities and intrigues of Britain, the distant possessions and overseas protectorates which she acquired – all in the end were bound up with that assumed imperative, the safety of the route to India.

But the route at its most direct – by land, then by sea and eventually by air – lay across the Ottoman Empire. Napoleon, remember, when he arrived in Egypt, was entering one of the dominions of the Sultan, however tenuous and reluctant its obedience might have become. From facts like this it was neither difficult nor illogical to deduce that the supreme interest of Britain depended on the goodwill of the Ottoman Empire and that the break-up of that Empire would be dangerous to Britain.

In the nineteenth century that logic was held to justify more than the proconsular status and behaviour of Britain's long-serving ambassador extraordinary and plenipotentiary to the Sublime Porte, Stratford Canning, raised in 1852 to the peerage as Viscount Stratford de Redcliffe. It did much more. It justified a war with Russia, at the height of which John Bright in the House of Commons was to exclaim 'perish India!' – a war which, indirectly and ironically, by denuding India itself of British forces, contributed to the greatest crisis of British rule in India, the mutiny of the Bengal Army in 1857.

If any one event in the murky train which led to the Crimean War was decisive, it was the alarm created in Britain by the destruction of the Turkish navy at Sinob by Russian ironclads in 1853. That war turned the balance of power in Europe on its head. Napoleon III's ambitious France, and Britain, its fellow guarantor of the European balance, found themselves aligned against Russia, their natural coadjutor in maintaining European equilibrium. In fact the remarkable phenomenon of Britain's inveterate inclination to envisage Russia as her enemy seems to be traceable to the Crimea. It was to the preservation of a very different balance of power, the balance which protection of the route to India and of the possession of

India appeared to demand, that the British effort in the Crimean War was directed. In that objective the war succeeded, but only at the ultimate cost of tilting the European balance in favour of Germany.

It is tempting to speculate how different would have been the fate of Europe in the twentieth century without the consequences of Britain's obsession with India. The two great conflicts which engulfed the continent in 1914 and 1939 are traceable to the breakdown of the European balance of power, a breakdown to which the abstention or ambiguity of Britain contributed. British fear, suspicion and hostility towards Russia certainly delayed the Entente with France at the beginning of the century. If it were permissible to extend conjecture into our own times, one might adduce the same underlying cause for the Russo-German Pact of 1939 and all the subsequent miseries which that event entailed upon Eastern Europe.

It is one of history's cruel ironies that the attempt to force the Dardanelles which failed disastrously amid the bloodshed of Gallipoli was designed to rescue Russia from isolation and so achieve the encirclement of Germany and Austria. After centuries during which British policy had aimed at holding Russia aloof from the Mediterranean, British arms and British sea power were engaged in the endeavour to provide entry for Russia to those forbidden waters. In the past access to India had appeared to demand that the Mediterranean be controlled by Britain from both ends: a *mare clausum*. At the western bottleneck the fortress rock of Gibraltar stood sentry; but the eastern bottleneck at the Dardanelles continued to cast an ominous spell, and now, with two German warships, the *Goeben* and the *Breslau*, cooped up at Constantinople, Britain succumbed to the fatal temptation to pick a quarrel with Turkey and thus to subvert the historic rule of British policy and range the Ottoman Empire in the ranks of our enemies.

Even after the First World War and the disappearance in 1917 of Russia's threat to the Ottoman Empire, another and a curious reason still remained for Britain to consider itself involved with the destiny of Turkey through the interests of the Indian Empire. The large Muslim population of India was an important factor in the evolution of empire into self-government which eventually came about through the creation of Pakistan. For that population the Caliphate still held by the Ottoman Sultan was a cynosure only less powerful than Mecca itself; and Britain at the beginning of the 1920s was fearful of anything which might cause it to be associated with action prejudicial to the Sultan. This too was a factor destined to vanish when, as an indirect consequence of Turkey's share in the defeat of the Central Powers, the Ottoman sultanate itself came to an end and Turkey became a secular state with a new constitution.

The revolution in Turkey coincided with a less dramatic but ultimately perhaps no less radical rearrangement of political power in Britain. The continuing wartime coalition government under Lloyd George had blundered into supporting Greece's attempt by military force to prosecute claims on territory in Anatolia. It was the near humiliation which Britain suffered in consequence at Chanak (i.e. Canakkale) in 1922 that sealed the downfall of Britain's wartime coalition government and thereby ushered in a new pattern of British party politics which has continued down to the present.

I have come to the threshold of a further question: has Britain even now outlived its obsession with India? In strict, mechanical logic, the end of the Indian Raj in 1947 ought to have entailed a fundamental revision of British foreign policy, disposing of any carry-over from the old obsession. Surveying events since 1945, I find it difficult to resist the conclusion that no such revision of British policy took place. Britain continued to assume after 1945 that it was still under the necessity of playing the role of a great power in the Middle East. It is an assumption which outlasted even the Suez catastrophe of 1956, and it can still be seen today haunting Anglo-American policy in Mesopotamia, where, if the United States imagines it has unfinished business, there is no excuse for Britain to indulge the same illusion.

I have, I realise, travelled a long way from Gallipoli; yet I have not gone over the edge of the map. My theme being that of Anglo-Turkish relations over the centuries since the Peace of Karlowitz, I have a conclusion still to draw. If Britain has ceased to be linked or even identified with her former Indian empire, the British national interest has become detached from those concerns which preservation of the route to India and of the Indian empire once dictated. Britain is no longer an interested player in the Middle East, any more than Britain is any longer a Mediterranean player. Her interest as an Atlantic archipelago in the balance of power on the adjacent European continent need be distorted no longer by an irrelevant perspective.

For Britain Turkey has ceased to be a piece on the chessboard of power, to be moved and steered in the light of British necessities. The two countries are free to view one another, with concern and tolerance, as those whose interests neither conflict nor intersect, countries which must obey the imperatives of their own respective geographical situations, uncomplicated by the ideas, the assumptions and the illusions of circumstances which vanished long ago.

Postscript

Today [1993], more than ever, that lesson needs to be well remembered. Today Britain is teetering on the brink of physical involvement in the Balkan scene, a scene physically and emotionally close to the history of Turkey, but a scene to which Britain no longer belongs by position or interest. I trust that illusions bred by memory of past power and glory will play no part in shaping Britain's decision.

TEN

ECHOES OF GALLIPOLI

Leonard Thornton

27 April 1994

They say: We leave you our deaths. Give them their meaning.
We were young, they say. We have died. Remember us.

Archibald MacLeish, 1892–1982

I speak as an unregenerate anglophile, a result of youthful exposure. I happened to be in this country with my New Zealand gunner regiment in the dramatic six months that followed Dunkirk and never recovered from my admiration for the British people at that time. Close collaboration in postwar years confirmed the affection and esteem felt by so many in New Zealand, and I hope will assuage any measured criticism that I may offer now.

I was surprised and pleased to learn that Gallipoli is specifically remembered in Britain. It has currency in the Antipodes but, for the people of the United Kingdom who have so many triumphs and tragedies to recall, its survival invites questions. Thus I shall endeavour to explain the nature of the New Zealand environment as the Empire (which it then was) approached the unprecedented expeditionary gamble of an invasion of Turkey, and cover the New Zealand part in the struggle. I will review resultant public attitudes in the Antipodes then and now and, finally, I shall suggest what is left to us from that dire and distant confrontation.

I have titled my address 'Echoes of Gallipoli'. I chose that because echoes are all around us through the active day, whether we are aware of them or not. They may be reassuring or threatening, clear or confused, clamorous or muted, significant or trivial, momentary or sustained – all words which can be applied to the impressions, the images and the legends which remain to us from a conflict occurring before most of us were born. Perceptions will not be held in common, nor are they immutable. A modern writer[1] has pointed out that: 'Wars, battles and armistice days are long remembered, but the psychology of war is quickly forgotten; or at least the recollection of what was the state of mind gets modified to fit the preferences of later years.'

It is to those preferences that we must address ourselves towards the end of my lecture.

Antecedents

When the frenzy of that first global war gripped the world in 1914, the British Empire was a vital force in New Zealand's reckoning. We had adopted Dominion status in 1907 but still cherished the strongest affiliations. We were almost wholly of British stock unto the third generation, apart from the indigenous Maori section of the population, which anyway felt a special relationship with the Crown. The structure of government, the law, education, even religious observances and social patterns were firmly based in British originals. There were mutual advantages in trade, of course, and on our side there was a long-standing anxiety about the security of our farthest-flung frontier of Empire. As evidence of our faith in the Royal Navy as the bulwark of our defence, we had readily agreed to meet the cost of a British battlecruiser. The same sense of obligation persuaded the NZ government to give an undertaking that we would, on call, provide troops for the defence of Empire, as we had done in a modest way in South Africa at the turn of the century. Six thousand five hundred men took part there and returned as popular heroes. It was felt by the public that we had done the right thing. We had twice as many deaths from disease and accident as from hostile action, and even then the total was limited to two hundred and thirty.

In support of the new military undertaking, universal compulsory military service was introduced in 1909. We were Empire-minded, but not entirely simple. At an Imperial conference held in 1911 the New Zealand delegates pressed for the creation of a forum which would allow the 'colonies' to influence policy in matters which could affect them, such as a decision to go to war. The British government, well inured to dealing with recalcitrant allies, was not in favour – and the other members were shrewd enough to see that policy participation could well lead to increased financial and other obligations. The proposal lapsed, and the New Zealand public happily went back to an uncritical acceptance of British policy-making.

When peace expired in 1914, and we were included without consultation in a declaration of war, there was no hesitation in New Zealand. The public had no understanding of the antecedents or causes of the war, nor its likely demands; it was sufficient that the Empire was threatened. Young men flocked to the colours to join what was to be known as the Expeditionary Force. Many came direct from farm, factory or office with little or no military training; only a smattering of regulars were available and there was no logistic back-up; that would be provided by Britain, as would higher command and naval support.

Full of enthusiasm, and concerned only that the war might end before they could get to grips with the enemy, the New Zealand force sailed, 8,500 strong, to be grouped with a neighbourly contingent from Australia and make up the Australia and New Zealand Army Corps. A new word emerged in English usage.

The prospect of being brigaded with the Australians was generally welcomed, but that is not to say that the relationship was an immediate and close brotherhood. Differences in temperament and background produced a kinship which might be called cousinly rather than brotherly. The Anzacs reserved the right to criticise each other[2] and to differ, but when faced with outside opposition from friend or foe such differences were forgotten. Certainly each group developed the greatest respect for the fighting qualities of the other as soon as battle was joined.

Meanwhile the Force had no idea where it was headed and there was some surprise at being disembarked in Egypt to complete assembly and training, and to be available wherever needed. Unfortunately the next leg of their journey, the last for many, had a destination that was no secret from anyone, including the Turks. Liman von Sanders, the German general advising the Turkish high command, records in his 1919 account:[3] 'The British gave me full four weeks to prepare. Their preparations were excellent . . . except that they underestimated the powers of resistance of the Turkish soldier.'

The second statement must be seen as self-serving, for it has to be said bluntly that the British preparations were very far from excellent. I do not propose to expand on that here except to say that one's sympathy goes to Sir Ian Hamilton, pitchforked into the job of preparing an operation for which the British Army had had no experience and for which he was given inadequate resources and insufficient time. Brave, scholarly and civilised, he was not the man to thump the table and demand performance from his subordinates – or his superiors.

There were misgivings about the mission at the time in London,[4] at political as well as military levels, and also in the theatre.[5] Wisdom after the event made Hamilton the scapegoat for the inadequacies of many, but to my mind his principal failing was in not refusing the mission or at least insisting on more time for preparation. In the assault force, however, there was no sign of doubt or hesitation, but only youthful exuberance as the ships steamed out of Mudros harbour on 24 April 1915 'with bands playing and flags flying'. Aubrey Herbert[6] and others record that 'cheers went from one end of the harbour to the other'. A remarkable scene; I must say that in all the years of the Second World War I never knew British – far less New Zealand – troops utter a spontaneous cheer for the cause, even if they felt things were going well!

The Experience: First Phase

In this case things did not go well, either for the 29th British Division at the top of the peninsula, or for the Anzacs – in Hamilton's view a somewhat wild and amateurish lot – who were given the supporting role of cutting the peninsula in two to prevent the movement of Turkish forces from the north to contest the British/French landings. The plan took little account of the sheer size of the objective or of the possibility that the Turks might not be pushed aside like a scattering of Afridi tribesmen.

The sequence of events is well known. Before dawn on 25 April, and immediately preceding the southern landings, the Australians were put ashore on the wrong beach, a tiny strip of sand later known as Anzac Cove. The error of navigation was probably a blessing in disguise. After studying the ground I am inclined to agree with Aubrey Herbert's view[6] that 'This was the one bright spot. Had we landed where intended we should have been wiped out.' Where they did land, there were relatively few Turkish defenders, and the Australians drove them off without too much difficulty. However the terrain was steep and extremely convoluted, and when the assault force began to run into hastily committed enemy reserve units it was soon widely scattered, quite disorganised, and in urgent need of help.

The New Zealanders were not part of that first dramatic charge, but in reserve; they began landing just before noon, and were committed piecemeal to the action in a desperate attempt to stabilise the situation. They too were soon hopelessly entangled in the ragged forward line. When nightfall came at last, the prospect seemed grim, and the Anzac commanders contemplated withdrawal – judged to be quite impracticable. Of the three thousand New Zealanders landed, six hundred had become casualties, and many of their officers and junior leaders were among those killed. This was not at all in line with anticipations of a glorious victory.

I forbear to describe what happened to the wounded; suffice to say that the medical plan, formed at the last minute and predicated on 'slight' casualties, was grossly inadequate. The resultant suffering was extreme, and many lives were lost unnecessarily. Somehow the Anzacs managed to hold on to their tiny lodgement, the minimum they needed to survive at all, and the maximum that they could hope to make secure.

As soon as the situation was under control – with some help now from the Naval Division – two Anzac brigades were shipped south to bolster a British/French offensive. They attacked across open country at 10.30 in the morning against nine entrenched Turkish battalions well supplied with machine guns. When the attack petered out, the divisional commander ordered them to do it again over the same ground at 5 p.m. They did so, and were repulsed without gaining any territory; they lost a further 30 per cent of their depleted strength, killed or wounded, and the survivors shipped back to Anzac Cove. R.R. James[4] tells us that the confidence of the divisional commander at Helles was quite unshaken by failure and dreadful losses; he even remained popular with the British soldiery. Perhaps it was just as well that he shortly succumbed to sunstroke and was evacuated!

Second Phase: Suvla

Now the long slog of endurance began: three months of shortages of water, fresh food, sleep, medical supplies, even ammunition; the wags said this was balanced by a surfeit of lice, dysentery, flies and danger. The Anzac lodgement survived by the skin of its teeth. The New Zealanders justly claim that it was one of their officers, a high-country sheep-farmer, who first pointed the way out of the fouled encirclement. In daring scouting missons, often in daylight, our Major Overton discovered that the high features to the north of the Anzac perimeter were relatively undefended, and that there were few Turks in the wide plain lying between those heights and the sea. Hamilton, to his credit, recognised the opportunity and made his plans accordingly, though it was to be two months before he could gather the necessary strength for a fresh assault. This would take shape as the Suvla landing, beginning on the night of 6 August.

In the new offensive a major task was entrusted to the Anzacs. Reinforced by a British division smuggled ashore in darkness a few days beforehand, they were to capture a vital hill feature, while a newly created British corps launched a seaborne attack on their flank. Initially, things went well. The foothills were cleared in a brilliant night attack by the New Zealanders (including some Maori sub-units for the first time) and the way was open for the main assault.

However the terrain was exceptionally confusing, as you will know if you have ever walked it, and by dawn many of the attacking units were hopelessly lost, well short of their objectives. Major Overton, acting as guide – perhaps the one man who could least be spared at that moment – was killed by a sniper. The New Zealand infantry were within striking distance of their night objective, a high point on the main ridge known as Chunuk Bair, but now they suffered what are politely described as 'command problems' – or in other words, disagreement among the senior officers. A belated daylight attack decimated the battalion committed, and the objective remained in Turkish hands. This had disastrous results for an Australian regiment in the old Anzac perimeter, who were ordered to make a supporting attack across the notorious Nek, already the scene of many grisly encounters. Almost two-thirds of them were either killed or wounded as wave after wave were ordered forward.

The New Zealanders managed to capture their hilltop during the following night, gaining a tantalising glimpse of the narrows in the distance, though with a lot of Turkish-held territory still ahead of them. Elements of the Warwickshire Regiment and 10 Gurkhas secured lodgements elsewhere along the ridgeline and hung on during the following day. The New Zealanders fought a long hand-to-hand battle for their summit, and were eventually forced back 50 metres to a reserve trench. That struggle, in which the commanding officer, Malone, was struck down by one of our own shells at a critical stage, has a prominent place in our Gallipoli legend. (So much is this so that recently there was agitation for posthumous recognition of Malone's gallantry and the award of a decoration 'denied' to him 75 years before. The appeal lapsed.)

Hamilton's plan achieved little. The great Suvla landing failed to develop momentum and became stranded not far from the beaches, a victim of inexperience and hesitant leadership. The lodgements on the hill feature, taken over by fresh troops during the night, were driven off in a massive counter-attack organised by a young officer named Mustafa Kemal, later to became Kemal Atatürk. Allied confidence began to leak away. The New Zealanders were now down to a handful of 'originals' and even the comparative newcomers were debilitated by the conditions of their existence. With some equally tired Australians they were ordered into a fresh attack two weeks later, this time to capture a low feature, known as Hill 60, which would secure the 'hinge' between Suvla and the Anzac perimeter. The advance was made over open fields in daylight, with little fire support. A couple of hectares was the gain, but Hill 60 remained in Turkish hands, and the cost was a thousand casualties. 'Land is very dear here', said a participant.[2]

That was the final disappointment. The necessary decisions were taken and, surprisingly enough, such meticulous planning and security processes were followed that it proved possible to extract the entire Anzac/Suvla force without loss just before Christmas 1915, and the troops from Helles in early January. It was a miraculous escape; but the unpalatable fact remained that the dogged Turkish defence had succeeded in the face of a major and sustained Allied endeavour, and the men took it badly.

Reckoning

As to what the expedition achieved in the awful balance of profit and loss, the answer has to be very little, politically, strategically or tactically. As one of our soldier-historians said of a much later battle, 'nothing was right except the courage'.[7] Reactions among the participant nations differed. In the United Kingdom there were political ructions and a massive enquiry[8] was held. In Australia heroic accounts were early in circulation and a legend established itself. For the Turks, success was shortly obscured by the humiliation of losing an empire; for many years they seem to have seen Gallipoli principally as the historic opportunity for the emergence of Kemal, to become the father of modern Turkey.

In New Zealand the reaction was slow and muted. Early press accounts of the battles relied primarily on despatches written by an Australian correspondent. The New Zealand representative had evidently found it difficult to get to Gallipoli and had written his version from Cairo.[9] Fortunately an enterprising staff officer at Hamilton's headquarters, monitoring the Australian despatches, prudently added the phrase 'and New Zealand' whenever he encountered the words 'the Australian'! The public was at first sheltered from a full realisation of the casualty figures through poor communication channels and the inadequacies of the records system. It was several weeks before private advice of deaths or woundings began to reach families, and questions were asked in Parliament. Confidence in ultimate victory remained unshaken, and on 4 August, the anniversary of the outbreak of war and a few days before the New Zealanders suffered their heaviest casualties on Gallipoli, a 'loyal motion' was passed in Parliament[10] without debate, pledging continuing support for the 'common and sacred cause of the Allies'. Hansard reports that after this touching evidence of Empire solidarity, 'the members rose in their places and sang the national anthem'. It is hard to visualise such a scene!

It was not until September that the New Zealand force commander, Godley, made his first report of casualties, then estimated at over 1,800. In December he wrote privately to the Minister of Defence:[2] 'Our impotence here fills one with shame, especially in view of the magnificent gallantry displayed.' Like him, I do not want to make too much of the casualty figures that eventually emerged, partly because all were suffering, partly because our part in the campaign was numerically small. Overall each side had about a quarter of a million killed and wounded; von Sanders tells us that the Turks had 60,000 killed but the true figure was probably half as many again. Britain lost 25,000 out of 400,000 engaged, the French 10,000 or one in eight, the Australians 7,600 and the New Zealanders 2,500. The Australian and New Zealand percentage figures were even higher than the French.

There are two things that should be said about such figures: the first is that from the Antipodes we provided only front-line troops, whereas the major participants also supplied logistic support units which do not usually engage directly with the enemy and thus suffer smaller losses. Any implication that the Anzacs 'fought harder' than their Allied comrades must be treated with reserve. Secondly, and more significantly, the number of fatalities was very much higher than either the participants or their home folks had expected – much higher, percentage-wise, than those suffered in the Second World War. But in spite of that and of the dreadful battlefield conditions endured, morale among the Anzacs remained tolerably high throughout. By the end of the First World War, New Zealand had mobilised a higher percentage of its male population than any other part of the Empire except Britain, and had suffered higher proportional casualties than any.

To turn to other aspects of the Gallipoli balance sheet, one can say that some military lessons were learned which should not have been needed – the importance of proper planning and secrecy, the need for adequate medical and health services, the hazards of the opposed landing, and the tactical unwisdom of daylight attacks against entrenched infantry supported by well-placed machine guns. (The last seems to have been forgotten again for the Battle of the Somme).

I like to think that there was significant military profit in the presence on Gallipoli of three young officers who later came to fame, and did better than their predecessors. I refer to Field Marshals Slim, with the Royal Warwickshire Regiment, and Harding, with a Territorial Division, and my old boss, Lord Freyberg VC, with the Naval Division. No doubt there were others who recognised certain imperatives. But I do know that the New Zealanders were to be grateful in the Second World War for General Freyberg's insistence on sound planning and coordination, his enthusiasm for night operations rather than daylight attacks, and his reliance on ample and skilled medical services. All of these sprang in the first instance from his own experiences at Gallipoli and helped to make him the outstanding and respected field commander he was.

Reactions in the Antipodes

Benefits of a broader nature arose from the Gallipoli experience in terms of self-awareness or national pride, and in relationships. Here again I want to refer essentially to New Zealand reactions, although it is not easy to differentiate between our response and that of Australia. I mentioned earlier that the Dardanelles campaign might not necessarily appear a major event in British eyes (I note that Bernard Montgomery devotes half a page to it in his 500-page *History of Warfare*) but it was truly significant for the Antipodes. Its importance was magnified at the expense of subsequent events in the same war, its heroics enshrined and its humiliations ignored. The negative aspects of the campaign went unregarded for many years, until another war and the perspectives of history permitted a re-examination of the legend.

Our reactions should be judged in their contemporary setting and not against 'the preferences of later years'. We had shown an express desire to play an active part in the defence of Empire, no matter what the circumstances, and in the event sought to show that we were worthy of our inheritance and could foot it with the best: the 'best' in this context being the British regulars. Subsequently we wanted to believe that we had done so, and to some extent circumstance encouraged us to believe it. R.R. James[4] records: 'The New Zealanders had already acquired [in May] a remarkable reputation . . . they combined the élan and dash of the Australians with the meticulous professionalism of the British troops.'

The men who returned – and there were not a lot of them – did not speak frankly of the errors and terrors they had experienced. This is not uncommon in men returning from the extreme of human experience to the humdrum of domestic reality. But there was another factor: even if there had been grievances about the way the campaign was handled, to express them openly while the struggle for the survival of Empire continued would have been seen as disloyal, unworthy and possibly seditious. So they kept silent, and by the time it was all over the glorious legend was established. The loss of life had been so great that it was necessary to find justification in the heroic rather than admitting tragic failure. Herbert, continuing service in France in 1916, noted that 'All the men from Gallipoli talk of it with something like reverence'.

New Zealanders at home were I think influenced by strong reactions across the Tasman. Robert Hughes, in an exceptional book[11] about the Australian colonisation, offers the suggestion that: 'one of the reasons why Australians after 1918 embraced with such deep emotion the mythic event of Gallipoli, our Thermopylae, was that there seemed to be so little in our early history to which we could point with pride. "History" meant great men, stirring deeds, and worthy sacrifices; our history was short of these.'

Both countries felt that they had not only played a worthy part but had done so in their own style, reflecting their national characteristics. W.P. Morrell, a New Zealand historian, wrote[12] in 1935: 'The men who fought, fought for Empire, but also for New Zealand. . . . By the very fact of coming to the Old World and coming in a body they could not but realise that they had as New Zealanders their own individuality.'

Another, Alan Mulgan, twenty years later acknowledged[13] the adoption of that view by his countrymen: 'Gallipoli taught us to think more of ourselves and more about ourselves. New Zealanders began to see more clearly that their country was not just another Britain but a different land with a history and destiny of its own.'

Neither that claim nor the justification for it were challenged during the interwar years, but today there are some who protest that military achievement is a sterile basis for nationhood. That is a question of perspectives again; certainly the contemporary view was that a national identity had been established at Gallipoli. Its anniversaries became the occasion for tacit acknowledgement of that claim as well as a commemoration of the fallen.

The first memorial service was held in 1916, and by 1920 an Act had been passed declaring that Anzac Day would be a public holiday – later amended to read 'treated as a Sunday'. Ten years later I was to find that in my school Anzac Day was a major date in our calendar, marked by the assembly of the entire school, holiday or not, and the ceremonial reading of the lengthy list of fallen Old Boys, while wreaths were laid at a memorial shrine. On ordinary days we often intoned, in diminuendo, that verse of the school song which commemorated

> Some yet nearer felt, whose blood an Empire bridges,
> On Flanders' riven belt and Anzac's tortured ridges.

I am pleased to hear from the current headmaster that substantially the same procedure is followed to the present day; I understand however that this is scarcely a common practice in other schools.

It was not until 1945 that the Anzac Day Act was extended to embrace those who fell in other wars and other services, making it clear that it should now be regarded as the equivalent of Memorial Day, the old Armistice Day. The latter is no longer generally observed in New Zealand, though special ceremonies were held last year to mark the seventy-fifth anniversary. That is also the official position in Australia; however they have differed slightly from us in that their observances generally include remembrance and tribute to all who served, and not solely the fallen. Perhaps there is another difference: one of their historians[14] recently stated that the Gallipoli landing is often the main focus of Anzac Day speeches even today, with scant recognition of the participation of others, or of other wars. If that be true, it serves to illustrate the significance of Gallipoli to subsequent generations there.

We in New Zealand have not been entirely scrupulous. I sometimes feel that Anzac Day takes on too much of an 'army' connotation at the expense of the other services. Nor have we been particularly generous about our Allies. Most New Zealanders, in modern times, are genuinely astonished to learn that the French not only took part in the campaign but contributed nearly twice as many men as the Australians and New Zealanders combined. Most will acknowledge that the British were there, but would reject the assertion that they outnumbered the Anzacs by a factor of ten to one.

It is a common failing to emphasise the achievements of one's own fighting services at the expense of allies, if only because national pride demands that our men and women should have been the best. History seems to show that criticism goes beyond simple xenophobia and is an inescapable part of military alliances. Individual Anzacs certainly offered criticism of other nationals, including the British, during and after Gallipoli, but I very strongly disagree with an English historian who recently suggested[15] that such complaints survived to become a permanent national disenchantment with things British. He instances anti-British comments heard during international rugby or even cricket tests; I advise him to listen sometime to the flow of remarks from the benches when we are playing the Australians, who are supposed to be our best mates! I indicated earlier that in my long experience I have seen no evidence of any such general animosity – that in fact the reverse is the case.

In summary, then, one can say that in New Zealand the observance of Anzac Day continues to attract a reasonable if declining public response. (Remembrance of service and sacrifice in times of war tends to recede as recollection of war itself recedes.) Most popular are the dawn services held in virtually all of our population centres; they relate now to all services and to all wars, but if only because of the dawn setting there is still an implied connection with Gallipoli. The vital legend has faded a little, to be succeeded by a more objective approach to its realities. Indeed some authors, playwrights and film-makers, seeking a dramatic effect, have overemphasised the tragic aspects, at some disservice to history.

In the Modern World

This brings us to the shadowy question of what significance and thus what observance, if any, should be attached to the Gallipoli tradition for the future. There can be no consensus, and my views are of course affected by my generation and background. We can agree, no doubt, that Gallipoli has had a remarkably persistent echo, distorted here and there by and between the participant-inheritors, and attenuated by subsequent and comparable dramas. At the one extreme the total crusaders for peace would like us to regard it historically as an unjustified aggression against a non-threatening opponent by an overconfident and underperforming European alliance, into which uncritical mercenaries (a nod here to the old India and the French dependencies) and simple colonials (the Australians and New Zealanders) were delivered for slaughter. No-one with any knowledge of the campaign and its vast literature would today regard it as a military triumph or seek thereby to glorify war; quite the reverse.

It has to be admitted that the management of the Gallipoli campaign was faulty from the start – and I have indicated that the Anzacs contributed their own tactical errors. It cannot be approached with any degree of professional satisfaction, as most critics will agree; but few have sought the reason. A young New Zealand writer who served with pride in British combat units in the Second World War put his tongue in his cheek and 'explained' in 1946:[16] 'After the Great War the British appear to have decided that their Army was inefficient, but that this was something like an act of God or a decision of nature that shouldn't be altered. . . . When you have a lot of deaths to think about, the argument gets less than literary.'

Later he added, 'I had seen enough of war to know that the first essential of command is competence.'

I am sure no-one would contest that last statement, but it does not touch on why that essential was not pursued more vigorously. A thoughtful Englishman, Lord Moran, famed physican to Winston Churchill through the Second World War, offers an explanation of sorts. Reflecting in 1945 on his own experiences in the trenches in France,[17] he has this to say: 'If we had weeded out inefficiency without mercy or remorse . . . the war might now be over, but we should have had to change our character to win. Toleration was as far as we had got towards a religion.' This spirit, he went on to say, was not found among the Dominion troops.

Be all that as it may, there are few Empire loyalists left who will hear only the echoes of glory in the history of the campaign. Nevertheless there are stirring echoes that sound still against the discordancies of suffering and defeat. How can one forget the astonishing phenomenon of 'five VCs before breakfast' won by the Lancashire Fusiliers at W Beach? Is the French recollection of the battle simply one of loyalty to an alliance under strain, or do they remember the actions of their regular and colonial units at Helles in words we have adopted from their language – élan and esprit de corps? Today the Turks celebrate not only the emergence of their great leader but also the dogged and unquestioning courage with which a conscripted peasant army fought and died to defend the homeland. For Australia, if I may presume to speak for it, and for New Zealand, the principal image of Gallipoli is still of heroism and not of 'exploitation' or even loss.

Throughout the interpretations of the Dardanelles campaign offered during the nearly eighty years which have elapsed, there runs one common strain – the indestructibility of the human spirit. It was J.M. Barrie who said in 1922: 'Courage is the thing. All goes if courage goes.' Stating the obverse he might equally have said 'All stands if courage stands'. A proper study for the historian of today is what enabled the Gallipoli participants – on both sides – to endure so much. Lord Moran, a traditionalist at heart, believed that it was a combination of concern for the good name of the regiment and confidence in leaders, efficient or not. He may have been right, but surely only for the old regular army. It was not generally true of the 'colonials'; for them, 'sticking it' was a question of not being found wanting by greater powers or by their comrades. In the loneliness of being far from their own homelands both inclinations were accentuated. There was the background knowledge that they would have to live with their mates in the small communities back home, when all was over. So 'mateship' was all-important; you could not let your mates down by giving in to fear or by failing to support them in battle.

Out of such reactions, endurance arose, and its active form – courage. It is of course true that in 1915 the issues must have seemed simpler, perhaps even the issue of life and death. Personal and corporate loyalties were more distinct, expectations were lower, existence more physical, and communities more structured. Even so, theirs was a remarkable performance when all is said. The evident courage in adversity, gallantry in the forlorn hope, consistent bravery beyond the demands of discipline or reason caused and causes the echoes of Gallipoli to ring out across the years. War makes its special demands on courage; but surely both courage and self-discipline are more than ever needed in the ordinary and troubled world of today. As long as that is true, you are right and we are right to celebrate and sustain the Gallipoli example and tradition.

I should like to offer one final Antipodean thought. I accept that, as the decades roll, a great many things change, sometimes because that is necessary and sometimes with beneficial results. But I also believe that we should seek to preserve traditions we have valued even if they no longer have practical effect. Among these I place very high the British part of our heritage, with pride and not contrition, although I acknowledge that other influences and sentiments are working in the national psyche today. I am disturbed when there are suggestions that the loyalties of the old Commonwealth infringe upon our independence or our identity. Surely these are issues which have been dead for more than half a century. We should seek to sustain the links that remain, not weaken them by innuendo. If shared memories and observances such as the Gallipoli drama help in that process, as I believe they do, then long may memory hold open that door for us and for you.

Notes

1. *Economist*, 23/29 January 1993.
2. Christopher Pugsley, *Gallipoli: The New Zealand Story*, 1984.
3. Liman von Sanders, *Five Years in Turkey*, 1928.
4. R.R. James, *Gallipoli*, 1965.
5. Compton Mackenzie, *Gallipoli Memories*, 1929.
6. Hon. Aubrey Herbert, *Mons, Anzac, Kut*, 1919.
7. H.K. Kippenberger, *Infantry Brigadier*, 1949.
8. HMSO, *The Final Report of the Dardanelles Commission*, 1917.
9. *New Zealand Parliamentary Debates for 1915*, Vol. 174.
10. *New Zealand Parliamentary Debates for 1915*, Vol. 172.
11. Robert Hughes, *The Fatal Shore: A History of the Transportation of Convicts to Australia, 1787–1868*, 1987.
12. Alan Mulgan, *The Making of a New Zealander*, 1958.
14. Press article, Professor Inglis, Historical Studies Division, ANU, 1992.
15. G. Moorhouse, *Hell's Foundations*, 1992.
16. John Mulgan, *Report on Experience*, 1947.
17. Lord Moran, *The Anatomy of Courage*, 1945.

ELEVEN

CHURCHILL AND GALLIPOLI

Martin Gilbert

26 April 1995

'What about the Dardanelles?' was a cry that pursued Winston Churchill on public platforms for four decades. He was not yet forty when Europe plunged into war and Turkey hovered on the brink of joining the Central Powers.

It was on 26 August 1914, while Turkey was still neutral, that Churchill's naval representative in Constantinople, Admiral Limpus, wrote to him:

> In giving my reasons to the authorities here why Turkey should not join the German Group, I have studiously omitted all talk of action that England might take . . . or might encourage Greece to take, such as a landing between Smyrna and the Dardanelles, taking the forts on the south side of the straits, admitting torpedo craft to the Marmara, cutting off and starving first the Gallipoli peninsula, and soon after cutting all communications between Constantinople and the south. But they are each and all things which, methodically undertaken and persistently carried out, would succeed, and would annihilate the remaining power of Turkey.

A week later, the British Military Attaché in Constantinople, Major Cunliffe-Owen, reported by telegram to the War Office on 'the question of our Fleet entering the Straits'. He believed that 'if mines can be negotiated, there should be little apprehension of difficulty in running past the short defences and, once off Stamboul, position would be a commanding one, completely paralysing all military movements between European and Asiatic shore'.

Cunliffe-Owen added, however, that 'to command situation properly at Dardanelles requires also use of military force and point arises whether substantial enterprise should be attempted in quite a subsidiary theatre of war'. On 4 September Churchill informed the British commander of the Greek Navy, Admiral Mark Kerr: 'The right and obvious method of attacking Turkey is to strike immediately at the heart. To do this, it would be necessary for a Greek army to seize the Gallipoli peninsula under superiority of sea predominance, and thus to open the Dardanelles, admitting the Anglo-Greek Fleet to the Sea of Marmara, whence the Turco-German ships can be fought and sunk, and where, in combination with the Russian Black Sea Fleet and Russian military forces, the whole situation can be dominated.'

Churchill regarded Greek participation as crucial. 'I am very unhappy about getting into war with Turkey without having Greece as an ally', he wrote to Sir Edward Grey on 23 October. Even if the Greek army 'were paralysed by Bulgarian and Turkish attack', he wrote to Grey a few weeks later, 'a Russian Army Corps could easily be brought from Archangel, from Vladivostok, or, with Japanese consent, from Port Arthur, round to attack the Gallipoli position. No other military operations are necessary. The price to be paid in taking Gallipoli would no doubt be heavy, but there would be no more war with Turkey. A good army of 50,000 men and sea-power – that is the end of Turkish menace.'

On 29 September the Turks mined the Dardanelles waterway, and Russia lost her only warm water link with her Entente allies. A month later two German warships, the *Goeben* and the *Breslau*, flying the Turkish flag but still commanded by a German admiral, bombarded Russia's Black Sea ports. The reaction of the British Prime Minister, H.H. Asquith, was emphatic. 'Few things would give me greater pleasure,' he wrote privately to his friend Venetia Stanley, 'than to see the Turkish empire finally disappear from Europe.'

On 2 November, after Britain had declared war on Turkey, Churchill, with the approval of his new First Sea Lord, Jackie Fisher, instructed the British admiral in the Eastern Mediterranean, Admiral Carden, to carry out a naval demonstration at the Dardanelles: 'Without risking the ships,' Carden was told, 'demonstration is to be made by bombardment on the earliest suitable day by your armoured ships and the two French battleships against the forts at the entrance of the Dardanelles.' The following day, British and French warships bombarded the outer forts of the Dardanelles for ten minutes, at a range of just over seven miles. A shell which hit the magazine of the fort at Sedd-el-Bahr destroyed almost all its heavy guns.

Subsequent critics of this bombardment declared that it alerted the Turks, and caused them to move their main defences closer to Chanak, in the greater security of the narrows. But no serious work was done on the Turkish fortifications between this initial bombardment and the Allied naval attack more than four months later. German fortifications experts who had already arrived at the Dardanelles for the specific purpose of strengthening its land defences needed no warning from the Allies of where an attack was likely to come.

Even before the Allied bombardment of the outer forts, most military supplies reaching Turkey were sent direct to the Dardanelles. Nor was the installation of three torpedo tubes at the narrows the result of the bombardment of 3 November, but of a suggestion which Admiral Limpus himself had made while still responsible, among his duties with the Turkish admiralty, for advising on the naval defences of the Dardanelles.

The effects of the bombardment of 3 November were studied at the Admiralty by Admiral Sir Henry Jackson, and used by him to form the basis of plans for a major naval assault. At the same time, Churchill began discussions with Fisher, Jackson and Admiral Oliver on the best method of forcing the Dardanelles, using some of Britain's older battleships which, while of no value to Jellicoe's Grand Fleet in the North Sea, could still fire their guns against a static land target, and fight a naval power like Turkey which possessed no superior ships.

At the first meeting of the newly formed War Council on 25 November, held at 10 Downing Street with Asquith in the chair, military intelligence reported that a large Turkish army was moving south through Palestine to attack the Suez Canal. Colonel Hankey, secretary to the War Council, recorded the subsequent discussion: 'Mr Churchill suggested that the ideal method of defending Egypt was by an attack on the Gallipoli Peninsula. This, if successful, would give us control of the Dardanelles, and we could dictate terms at Constantinople. This, however, was a very difficult operation requiring a large force.' During the discussion, Fisher asked 'whether Greece might not perhaps undertake an attack on Gallipoli on behalf of the Allies'. Grey then explained that the King of Greece had refused to endorse his Prime Minister's earlier offer of 60,000 Greek troops for such an attack.

Churchill had already stressed the need for a large military force in any operations against the Dardanelles. On 30 November, Admiral Oliver suggested that troop transport should be kept in Egypt sufficient to transport a division of troops to the Dardanelles should it become possible to assemble the men in future. Churchill passed this request to Kitchener with the note: 'Had we not better keep enough transports congregated for 40,000 men . . .'.

Throughout December, with Greece unwilling to provide the men, and no other troops then available, the Gallipoli peninsula was left unmolested. This did not please Churchill. 'His volatile mind', Asquith wrote to Venetia Stanley on 5 December, 'is at present set on Turkey and Bulgaria, and he wants to organise a heroic adventure against Gallipoli and the Dardanelles: to which I am altogether opposed . . .'. Asquith's mind soon moved, however, in Churchill's direction, for on 28 December, Colonel Hankey, whose judgement Asquith respected, suggested striking at Germany through her allies, 'and particularly through Turkey'. What Hankey advised was to 'weave a web around Turkey which shall end her career as a European Power'.

Hankey proposed a Bulgarian attack on Turkey, in return for territory in Thrace. Greece would be offered southern Albania. Serbia (which had just driven the invading Austrians from Belgrade) would be offered Bosnia, Herzegovina and northern Albania. Three British army corps would participate. This force, Hankey believed, in conjunction with the Greeks and Bulgarians 'ought to be sufficient to capture Constantinople'. Three months were needed. Success would restore communication with the Black Sea, 'bringing down at once the price of wheat, and setting free the much needed shipping locked up there'. With Constantinople conquered, the Entente powers, joined by Serbia and Roumania, would march simultaneously into Austria-Hungary.

Such was Hankey's plan. Churchill supported it in a letter to Asquith on 31 December. A day later, the Russian Commander-in-Chief, the Grand Duke Nicholas, asked for a British demonstration against the Turks in the west to relieve the pressure in the Caucasus. Kitchener wrote to Churchill: 'the only place that a demonstration might have some effect in stopping reinforcements going east would be at the Dardanelles'. Churchill discussed Kitchener's letter with his Admiralty War Group on 3 January 1915. If such an attack took place, it would have to be with old battleships not needed in the North Sea. Before the war, Churchill had allocated funds to maintain these ships. This gave the War Group confidence that a plan might be worked out for naval action within the next few months, assuming that Admiral Carden felt a purely naval enterprise had some chance of success.

Shortly after mid-day on 3 January, Churchill signalled Carden: 'Do you consider the forcing of the Dardanelles by ships alone a practicable operation? It is assumed older battleships fitted with mine bumpers would be used preceded by colliers or other merchant craft as bumpers and sweepers. Importance of results would justify severe loss. Let me know your views.'

While the Admiralty waited for Carden's reply about a naval move to help Russia, Fisher, who had been impressed by Hankey's memorandum of 28 December, put forward his own 'Turkey plan', as he called it, writing to Churchill: 'The Greeks to go for Gallipoli at the same time as we go for Besika, and the Bulgarians for Constantinople, and the Russians, the Serbians and Roumanians for Austria . . . Sturdee forces the Dardanelles at the same time with "Majestic" class and "Canopus" class! God bless him!'

Fisher envisaged a combined military and naval operation against Turkey, based on an alliance of all the Balkan States. Churchill had been evolving an entirely different plan for the early months of 1915. This was an amphibious landing on the German North Sea coast, against either Oldenburg or Schleswig-Holstein. He therefore replied to Fisher: 'I think we had better hear what others have to say about the Turkish plans before taking a decided line. I would not grudge 100,000 men because of the great political effects in the Balkan peninsula: but Germany is the foe, and it is bad war to seek cheaper victories and easier antagonists.'

The possibility of British naval action at the Dardanelles depended on the view of the admiral on the spot. Carden's reply, which arrived early on the afternoon of 5 January, stated that he might be able to force the Dardanelles by ships alone. His signal read: 'With reference to your telegram of third inst., I do not consider Dardanelles can be rushed. They might be forced by extended operations with large numbers of ships.'

The War Council met later that afternoon. Carden's telegram, suggesting the possibility of an entirely naval effort to force the Dardanelles, had not deflected Churchill's belief that with the seizure of a North Sea island and the invasion of Germany through Schleswig-Holstein all other theatres of war and all other strategic possibilities would become secondary. But when Kitchener spoke of the need for action at the Dardanelles, to help Russia, Churchill read the War Council the 'might be forced' telegram he had received from Carden an hour before.

Returning to the Admiralty, Churchill found that the 'extended operations' Carden favoured were supported by Admiral Oliver, and also by Admiral Jackson, who had been impressed by the effects of the bombardment of 3 November, and believed that a systematic bombardment from the sea, fort by fort, would enable ships alone to force the Dardanelles.

On the following afternoon, supported by the views of Oliver and Jackson, Churchill telegraphed to Carden: 'Your view is agreed with by high authorities here. Please telegraph in detail what you think could be done by extended operations, what force would be needed, and how you consider it should be used.'

At the War Council on 8 January, Kitchener was emphatic. 'The Dardanelles', he said, 'appeared to be the most suitable objective, as an attack here could be made in cooperation with the Fleet. If successful, it would reestablish communications with Russia; settle the Near Eastern question; draw in Greece and, perhaps, Bulgaria and Roumania; and release wheat and shipping now locked up in the Black Sea.' Hankey, though not a member of the Council, added that success at the Dardanelles 'would give us the Danube as a line of communication for an army penetrating into the heart of Austria and bring our sea power to bear in the middle of Europe.'

The minutes of the meeting show that Churchill's thoughts were still dominated by the North Sea:

Mr Churchill said he fully agreed in the proposal to study the suggested operations in the Mediterranean. He urged, however, that we should not lose sight of the possibility of action in Northern Europe. As an instance of the attractiveness of such operations, he mentioned that the distance from Emden to Berlin was exactly half the distance from Sir John French's headquarters to Berlin. Was there no possibility that Holland might enter the war on the side of the Allies? . . . If Holland could be induced to enter the war the advantages would far outweigh those of the Mediterranean; we could then have an island as a naval base without fighting for it, and our armies, in conjunction with the Dutch, could attack towards Essen.

Fisher continued to advocate action against the Turks. 'If the Greeks land 100,000 men on the Gallipoli Peninsula, in concert with a British naval attack at the Dardanelles', he wrote to a friend at the Foreign Office on 11 January, 'I think we could count on an easy and quick arrival at Constantinople.' A day later the need for troops as an adjunct to a naval attack was dispelled by a second telegram from Carden, for the admiral now stated that it might be possible, by ships alone, to force the Dardanelles in about a month.

Carden outlined four phases of action: the 'total reduction' of the Turkish defences at the entrance to the Dardanelles; clearing the Turkish defences inside the straits up to and including Kephez Point; the reduction of the defences at the narrows and at Chanak; and, finally, clearing a passage through the minefield, advancing through the narrows, reducing the forts above the narrows and advancing into the Sea of Marmara. Carden envisaged the attack ending with four battleships, two battle-cruisers and twelve destroyers securely inside the Marmara.

The implication of this signal was clear. The Royal Navy could, by ships alone, achieve a master stroke of the war. By ships alone the pressure on Russia could be relieved. Without transferring troops from Flanders, Britain would turn the southern and weakest flank of the Central Powers, and ensure that Greece, Bulgaria and Roumania, even Italy, hasten to join the Entente.

Up to that moment Churchill had doubted the possibility of forcing the Dardanelles without troops. But he had never doubted that, once the Dardanelles were forced, British naval power would suffice to encompass the Turks' defeat. The naval force which Carden proposed to take into the Sea of Marmara would inevitably defeat the Turkish Fleet, even with the *Goeben* and the *Breslau* at its head. If the arrival of the *Goeben* and the *Breslau* off Constantinople had turned the balance in Germany's favour at the outbreak of war, it seemed impossible that the Turks could resist the overwhelming strength of Carden's fleet.

Much of Turkey's war-making power was at Constantinople, exposed to attack from the sea. Turkey's sole shell factory was on the shore of the Sea of Marmara. Her principal gun and rifle factory was likewise vulnerable to naval attack. West of the city, the railway linking Constantinople with the fortress of Adrianople and the fortified lines of Chatalja ran for several miles along the shore. On the Asian side, the railway into Anatolia did likewise. Both could easily be cut by ships in the Sea of Marmara.

On 12 January the Admiralty War Group, headed by Fisher, discussed every aspect of Carden's proposals. Neither Jackson nor Oliver, who subsequently criticised Carden's plan before the Dardanelles Commission, did so that day. Fisher made no protest. Jackson not only concurred in the proposals but urged their rapid implementation. Each member of the group realised the enormous difficulties involved; each turned his own knowledge and expertise to the search for methods of overcoming the difficulties.

The victory at the Falkland Islands six weeks before, by completing the destruction of German naval power outside German waters, had released large numbers of ships for the new enterprise. Fisher himself suggested that, in addition to the old ships which Carden considered sufficient, the newest and most powerful ship in the fleet, the *Queen Elizabeth*, should be sent out to the Dardanelles. Her 15-inch guns had not yet been fired but could be tested, Fisher argued, not on dummy targets off Gibraltar, but on the Turkish forts at the Dardanelles. 'If this is practicable,' he wrote to Oliver, 'she could go straight there, hoist Carden's flag and go on with her gunnery exercises.'

'This had not occurred to me before', Churchill told the Dardanelles Commissioners in 1916, 'but the moment it was mentioned its importance became apparent. We all felt ourselves in the presence of a "new fact". Moreover the *Queen Elizabeth* came into the argument with a cumulative effect.'

When the War Council met at noon on 13 January, the main discussion was how to help Sir John French by naval action along the Belgian coast, culminating in the seizure of Zeebrugge. When the Council finally turned its attention to the Dardanelles, Churchill outlined the details of Carden's plan. He explained that the three modern and twelve old battleships which Carden believed necessary could be spared for the task 'without reducing our strength in the main theatre of war'. He described the discussions that had already taken place at the Admiralty, and expressed his belief 'that a plan could be made for systematically reducing all the forts within a few weeks'.

The effects of this action would, Churchill told his colleagues, be impressive: 'Once the forts were reduced, the minefields could be cleared and the Fleet would proceed up to Constantinople and destroy the *Goeben*.' Hankey recalled in his memoirs how 'The idea caught on at once. . . . The War Council turned eagerly from the dreary vista of a "slogging match" on the Western Front to brighter prospects, as they seemed, in the Mediterranean. . . . Even French . . . caught something of the tremendous enthusiasm.' According to Hankey's minutes of the meeting, Lloyd George declared that he 'liked the plan', and Kitchener said that he 'thought it was worth trying'. Discussion then turned to other possible areas of British naval and military action. Grey wanted the Navy to attack the Austrian port of Cattaro, on the Adriatic, to influence Italy to join the Entente. Lloyd George again suggested a British naval assault up the Danube, into the heart of Austria-Hungary.

Zeebrugge, the Dardanelles, Cattaro and the Danube; each had its advocates. It was Asquith who then drafted the War Council's conclusions. In them, he set out two tasks for the Navy. The first was 'That the Admiralty should consider promptly the possiblity of effective action in the Adriatic, at Cattaro, or elsewhere, with the view (*inter alia*) of bringing pressure on Italy.' The second was 'That the Admiralty should also prepare for a naval expedition in February to bombard and take the Gallipoli peninsula, with Constantinople as its objective.'

'The Council is now over,' Asquith wrote to Venetia Stanley, 'having arrived harmoniously at four conclusions suggested by me which will keep both navy and army busy till March. . . . I maintained an almost unbroken silence till the end, when I intervened with my conclusions.' The second of Asquith's naval conclusions, to 'bombard and take the Gallipoli peninsula', constituted the decisive authority for action.

Asquith's first naval conclusion had instructed Churchill and his admirals to plan for an attack on Austrian naval positions in the Adriatic. But Fisher and Oliver both felt that any British naval involvement in the Adriatic might weaken the chances of success at the Dardanelles. Churchill put their objections to Asquith, Grey and Kitchener: 'We consider that no useful means can be found of effective naval intervention in the Adriatic at the present time . . .', he wrote. 'The attack on the Dardanelles will require practically our whole available margin. If that attack opens prosperously it will very soon attract to itself the whole attention of the Eastern theatre, and if it succeeds it will produce results which will undoubtedly influence every Mediterranean power. In these circumstances we strongly advise that the Adriatic should be left solely to the French and that we should devote ourselves to action in accordance with the third conclusion of the War Council, viz: the methodical forcing of the Dardanelles.'

Asquith accepted this, telling Venetia Stanley he hoped that what he called 'our Gallipoli enterprise' would help compel Italy to enter the war on the side of the Entente.

On 25 January Admiral Oliver completed a comprehensive scheme for the rapid concentration of six battleships at the Dardanelles. It was Fisher who then suggested adding two more battleships, *Lord Nelson* and *Agamemnon*. They too were ordered to proceed to the eastern Mediterranean. But on the morning of 28 January, shortly before the War Council was due to meet, Fisher wrote to Churchill, announcing, astoundingly, that he was resigning as First Sea Lord. The North Sea Fleet was being denuded of essential warships, Fisher said, because of the demands of the Dardanelles.

Asquith asked to see Fisher and Churchill in his study at Downing Street. If the Zeebrugge and Dardanelles operations were in conflict for naval resources, he told them, then Zeebrugge should be dropped. The three men then went downstairs to the Cabinet Room, for the War Council. When, all of a sudden, Fisher tried to leave the room, Kitchener stopped him, pointing out, as Fisher himself later recorded, 'that he (Lord Fisher) was the only dissentient, and that the Dardanelles operation had been decided upon by the Prime Minister.' Fisher returned to the Cabinet table. Asquith then asked members to say what importance they attached to the Dardanelles operation. The minutes recorded:

> Lord Kitchener considered the naval attack to be vitally important. If successful, its effect would be equivalent to that of a successful campaign fought with the new armies . . .
>
> Mr Balfour pointed out that a successful attack on the Dardanelles would achieve the following results:
>
> It would cut the Turkish army in two;
>
> It would put Constantinople under our control;
>
> It would give us the advantage of having the Russian wheat, and enable Russia to resume exports;
>
> This would restore the Russian exchanges, which were falling owing to her inability to export, and causing great embarrassment;
>
> It would also open a passage to the Danube.
>
> It was difficult to imagine a more helpful operation.
>
> Sir Edward Grey said it would also finally settle the attitude of Bulgaria and the whole of the Balkans.

Grey was emerging as the keenest for action. At a second War Council on 28 January, he pressed for the earliest possible date for the naval attack at the Dardanelles. 'The Austro-German objective now', he wrote to Churchill on 31 January, 'is to overawe Roumania and Greece, to attract Bulgaria and to steady the Turks by an offensive against Serbia. If we can succeed in forcing the straits, or even creating a scare at Constantinople before this offensive can make headway, we shall have done much to discourage if not to paralyse it.'

Asquith also wanted rapid action at the Dardanelles, writing to Venetia Stanley: 'I can't help feeling that the whole situation in the Near East may be vitally transformed, if the bombardment of the Dardanelles by our ships next week (Secret) goes well. It is a great experiment. . . . If it is successful, it will smash up the Turks, and, incidentally, let through all the Russian wheat which is now locked up and so lower the price of bread. But it is full of uncertainties.'

Opinion at the Admiralty had begun to veer towards the use of troops as well as ships at the narrows. 'Not a grain of wheat will come from the Black Sea,' Fisher wrote to Churchill in the early hours of 16 February, 'unless there is a military occupation of the Dardanelles.' Churchill put forward this view at an emergency meeting of the War Council on the same day. It was agreed that the 29th Division, and 50,000 Australian and New Zealand troops then in Egypt, should be held in readiness for a Gallipoli landing. Kitchener's words to Churchill were: 'You get through! I will find the men.'

Then, at the War Council three days later, Kitchener announced that he would not allow the 29th Division to go. Churchill appealed against this, but in vain. Lloyd George, Grey, Balfour and Asquith each supported Churchill, but their arguments were to no avail.

The bombardment of the outer forts of the Dardanelles began on the morning of 19 February. At the War Council five days later Kitchener stated that 'if the Fleet succeeded in silencing the forts, the garrison of Gallipoli would probably be withdrawn'. If they did not withdraw 'they would run the risk of being cut off and starved out'.

Churchill then explained to his colleagues his reasoning for still wanting the 29th Division: 'If the fleet got through the Dardanelles', he said, 'they could be put into Constantinople. Or they could be put into European Turkey towards the Bulgarian frontier; Bulgaria could then be invited to take possession up to the Enos–Media line as a condition of joining the Allies. The Allied forces could then be sent up through Bulgaria to Nish. Another plan would be to send them to Salonika in order to influence the Balkan States. Or they might be sent up the Danube if Roumania joined the Allies.'

Lloyd George also wanted troops used 'after the navy had cleared the Dardanelles, to occupy the Gallipoli Peninsula or Constantinople'. But Kitchener was emphatic that the navy could defeat the Turks at the Dardanelles without military support, telling the War Council that as soon as the forts 'were clearly being silenced one by one' the Turkish garrison on the Gallipoli peninsula would evacuate its position, and that 'the garrison of Constantinople, the Sultan, and not improbably the Turkish army in Thrace, would also decamp to the Asiatic shore'. With patience and wise negotiation, Kitchener argued, the remaining Turkish forces in Europe 'would probably surrender'.

Why then was it necessary, Kitchener asked, to send out to the Dardanelles 'the large forces contemplated by Mr Churchill'? Before Churchill could answer, Grey spoke in support of Kitchener, emphasising the moral effect of large naval guns. Once success was achieved at the Dardanelles, he said 'we might have a coup d'état in Constantinople'. This would obviate the need for any military activity against the Turks, who would either return to their former neutrality, or even agree to join the Entente against their German ally.

Churchill made one more effort to secure troops. If Britain could offer the Balkan states the prospect of victory against the Turks, he said, it might bring a million Balkan soldiers into the Allied Army. Surely, he asked, the presence of 100,000 British troops would be worthwhile if it achieved its objective? Kitchener could not be convinced. He did not envisage a strong Turkish resistance. When Asquith asked whether the Australians and New Zealanders 'were good enough' for an important operation of war, Kitchener replied 'that they were quite good enough if a cruise in the Sea of Marmara was all that was contemplated'.

Unwilling to overrule Kitchener, Asquith confided his inner thoughts to Venetia Stanley. 'One must take a lot of risks in war', he wrote to her after the War Council, 'and I am strongly of the opinion that the chance of forcing the Dardanelles, and occupying Constantinople, and cutting Turkey in half, and arousing on our side the whole Balkan peninsula, represents such a unique opportunity that we ought to hazard a lot elsewhere rather than forgo it.'

Churchill continued to press for the 29th Division, hoping to make up a total of 115,000 men, including the Australians and New Zealanders. At the War Council on 26 February he appealed again, telling his colleagues: 'In three weeks' time Constantinople might be at our mercy. We should avoid the risk of finding ourselves with a force inadequate to our requirements and face to face with a disaster. At the previous meeting Lord Kitchener had asked him what was the use to be made of any large number of troops at Constantinople. His reply was that they were required to occupy Constantinople and to compel a surrender of all Turkish forces remaining in Europe after the fleet had obtained command of the Sea of Marmara. With an army at hand this could be accomplished either by fighting, or by negotiation, or by bribery . . . .'

If Bulgaria subsequently joined the Allies, Churchill told the War Council, 'we should be in a position to push the troops up through Bulgaria to Serbia. Or, if Roumania came in, they could be sent up the Danube, or by rail through Roumania. The actual and definite object of the army would be to reap the fruits of the naval success.' Kitchener reiterated his belief that the naval attack would secure victory. He was convinced, he said, 'from his knowledge of Constantinople and the East, that the whole situation in Constantinople would change the moment the fleet had secured a passage through the Dardanelles'.

Balfour, a former prime minister, spoke in Kitchener's support. 'If the purely naval operation were carried out,' he said, 'the following results would be attained: the command of the Sea of Marmara would be secured; the Turkish troops remaining in Europe would be cut off; the arsenal and dockyards at Constantinople could be destroyed; the condition of the Turks would become worse every day they held out; the Bosphorus could be opened; a line of supply for war-like stores opened up with Russia, and wheat obtained from the Black Sea.'

Hankey, Lloyd George and Asquith each then supported Churchill's appeal for the despatch of the 29th Division, but Kitchener now insisted that he must have a means of reinforcing the Western Front if the Russian front collapsed. Churchill entered a powerful caveat. 'The 29th Division would not make the difference between failure and success in France', he said, 'but might well make the difference in the East. He wished it to be placed on record that he dissented altogether from the retention of the 29th Division in this country. If a disaster occurred in Turkey owing to the insufficiency of troops, he must disclaim all responsibility.' That evening Churchill wrote to his brother Jack: 'The limited fund of life and energy which I possess is not much use to influence these tremendous events.'

The outer forts of the Dardanelles were bombarded on 25 February. The bombardment was a success. Plans for minesweeping up to the narrows went ahead. The prospect of victory was a powerful stimulant to plans and forecasts, even for Churchill, deprived of the first-class troops of the 29th Division. On 28 February he turned his mind to the conditions of Turkey's surrender, writing to Grey: 'Should we get through Dardanelles, as is now likely, we cannot be content with anything less than the surrender of everything Turkish in Europe. I shall tell the admiral after destroying the Turco-German fleet to push on at once to attack Bosphorus, and thus cut off the retreat of the army. Their capitulation is then only a question of time.'

The Turks must surrender all their forces, and all arms, arsenals, armaments and ships in European Turkey, as well as the fortress of Adrianople and all military positions controlling the Bosphorus. The Allies would occupy and administer all Turkish territories in Europe.

All German officers and men in Turkey would become Allied prisoners of war. Churchill added: 'I look forward with much hope to the delivery of Adrianople by the British to the Bulgarian army. But celerity and vigour are indispensable. Remember,' he told Grey, 'Constantinople is only a means to an end – and the only end is the march of the Balkan States against the Central Powers.'

Minesweeping began on 1 March. A week later Carden warned of the problems in locating the Turkish mobile howitzers. But at the War Council on 10 March the prospect of a swift victory still captivated those present. Lloyd George wanted Britain to acquire Palestine. Kitchener said Palestine 'would be of no value to us whatsoever' and urged the annexation of Alexandretta. The Colonial Secretary, Lewis Harcourt, rejected this, wanting Britain to acquire instead the port of Marmarice, on the Turkish coast opposite Rhodes. Churchill expressed no territorial desires (and thought that Palestine might be given to 'neutral, and now noble' Belgium). The Viceroy of India, Lord Hardinge, had also welcomed victory over the Turks. It would enable 'a stream of grain' to leave the Black Sea, he said, with the result that India's difficulties in obtaining adequate food would be 'much alleviated'.

Fisher sent his own plan to Churchill on 12 March. 'Carden to press on!' he wrote, 'and Kitchener to occupy the deserted Forts at extremity of Gallipoli and mount howitzers there! . . . Invite Bulgaria by telegram (direct from Sir E. Grey) to take Kavalla and Salonika provided she at once attacks Turkey and tell Greece "Too late"! and seize the Greek Fleet by a "coup" later on. They would probably join us now if bribed!'

Shortly before the first naval attempt to break through into the Sea of Marmara, Kitchener sent Sir Ian Hamilton to command what he optimistically designated the 'Constantinople Expeditionary Force'.

Churchill at once sought some simultaneous military operation by the 30,000 Anzac and 10,000 Royal Naval Division troops that were already in the eastern Mediterranean. Hamilton agreed. 'I don't see how these concealed howitzers are to be tackled without storming the plateau', he wrote to Churchill while in the train on his way to Marseilles. Kitchener insisted, however, on deferring any military action until the 29th Division, which he had finally agreed should go to the Dardanelles, had arrived.

On 13 March Fisher ordered two further battleships, *Queen* and *Implacable*, to strengthen Carden's fleet. Three days later, on the eve of the naval attack, Carden was taken ill. He was replaced by his second-in-command, Admiral de Robeck, who was willing to go ahead without delay.

The naval attack on 18 March put all speculation to the test of naval action. Hamilton watched the attack from on board ship, but with no plans to put ashore the 59,000 men, including French troops, who were then at Lemnos. When the naval attack was called off, after stumbling upon the hazards of a small, undetected minefield (with the loss of 60 British and 600 French sailors), de Robeck told the Admiralty that further minesweeping, and a second naval attack, would be resumed within three to four days. He was willing, he said, 'to resume a vigorous offensive' before the army was ready to land. Fisher, still an enthusiast, ordered two more battleships, *London* and *Prince of Wales*, to reinforce de Robeck's fleet.

No second attempt was made to force the narrows by ships alone. Within forty-eight hours, after consultation with Hamilton, de Robeck decided that troops must land simultaneously with the next naval attack (as Churchill had wished for 18 March). General Birdwood, the Anzac commander, wanted to attempt this at once. But Kitchener's orders were still that Hamilton must wait for the 29th Division, and no further naval action took place until the military landings on 25 April.

Two weeks after the military landings, which fell within Kitchener's sphere of authority, and before any decisive outcome, a political crisis erupted. It centred on the shortage of shells on the Western Front, but was accelerated when Fisher, agitated by Churchill's continued despatch of surplus naval vessels to de Robeck, walked out of the Admiralty building, alerted the Conservative opposition to the fact that he had left, and went into hiding. Asquith, who was at that very moment in the throes of a desperate personal crisis, ordered Fisher by letter to return to his post 'in the King's name', but Fisher remained in hiding. Desperate to end the political crisis, Asquith agreed to bring the Conservative leaders into his government.

One Conservative demand was that Churchill leave the Admiralty. Churchill begged Asquith to allow him to defend his conduct of naval affairs, including the Dardanelles, but Asquith refused to allow this. The shadow of the Dardanelles was to hover over Churchill's career for more than a quarter of a century. While still in Asquith's government he spent several hundred hours preparing his evidence for the Dardanelles Commission but, despite his pleas to Asquith, his evidence was never made public. The government agreed to publish only a general report. The documents (many of which I have used here), submissions and cross-examinations were not made public.

Churchill's final letter to the Dardanelles Commissioners, in which he dwelt on the land campaign which was so often, and wrongly, associated with his executive authority, was relegated, with all his evidence and submissions, to the status of a secret document. In it he made a comparison with the Battle of the Somme.

For the sake of a few miles of ground devoid of strategic significance, nearly 600,000 British casualties have been sustained and the efficiency of our Army in the West sensibly and permanently diminished. . . .

Nevertheless with a good Press sedulously manipulated and employed and the effective support of the governing forces, these operations have been represented as a long series of famous and memorable victories and the initial disaster of the 1st of July has been established in the public mind as a brilliant triumph. A fifth of the resources, the effort, the loyalty, the resolution, the perseverance vainly employed in the Battle of the Somme to gain a few shattered villages and a few square miles of devastated ground, would in the Gallipoli Peninsula, used in time, have united the Balkans on our side, joined hands with Russia, and cut Turkey out of the war. The choice was open to us; we have built our own misfortune and no one can tell what its limits will be.

Churchill concluded:

Public opinion is unable to measure the true proportion of events. Orthodox military opinion remains united on the local view that victory in 1915 could only be found by pouring out men and munitions in frantic efforts to break the German entrenchments in the West. The passage of a few years will throw a very different light on these events. They will then be seen in a truer proportion and perspective. It will then be understood that the capture of Constantinople and the rallying of the Balkans was the one great and decisive manoeuvre open to the allied armies in 1915. It will then be seen that the ill-supported armies struggling on the Gallipoli Peninsula, whose efforts are now viewed with so much prejudice and repugnance, were in fact within an ace of succeeding in an enterprise which would have abridged the miseries of the World and proved the salvation of our cause. It will then seem incredible that a dozen old ships, half a dozen divisions, or a few hundred thousand shells were allowed to stand between them and success. Contemporaries have condemned the men who tried to force the Dardanelles – history will condemn those who did not aid them.

Churchill's part in the Dardanelles–Gallipoli story is surely a creditable one. He also understood the human aspect which inevitably overshadowed, and still overshadows, the campaign. Two months after being removed from the Admiralty he wrote to a soldier friend: 'I am hopeful that the truth may be published. But failure and tragedy are all that are left to divide.'

The courage of those who fought – 'these prodigies of devotion' Churchill called them – can never be overshadowed by the hesitations, mistakes, miscalculations, idiosyncrasies and short-sightedness, or even by the vision, of those who conducted the war from Whitehall.

1. The battleships *Queen* (leading), *Triumph, Prince of Wales, Bacchante* and *London* on passage to the Anzac landing. (Australian War Memorial)

2. Winston Churchill and Lord Fisher at Whitehall. (Hulton Getty Picture Collection)

3. V Beach on 25 April 1915. A photograph taken from the fo'c'sle of the *River Clyde*. In front of the ship is a dumb lighter on which are dead and wounded, mostly Munsters and Hampshires. Sheltering below the low cliff at the shoreline are men from the Royal Dublin Fusiliers; they are being fired on by Turks to the left of the photograph. (Imperial War Museum, London)

4. The *River Clyde*, with the jetty built after the landings to link it to the beach. (Judy Holdsworth)

5. Ari Burnu and Anzac Cove on the day of landing. (New Zealand PIcture Library, London)

6. Looking north from Cape Helles. (Imperial War Museum, London)

7. Mustafa Kemal (Atatürk).

8. Cliffs at Anzac. (Australian War Memorial)

9. A British soldier teasing a Turkish sniper. (Imperial War Museum, London)

10. 14th (KGO) Sikhs. (Imperial War Museum, London)

11. French troops on their way to Gallipoli. (Imperial War Museum, London)

12. A wounded Turkish soldier
receives water from a British soldier.
Imperial War Museum, London)

13. 1/6th Gurkhas. (Imperial War Museum, London)

14. 5th Royal Irish Fusiliers in the trenches. (Imperial War Museum, London)

TWELVE

GALLIPOLI:
A FRENCH PERSPECTIVE

Jean-Charles Jauffret

23 April 1996

The Gallipoli Campaign: the French point of view

Each time the training ship *Jeanne d'Arc* sails up the straits of the
Dardanelles, the crew throws a wreath where the sailors of the battleship
Bouvet perished on 18 March 1915. On the Sedd-el-Bahr side, a lantern-
tower watches over the French cemetery, in silent homage to the nearly
15,000 men from the expeditionary force who died there. There is only one
monument in France to the glory of the *poilus* of this glorious but
disappointing eastern campaign; it is placed on the Corniche in Marseilles,
the harbour from which most of them left. If the nation's memory is
deficient, despite the existence of a national association to preserve the
memory of the Dardanelles and Middle East fronts, it is because the
sufferings on the Gallipoli peninsula do seem pointless. This expedition was
characterised by a lack of preparation and a whole series of errors. We have
to re-examine the way it developed if we are to understand the French
point of view and French criticisms. We also need to evoke what daily life
on a few square metres of rocks and sand was like, since, as one of the
major French strategists, Ardant du Picq, remarked: 'Le combat est le but
final des armées, et l'homme est l'instrument premier du combat'.[1]

The French Strategic Concepts

After the victory of the Marne and the race to the sea, the Allies knew the
war would be long. Two strategies were in direct opposition or perhaps
complemented each other. One was direct, looking for a decision in the
main theatres of operations: on the Western Front, from Alsace to Flanders,
on the Eastern Front, from Eastern Prussia to Ruthenia, south of the
Carpathians. The other, of which the maritime blockade of Germany
already gave an indication, was indirect and sought to choke Germany's

allies by the use of sea power. It was also designed to restrict Germany's own supplies of raw materials and to recruit new partners into the Entente.

From his headquarters in Chantilly, General Joffre declared he was resolutely against any waste of energy. The enemy was occupying the territory of the homeland and had to be chased away whatever the price, which included asking the British to increase their help through extending their front. The Germans were within 80 km of Paris, and the front was more than 800 km long. All the French offensives until 1918 were conditioned by Joffre's instruction no. 8, signed on 8 December 1914: to compel the enemy to fall back on the narrow base of the Meuse by squeezing him on both flanks. Consequently, the French Commander-in-Chief was constantly asking for British reinforcements, especially for the Champagne offensive launched in February 1915, the second phase of which had taken place from 16 to 20 March before the Artois offensive opened on 9 May. Those costly operations, carried on without sufficient heavy artillery, could be explained by another imperative. Joffre had no choice but to attack: if not he would lose the war. Indeed, the Russians called for help on 2 January 1915. The Tsar's regiments had been severely defeated by the Turkish troops of Enver Pasha at the foot of the Lesser Caucasus and were in retreat on the European Eastern Front. This retreat had started with the defeats at Tannenberg and the Masurian Lakes in August and September 1914, not to mention the setback in front of Lodz, in Russian Poland, in November 1914. It was therefore necessary to help this failing ally by constantly attacking and thus preventing most of the German army from going east to scramble for the spoils. For this reason, Joffre did not want a single man withdrawn from the Western Front.

The reluctance of the Commander-in-Chief of the French army is thus understandable when, pressed by the politicians putting a brave face on things, he had to form an expeditionary corps for the Dardanelles. Now, in March 1915, at the most crucial time of the Champagne offensive, the French troops faced a serious manpower crisis. The eastern expeditionary corps (17,000 men), under General d'Amade's command, was formed of two brigades whose distinctive feature was that they were not taken from the armies engaged in the west. The Metropolitan Brigade, under General Vandenberg's command, had a regiment from the active list created for this purpose (on the model of the Madagascar expedition of 1895). It was the 175th Infantry Regiment formed in the Dauphiné region: there were men from the Grenoble, Saintes and Varennes-sur-Allier depots. This brigade also had a second regiment drawn from the army stationed in North Africa. Five Zouave and one Foreign Legion battalion formed that 1 March African Regiment. No Algerian infantryman was recruited because a holy war had been proclaimed by the Sultan-Caliph of Constantinople; the Algerian component consisted only of French settlers. The cavalry came from the 8th Regiment of African chasseurs. The second brigade, under the command of Colonel Rueff, was colonial, composed of four battalions of Senegalese infantrymen and of two regiments, one of which, the 6th Infantry Regiment, was formed of Europeans, most of them from Indo-China.

The way the Amade division was formed illustrated the broader strategic option. Contrary to what is generally believed, part of the French high command was favourable to an outflanking strategy. On 10 October 1914, General Galliéni, a prestigious colonial war chief commanding the Paris Army, who did not believe that a decision on the Western Front was possible, advised Aristide Briand, the Minister of Justice, to carry out a diversion through Salonika to march towards the Danube through the Balkans, with a second possible diversion in the gulf of Alexandretta.[2] This plan was known to Lloyd George, Chancellor of the Exchequer in the Asquith government, who agreed with it and so informed the British War Council on 1 January 1915.[3] Again, in October 1914, the French-Algerian General Franchet d'Espérey – in charge of the Vth Army, whose role was decisive in the victory of the Marne – who knew the Middle East well, showed President Raymond Poincaré (the linchpin of the Franco-Russian alliance) the advantage of a landing in Salonika in order to help the Serbs and also to help the Russians by taking the Austro-Hungarians in the rear. On 1 January 1915 Franchet d'Espérey was entertained at the Elysée and listened to by the President of the Republic and the Prime Minister, René Viviani. On 6 January, he gave Poincaré a memorandum, the historical importance of which was fundamental, since it contained the scheme for the victory of September–October 1918 in the Balkans. This plan, based on the hope of bringing the hesitating Balkan states (Greece, Bulgaria, Roumania) into the war on the Allied side, could be summarised in a few essential characteristics. It was based on the principle of a landing at Salonika – a Greek harbour with easy access and, moreover, opening into the only major valley running north-west/south-east. This, the Vardar valley, permitted a direct penetration into the Balkans from the Aegean sea. To summarise, d'Espérey wished to direct an expeditionary corps through Belgrade to Vienna and Berlin; to enlist the help of the Serbs, who at that moment held the upper hand over the Austro-Hungarians, in concentrating on the Danube a French army strong enough to cut the Turks off from their allies; and to establish a link with Russia through Roumania.[4]

In practice, the French and the British were each working independently to help the Russians. It was only at the end of 1914 that the French government was informed of Churchill's plan. The latter advocated a direct attack on Constantinople through the Dardanelles.[5] On 23 January the French War Minister, Alexandre Millerand, who was in London to talk to Lord Kitchener about British reinforcements for the Western Front, wired France in time for the cabinet meetings. The Navy Minister, Victor Augagneur, then informed his colleagues that the British Navy was preparing an operation in the Dardanelles. Three days later, while the Navy Minister was in London on a mission, and during a further cabinet meeting, Alexandre Millerand reported that he had been received by King George and by British ministers, among whom was Winston Churchill. Lord Kitchener seemed to favour the French project and had declared himself ready to send a division to Serbia.[6] On 30 January, Augagneur came back from London and presented the operation in the Dardanelles as a diversion with which Winston Churchill wanted to associate the French. The French government agreed; Augagneur, who doubted whether the straits could be forced, thought England could not be diverted from her project, since she was taking all the risks. It was in fact an exchange of friendly gestures: the French cabinet agreed to participate in the Dardanelles expedition under British command against the promise of a reinforcement of five divisions to help prepare the Champagne offensive. By taking this decision rather hastily the French temporarily abandoned the Salonika project Aristide Briand cared about. Nevertheless, they managed to agree to the defence of the eastern Mediterranean with their British ally and hoped to see 500,000 Roumanians join their side. Indeed, marching on Constantinople meant cutting the umbilical cord of the famous Baghdad–Berlin railway and offered the possiblity of encircling the Central Powers by putting the Ottoman Empire out of the war. Such an operation would also protect Suez, the main artery for imperial trade and oil traffic, from another Turko-German offensive, such as that of 2 February 1915. Still further, it would offer a helping hand to the Russians through the Black Sea both by establishing a direct maritime link with the granary that the Ukraine represented, and by making possible some immediate supply of arms to the Russian Army, whose logistics were in a state of collapse.

Taking action was not as simple as the politicians had expected. The whole operation was based on an ambiguity. At the beginning of January, the Russians asked their allies for help without specifying where it was required. The Grand Duke Nicholas, Commander-in-Chief of the Russian Army, asked for two things. The French were asked for urgent delivery of artillery ammunition. The British were rather imprecisely asked to mount an operation in the Mediterranean to relieve Turkish pressure on the Caucasus. The British chose a support operation by the shortest route via the Dardanelles and the Sea of Marmara. The Quai d'Orsay let them do it, forgetting one of the axioms of Russian foreign policy summarised by Dostoyevsky in the following formula: 'Tôt ou tard, Constantinople devra nous appartenir'.[7] The Russian government did not really want to see the British and the French arrive in Constantinople as conquerors. This city was still the symbol of the Second Rome where the Russians thought they had a sacred mission to restore the Orthodox religion as its protectors throughout the Middle East. Moreover, the Russians feared that taking Constantinople would mainly benefit the Greeks, whose Prime Minister, Venizelos, was doing his best to bring Greece into the war on the Allied side. And the Tsar distrusted the Greek queen who was the German Kaiser's sister. All these factors add up to explain how the Allies committed their first major geostrategic error of launching a risky and ambitious operation without being sure Roumania would enter the war on their side and without any practical Russian support. Admittedly, Russia's offensive potentiality had been restricted since August 1914, but while the Allies had to endure continuous Turkish fire on the Gallipoli peninsula, the Russian Navy was shut away in the Crimean and Ukrainian harbours. The only important action by the Tsar's troops took place on 22 March 1915 in Galicia, far from Thrace and Gallipoli, when they took the Austro-Hungarian fortress of Przemysl in an offensive whose objective was Budapest. This brief breakthrough in the Carpathians ran out of steam through lack of ammunition and fresh troops. In May 1915 any hope of indirect support from the Russians disappeared. Their front was broken through at Gorlice, creating a general withdrawal that was the start of a long agony. The offensives of Brusilov in June 1916 and July 1917 did not succeed in checking it. Remembering this background is important in a total war where everything takes places on a continental scale. The isolation of the fighting men in the Dardanelles who progressively faced more and more Turkish battle formations can be better understood.

From the very beginning, the French and the British made another fatal error of judgement: a deplorable underestimation of the adversary. The Middle East and its exotic fragrances, the Turkish defeats of 1912 during the first war in the Balkans, the Turko-German failure at Suez in 1915, all made them forgret the rustic simplicity of the Ottoman army trained by such skilled German officers as Liman von Sanders. This second error led to a maritime offensive that was too quickly planned and met with setbacks similar to those suffered later by the land forces.

Nelson was Right

The first phase of the maritime Franco-British offensive illustrated this well-known maxim of Admiral Nelson: 'Tout marin qui attaque un fort est un fou.'[8] The success of Admiral Duckworth in forcing the straits in 1807, and the memory of the Franco-British-Russian naval victory in 1827 at Navarino against the ships of the Sublime Porte, helped to generate a disdainful attitude towards the Turks. Then the Allies became confused between gunboat policy and the preparation of a large-scale enterprise. On 3 November 1914, a Franco-British squadron opened fire against the forts in the Dardanelles in response to the bombardment of the Russian harbours in the Black Sea by the warships *Goeben* and *Breslau* which the Germans had given to the Turks. But the Allied bombardment also prompted the Ottoman Empire to fortify the straits, taking advantage of German know-how and material.

At the beginning of January 1915, despite Admiral Fisher's reservations, Winston Churchill managed to convince the British government of the need for a large-scale naval action in the straits along the lines of Admiral Carden's plan. By this time, the French were no longer interested in burden-sharing between the Allies. Thus the French, rather inconsistently but because they were happy to let their ally bear the brunt of the operation, carry a share of responsibility for the faults that developed in the command structure. The inconsistency arose because the London conference of 6 August 1914 had assigned the Mediterranean to the French fleet, while the Royal Navy took charge of the security of the Channel and the North Sea. After this conference, Admiral Boué de Lapeyrère was appointed Commander-in-Chief of the Franco-British forces in the Mediterranean.[9] But he was totally excluded from the preparations for the Dardanelles which were thus outside the control of the man supposed to be responsible for this central theatre of operations. This lack of initial coordination was to cause trouble when decisions had to be improvised during the expedition against the Dardanelles.

Admiral Guépratte was the commander of the French naval squadron in the eastern Mediterranean in March–April 1915 and, like his successors, dealt directly with the Navy Ministry in Paris. Once again mistakes were made through underestimating the adversary. The French thought that old armoured ships with a respectable main artillery (305 mm or 12 inch) would be sufficient; the *Bouvet*, the *Charlemagne*, the *Gaulois* and the *Suffren* were engaged. The British made the same miscalculation and added only one superdreadnought, the *Queen Elizabeth*. Considering the firepower of this brand new battleship, cautiously though it was used, it has often been wondered what would have happened to the Turkish forts if other battleships of this sort had been engaged. In fact, this was not possible. The Allies' room to manoeuvre remained limited because of the application of the Mahan principle of the fleet in being which immobilised most of the Franco-British maritime forces. The Grand Fleet could not release its big units in the North Sea from their station. This was because of the presence of the German High Sea Fleet, whose battlecruisers displayed an offensive spirit (Battle of the Dogger Bank on 24 January 1915). The ships of Boué de Lapeyrère kept a long watch south of the Strait of Otranto at the mouth of the Adriatic, to keep the Austrian Navy, which had six front-line battleships, three of them dreadnoughts, at a respectful distance. The Allies' main squadrons were thus pinned down by the Central Powers, and so they had no sizeable reserve that could be decisive in forcing the straits. This was the third strategic error made even before the appearance of the German submarine menace in the Mediterranean.

Admiral Carden's plan was put into effect on 18 February 1915: it aimed to neutralise the forts and to break through to Constantinople with the combined navies alone. The battleships opened fire from a great distance (almost 10 km) and battered the Turkish positions for five hours. The following day, and again on 25 and 26 February, they went closer. As from 19 February, the *Suffren*'s four 305 mm guns neutralised the Kum Kale fort on the Asian side of the Dardanelles. Admiral Guépratte sent in a company of marines to check the firing results and to carry out some additional demolitions. On 18 March, the well-known second phase of the operation took place: its purpose was to try to force the Dardanelles straits. In the preceding days the minesweepers and submarines were put into action. Admiral Guépratte, imitating the crusaders before the capture of Jerusalem in July 1099, said: 'J'entrerai à Constantinople avec mon cheval couvert de sang'.[10] Those old battleships fought hard but met with a strong Turkish resistance (forts, mines, mobile batteries) blocking the straits in their narrowest part. The *Bouvet* struck a mine that the Allied minesweepers had missed, and sank rapidly with the deaths of more than 600 men. The *Gaulois*, knocked out of the fight by shellfire, was saved by her captain who managed to run her aground. There were even more deaths among the British. But the results were derisory; this deployment of forces and all this heroism only achieved the destruction, among the important targets, of eight Turkish 176 mm guns. It was acknowledged afterwards that more decisive results could have been obtained since the Turkish guns had almost run out of ammunition. This was a bitter thought considering that on 18 March not all of the available ships were committed to the attack – there were about ten waiting in reserve. The decision of Lord Kitchener and the British War Council on 10 March 1915 to send the 29th Division to the Aegean made it easier to decide upon an amphibious operation following the naval failure. On the other side, Liman von Sanders, who had been nominated commander of the Turkish troops on Gallipoli, decided, from 25 March, to reinforce the straits' defence by unlimbering 200 Skoda guns.

The Tactical Deadlock

The failure of the naval attempt made the Allies suddenly rediscover the virtues of interservice cooperation. General Ian Hamitlon's 80,000 men, many of whom had been sent to the island of Lemnos in March, were by now training in Egypt. In Alexandria and Port Said the French soldiers under training were being closely watched by the enemy's intelligence agents. This colourful episode, which was revealed by Egyptian newspapers, had the serious consequence of depriving the operation in the Dardanelles of any element of suprise. On 10 April, the expeditionary corps left Egypt for Lemnos where the process of concentration ended only on 21 April. This delay was partly due to loading mistakes (shells and guns had been placed on the wrong cargo boats), but it confirmed the imminence of an attack for which the Turks had time to prepare. The troubles of General Hamilton, who was Commander-in-Chief of the Allied armies in the Mediterranean, had only just begun: for example he had no authority over his naval gunfire support. This lack of overall command can explain the choice of landing areas, over which the French were sceptical from the beginning. An attack on the European side of the Dardanelles was consistent with the traditional thinking of the French generals, but even with the support of naval fire it seemed risky to them because of the steep topography and the narrowness of the Gallipoli peninsula. They would have preferred to land on the Asian shore. General d'Amade proposed to launch the attack from the island of Mytilene, which is nearer the Asian mainland, rather than from Lemnos which the British chose. The landing could then have taken place in the Gulf of Adramit, still with the objective of Constantinople, but advancing via the holy city of Bursa. This proposal also had the advantage of cutting the railway line along the coast between Smyrna and Constantinople while ensuring for the Allies wide possibilities of manoeuvre once the bridgehead had been secured. The French also proposed a series of successive raids on the Asian coast, especially around Besika Bay, to compel the Turks to disperse their forces.

From these considerations, the idea of a deception operation was retained, and the French were entrusted with it, but nearer the straits. They were backed up by the naval guns and landed at Kum Kale on the Asian coast of the Dardanelles. The 6th and 8th Colonial Regiments, led by Colonel Rueff, took the old fort of Kum Kale with their bayonets. They took 575 prisoners at the expense of great losses and held out against a series of violent counter-attacks. With this effective action, the French pinned down the 3rd and 11th Turkish divisions. They nevertheless had to re-embark on 26 April when their diversionary operation came to an end, and from 27 April they had to face a deadly fire helping the British who were engaged on the narrow beaches and on the cliffs of the Gallipoli peninsula. Fighting in the south-east sector of the allied front, the French were exposed to the Turkish artillery based on the Asian side of the straits[11] and felt as if they had been left alone to take some fortified positions. Indeed, the naval guns were unable to penetrate either the Turkish trenches or the natural ravines that constituted many defensive positions. The 75 mm guns had too flat a trajectory of fire to get at the machine guns that were posted in these defences.

On 4 May General Gouraud arrived with reinforcements (156th Infantry Division) to replace General d'Amade who had been deeply affected by the losses incurred for little result. At a time when the French strength reached a peak of 42,000 men, the Senegalese battalions, which were formidable in attack but fragile in an extended defensive position under continuous bombardment, were withdrawn from the Dardanelles. General Gouraud, who was hoping for a decisive action, suggested to General Hamilton that he should renew the offensive on the Asian shore in order to regain some initiative of manoeuvre. But General Hamilton, whose headquarters had been installed on the island of Imbros since 1 June, preferred to keep his five reinforcemement divisions for the European side. As a means of getting out of the tactical deadlock, General Gouraud advocated either an attack at Gaba Tepe, the narrowest part of the peninsula, to take Gallipoli via Boghali, or a landing at the head of the Gulf of Saros to take Bulair and invest Gallipoli from the rear. The latter was a possible manoeuvre since the Allies were in control of the sea.

In fact, fierce fighting continued on the territory which the Allies had occupied but which was chronically lacking in depth. In order to extend it, the British and the French introduced trench warfare to Gallipoli, hoping that vigorous offensive pressure would produce a breakthrough of the kind that Joffre was trying to achieve on the Western Front. From 5 to 8 May, a new general attack took place to get out of the trap. The French incurred heavy casualties at the foot of the Achi Baba crest, in the small valley called Kereves Dere: 246 officers (75 per cent) and 12,632 men (57 per cent). For these, General Gouraud gained 500 metres of ground from the Turks.

The Dardanelles, like the Vieil-Armand, the Vauquois mound or Vimy Ridge on the Western Front, became a front in itself to which the soldiers clung as if it were a last rampart bathed in the sacred blood of their friends already killed in action. Like his predecessor at the head of the French expeditionary corps. General Gouraud, who was nicknamed 'le petit père' by his men,[12] asked for more active artillery support, all the more necessary since naval support had been reduced from 12 May after the British battleship *Goliath* had been torpedoed at the entrance to the straits. This setback was one of the factors leading to the resignation of Lord Fisher and the reconstruction of the Asquith government. On 18 and 19 May, 42,000 Turks launched a violent counter-offensive. On 4, 5 and 6 June, the Allies made another attempt to improve their position. General Gouraud launched his men against *Le Haricot*, a small hill whose capture would open the way to the larger objective of Achi Baba. Despite support from the guns of the cruiser *Latouche-Tréville*, this heroic action proved fruitless and costly, as were those of 21 and 30 June. Seriously injured, with an arm amputated on 30 June, Gouraud was replaced by General Bailloud, another officer with a background in the colonial army.

General Bailloud in his turn advocated skirting round the obstacle with a massive landing on the Asian shore: once again the commander of the French expeditionary corps met with a refusal. On 12 and 13 July another

French frontal attack failed because of a lack of artillery. One of the chronic weaknesses of this expedition is to be found in this shortage of artillery support as soon as the Navy, afraid of German submarines and Turkish drifting mines, became conspicuous by its absence. Turkish pugnacity in defence, Mustafa Kemal's spirit of initiative, the Russian defeats of May–July 1915 that allowed the Turks to transfer to the Dardanelles regiments that had been stationed at Erzerum or in the Lesser Caucasus, did not explain everything. We have to remember the frequent breakdowns in logistic support: one consequence of these was a lack of sufficient stocks of heavy large-calibre weapons with a high trajectory of fire, and such as there were could not be installed under the constant fire of the Turkish artillery.

On 6 and 7 August the last Allied offensive was launched: it was inspired by the plan that General Gouraud had devised on the old principle of pinning the enemy down in order to outflank him. While the British 9th Corps was landing at Suvla, the French units and a few British regiments applied pressure in the south of the Gallipoli peninsula in order to conceal from the Turks the main axis of attack towards Sari Bair, with which the Anzacs had been entrusted. This last effort was not successful, except to the extent that on 10 August the sectors defended by the British and the Anzacs around Suvla Bay were linked up. It was followed by a crisis of morale which itself revealed the unique character of the fighting at the Dardanelles.

The Man of Sacrifice: the eastern poilu

Francine Roussane has described the daily life of the soldiers at Gallipoli. It was marked by the disproportion between the size of the terrain, barely 2 × 4 km in the French sector, and the number of troops that were concentrated within it.[13] Let us list a few other facts. After the first excitement of the embarkation in Marseilles for Alexandria, with the band leading and the crowds cheering, after the initial curiosity of the *poilu* leaving for a remote theatre of operations, there were the discomforts of the trip and then the feeling of facing death while surrounded by beautiful landscapes 'aux tons pâles mollement fondus'.[14] The living and fighting conditions in the Dardanelles were exceptional even for trained troops. The artillery fire was more constant and more precise (from the Turkish guns firing from the Asian coast) than anywhere else. The fire came from the sea, covered the sky and lifted the ground. The Zouave Captain Canudo described this sunny hell in a few sentences:

We all live under this blazing dome. Innumerable, fierce diseases are snaking into the trenches, stretching their invisible and persistent tentacles into the air, into the food, into the rotten water. There is also the annoying whistling of the mosquitoes and the harrowing humming of the enormous flies and the numerous intolerable bites of the fleas and the lice . . . Diseases are snaking into the blazing trenches as billions of metal pieces and bullets cross the unbreathable air every moment. The horrible fury of shells and bullets, and their vertical ferocity while falling, constantly rend the space in millions of invisible crosses. We eat our bread kneeling on the ground. Our air is made up of dust and iron.[15]

Those formidable conditions were made worse by a constant thirst that raged more strongly than on the Western Front. Despite the arrival of tankers from Alexandria, the individual ration was reduced to a litre per day per man. The stench was such that fighting was suspended by mutual agreement in the evenings of 8 and 24 May to allow the evacuation of dead between the trenches. We may wonder how these men managed to cope with the situation. To the sense of duty, to the brotherhood of arms between the living and the dead of the same unit, to a measure of hatred towards the enemy could be added what Maurice Genevoix calls 'l'incommunicable'. The losses among the French troops, as well of those of the Anzacs and the British, reached a peak. Only one *poilu* out of three came back unscathed from the Dardanelles. Between 25 April and 1 July 1915, 430 officers and 20,042 men were put out of action within the French ranks.

The fact that doubts arose in many minds, frightened by the extent and the futility of the sacrifice for a land that was not theirs, can be easily understood. Lucien Tric, of the 6th Colonial Regiment, who came from the class of 1915 in the Ain department, recalled a feeling of stupor that has seldom been given expression. Injured during the attack on 8 May, he wrote: 'I stood there watching the men rushing foward, but the captain raced towards me with his gun pointing towards my head. What is going on? he asked. I'm wounded, I said. At a glance, he saw that my badge was not that of his regiment and my trousers were stained with blood, and without saying a word he hurried to catch up with his men.'[16]

After the final effort on 6 and 7 August and the discouragement that followed, the crisis of morale increased with a series of disappointments. The Dardanelles, which had been an active front, became a 'rotten front'. Epidemics, like dengue fever (caused by a virus transmitted by mosquitoes) and dysentery, came on top of the navy's withdrawal to Imbros on 25 May. Little help came from Italy (she entered the war on 23 May while refusing to intervene in the Near East). To the news of Russian defeats, confirmed by the ever-increasing number of Turkish troops in the trenches, were added anxieties about the Bulgarian threat. The Eastern Front, which had been opened to shorten the war, became a consuming fire in the Balkans because of the successive failures of the Allies. The plan to help the Serbs, sketched out by Galliéni and Franchet d'Espérey in 1914, became topical again. On 5 August,

General Sarrail formed the Armée d'Orient (Eastern Army). On 29 September, most of the French forces stationed in Gallipoli embarked for Salonika, even though Greece refused to enter the war on the Allied side. Twenty-one thousand French stayed in the Dardanelles under General Brulard's command and continued to do their duty, even if they did not feel like doing so, while retaining their esteem for the British soldiers. System D,[17] so dear to the African army, came into its own again. For example, Captain Weil improvised two anti-aircraft platforms with 75 mm guns to counter the chronic lack of anti-aircraft defence. In the small valley of Kereves Dere the piles of dead were so high and the limestone so hard that some communication trenches were built of stacked corpses to make up for the lack of sandbags. At times, during the rare moments of lull, some bathed on the Sedd-el-Bahr beach that was used as a rest area when the Orient Express or the Omnibus, two of the Turkish heavy guns, stopped firing; some managed to go fishing, others belonged to the archaeology section led by Professor Gauthier from Algiers University who had volunteered for the eastern expeditionary corps.

The end was near. In Chantilly, between 6 and 8 December 1915, an interallied meeting chaired by General Joffre decided on the evacuation of the Dardanelles.[18] The order was signed by Lord Kitchener on 26 December. By 9 January 1916, the Gallipoli peninsula had been evacuated with no casualties.

The Dardanelles Syndrome

On 15 September 1918 General Franchet d'Espérey broke through the Bulgarian front with a modified form of the plan he had drawn up in October 1914. He was enjoying a freedom of discretion that allowed him to use his spirit of initiative: the rarest military virtue. Within three days, going over the mountain, the Armée d'Orient advanced a distance of 25 km. On 29 September, the capture of Uskub (Skopje) opened up the Vardar route and Bulgaria surrendered. The following day the British and the Turks signed the armistice of Mudros while the French reached the Danube and the Serbs liberated Belgrade. The way to Vienna was opened, and only the armistice of 11 November checked the triumphant march of the Armée d'Orient, an army in rags but whose irresistible impetus had taken it nearly 700 km in less than five weeks, a march unequalled by any other Allied army in the war. On 13 November 1918, a Franco-British squadron lay off Constantinople; the bloodbath of Gallipoli had been avenged.

The time had come for assessments, for which the French were comfortably placed since they had been under British command in the Dardanelles. If a very strong feeling of solidarity prevailed at Gallipoli so long as the Allies were engaged in the same business, it would be wrong to believe that the failure did not feed a certain number of resentments. In August 1916, the historian

Ernest Lavisse had already advised the *Revue de Paris* to refuse an article on the Dardanelles expedition that was a serious indictment against the British.[19] Later on, the Vichy propaganda, stimulated by the tragedy of Mers-el-Kebir, made an inexhaustible theme of the French blood that had been so 'generously' shed by the British at the Dardanelles. This controversy has fortunately died down. It is now possible to set out the essence of the French criticisms without passion, starting by recalling the first synthesis made ten years after the tragedy of the Dardanelles. In 1990 Lieutenant-Colonel Allain Bernède[20] gave a remarkable presentation of the conclusions reached in 1925 by the École Supérieure de Guerre, whose commandant Desmazes observed the tactical mistakes made by the British Commander-in-Chief, while recognising the limits imposed upon his liberty of action by the very tight instructions written by Lord Kitchener. General Ian Hamilton, of whom it could not be said that a spirit of initiative was his strongest point, could not win sufficient room for manoeuvre, and was handicapped by the lack of a unified command structure, especially in respect of naval gunfire support from the end of May; most of the time he had to improvise with troops of varied backgrounds and with inadequate means. For lack of logistic resources the scope for exploiting the landings on the European side of the straits remained very limited. *Les Principes de Guerre*, published by General Foch in 1903, advocating good intelligence, single-mindedness in action, economy of force, freedom of action and concentration of means were scrupulously applied . . . by the Turko-Germans. The political choice of the Gallipoli peninsula did not take full account of the defensive qualities of the Turks, fired as they were by the need to defend their native soil. Consequently a naval operation was launched without sufficient means and without the aggressive confidence necessary for victory. The same lack of preparation could be found, according to the French, in the choice of the landing sites, in the shortage of high-trajectory heavy artillery and in logistics generally.

As far as the tactical plan was concerned, the only positive lesson that the École Supérieure de Guerre drew was the importance of rapid adaptation to the terrain and to the enemy troops, as the success of the Armée d'Orient would later confirm. By a strange irony of fate the British masters of indirect strategy desperately tried to apply a direct strategy on the Gallipoli terrain, while the French, though deeply involved in frontal offensives on the Western Front, favoured the indirect approach traditionally associated with the small wars of the British school. It could also be remembered, if a quick historiographic enquiry[21] were made, that the 539,000 men who participated in this expedition on the Allied side, more than a third of whom became casualties, at least succeeded in eliminating any threat to Suez. Their sacrifice also relieved the Russians in the Caucasus, checking a Turkish invasion by forcing them to withdraw men to defend the straits. Finally, the effort made in Gallipoli subjected the Turkish army to such strains that it was unable to resume the offensive in Mesopotamia, in the Hejaz or in Thrace. On the strength of her participation in the Dardanelles expedition, even though she had been a junior partner, France claimed a prominent position in the Middle East following the signature of the Sykes–Picot agreements in 1916 on the disposal of the remains of the Ottoman Empire. The French zone of influence in the Levant was confirmed by the recognition of their mandates over Syria and the Lebanon in 1920.

The shadow of the Dardanelles still haunts the French military memory. In his *Théories Stratégiques*, Admiral Castex, as early as 1929, referring to the Gallipoli fighting in particular, strongly qualified Mahan's concepts: he suggested that the sea was not necessarily more important than the land and that decisive battles were rare. The memory of the failure was so strong between the two wars that any study of combined operations seemed incongruous at a time when French military thought became ossified in the concept of the continuous front. The Navy, the Air Force and the Army each concentrated on its own kind of war. New types of warships such as the aircraft carrier were not thought through, and so the *Béarn* seemed more like a simple transporter of aircraft than a new capital ship. Indeed, she was laid up before the fighting in 1940. Everything had to be improvised for both Allied landings in Norway in 1940. At Dieppe, two years later, the obsessive fear of failure paralysed part of the British command. Only a new conception of amphibious warfare, developed in the Pacific and in the Mediterranean, succeeded in defeating the old syndrome of the Dardanelles that re-emerged for the last time in the Anzio landings in Italy in 1944.

Notes

1. Fighting is the ultimate goal of armies and men are the primary instruments of combat.
2. Gallieni parle . . . entretiens du 'Sauveur de Paris', ministre de la Guerre avec ses secrétaires (Marius-Leblond), Paris. Albin Michel, pp. 78–80.
3. Lloyd George, *Mémoires de guerre*, vol. 1, Paris, Fayard, 1934, pp. 352–71. This is an important historical question: Lloyd George was not alone in thinking that a direct blow on Constantinople was impossible. He also knew about General de Castelnau's idea of attacking through the Balkans (end of 1914) without any stroke against the Dardanelles (ibid.).
4. Poincaré, Raymond, *Au Service de la France*, vol. 6: *Les Tranchées, 1915*, Paris, 1930, pp. 2–4, 7. On this important historical point, also see Masson, Philippe, 'La Marine dans la Première Guerre Mondiale', chapter IX of the *Histoire Militaire de la France*, Paris, PUF, 1922, p. 240.
5. Gilbert, Martin, 'Churchill and Gallipoli', pp. 122–36.
6. Poincaré, R., op. cit., p. 31.
7. Sooner or later, Constantinople must be ours.

8. Any sailor who attacks a fortress is mad.

9. Pedroncini, Guy, 'Les alliés et le problème du commandement naval en Méditerranée de 1914 à 1918', colloquium on *La France et la Grèce dans la Grande Guerre*, Thessalonika, November 1989.

10. I will enter Constantinople riding my horse covered with blood.

11. Lieutenant Marcel Blanchard's account, Journal de marche, April 1915, *Revue Historique des Armées*, no. 2, 181, p. 157. Officer in the reserve, platoon commander then company commander in the 175th Infantry Regiment, agrégé d'histoire et de géographie, teacher in the Grenoble secondary school. Wounded on 28 April, he was sent back to his regiment at the beginning of June in the Dardanelles where he was again seriously wounded (loss of the left eye) and had his right arm amputated. Back in the civil service, he had an outstanding career as a Professor of Modern and Contemporary History at the University of Montpellier.

12. Tric, Lucien, *Souvenirs manuscrits des Dardanelles, 1915–1916*, T.114, Service Historique de l'Armée de Terre.

13. *Histoire de la France Militaire*, vol. 3, op. cit., pp. 186–96.

14. Blanchard, Marcel, letter to his brother Raoul, Sedd-el-Bahr, 25 May 1915, private archives.

15. Quoted by Paul Chack and Jean-Jacques Antier, *Histoire Maritime de la Première Guerre Mondiale*, vol. 2, Paris, Editions France-Empire, p. 229.

16. T.114, op. cit.

17. Système D – on se débrouillera (we'll muddle through).

18. Varillon, Pierre, *Joffre*, Paris, Fayard, 1956, p. 418.

19. 'Les Dardanelles à la pointe de l'Europe', in *Revue Historique des Armées*, op. cit., p. 129.

20. 'L'expédition des Dardanelles, 22 février 1915–9 janvier 1916. Les conditions d'engagement des forces terrestres d'après les dossiers de l'Ecole Supérieure de Guerre en 1925', contribution to the symposium on the Dardanelles, 75th anniversary of the expedition, Ankara, 8–9 March 1990, Middle East Technical University.

21. Among many titles, the following can be quoted: Delage, E., *La Tragédie des Dardanelles*, Paris, 1931; Charles-Roux, Fr., *L'Expédition des Dardanelles au Jour le Jour*, Paris, 1920; Deygas, Captain, *L'Armée d'Orient dans la Guerre Mondiale, 1915–1919*, Paris, 1932; Mordal, Jacques, 'L'expédition des Dardanelles, 3 novembre 1914–9 janvier 1916' in *Revue Historique des Armées*, no. 2, 1965.

THIRTEEN

WAR AND THE MAKING OF NATIONS

Michael Howard

24 April 1997

It is a truism to say that national self-consciousness, a sense of national identity, has almost invariably been moulded by memories of past wars, and sustained by celebrating them. In France the wars of the Revolution and Napoleon are commemorated by that most splendid of all war memorials, the Arc de Triomphe, where all the glories of France are celebrated every 14 July by spectacular military parades. For Britain national identity became defined during the century of naval and, very occasionally, military victories over France after 1689, culminating at Waterloo in 1815; although these British triumphs did not entirely blot out the Scottish sense of national identity forged in their own earlier wars against the English. For the Germans, it was the victories over the French in 1813–14 and again in 1870–1 that forged a nation out of a dozen separate states – a nation that it was to take two terrible wars to destroy. For the United States it took seven years of war against the British to create among the thirteen original colonies a sense of national identity, which is refreshed every 4 July and reaffirmed on every possible occasion with the singing of 'The Star Spangled Banner' – a rather redundant reminder of yet another war against the British. Imperial Russia constantly harked back to the victory of 1812, while for the former Soviet Union victory over the Germans in the Second World War stirred a sense of communal pride that might have created a great nation had it not been so disastrously squandered by the follies of Stalin and his successors. Other, less happy nations, are equally sustained by memories of defeats – the Hungarians by Mohacs, the Serbs – disastrously – by Kosovo, the Poles less by defeat in the field than by memories of constant betrayals. In the Far East, Japan came of age as a modern nation with her victory over China in 1895 and, more spectacularly, over Russia ten years later. For China, it was her victory over Japan between 1937 and 1945 and the subsequent eviction of the United

States from her soil that provided the foundation for that sense of national renewal on which Mao Zedong was to build. And for Australia and New Zealand there is, of course, Gallipoli.

Why should it be Gallipoli? After all, the campaign was a minor episode in a far greater conflict in which Anzac forces were to gain greater laurels and endure far worse sacrifices on other fronts. Strategically it was a disaster. Most historians now agree that, even if the campaign had succeeded in its objective, it would have made little difference to the outcome of a war that could be won only by the defeat of the main German armies on the Western Front. Tactically all that the Allied forces succeeded in doing was to ward off total catastrophe and escape with whole skins – apart, that is, from the 33,000 Anzacs, 120,000 British and 27,000 French troops who were killed, wounded or invalided out during the course of the campaign. It was a horrible experience; but if one wanted to celebrate horrible experiences that of Pozières in the Battle of the Somme was perhaps even worse; and if one wanted to do the natural thing and celebrate a victory, it would be hard to beat Villers-Bretonneux. The whole Dardanelles campaign was a shambles. Why not forget it, and leave the military historians to pick over its bones?

There are two reasons why Gallipoli has remained so fixed in the Australian (and New Zealand) national consciousness, both perhaps fortuitous. The first was the decision of the Australian government to celebrate the anniversary of the Gallipoli landings on 25 April 1916 as Anzac Day, before Australian forces had gone on to their further achievements on the Western Front. Celebrations were held not only throughout Australia but in London, where a service of commemoration was held at Westminster Abbey in the presence of the King and Queen and Lord Kitchener. In these ceremonies there were constant references to Australia and New Zealand having 'endured their baptism of fire', 'proved themselves as Nations' and 'come of age'; war being seen, in those Social-Darwinian days, as a rite of passage through which all peoples had to pass in order to prove their fitness for nationhood. Whatever adolescent uncertainties the Australians and New Zealanders may have felt about their identity before 1914 – and there were many – the experience of Gallipoli had resolved them. Whatever happened thereafter, the pattern of celebration had been established and was not subsequently to be changed. Anzac Day, 25 April, was to be the equivalent of 14 July in France or 4 July in the United States; the day on which subsequent generations were to celebrate the birth of a nation.

The second reason that the memory of Gallipoli was to become so deeply embedded in the national consciousness was the work of that dedicated and remarkable man, Charles Bean, who set himself quite deliberately to create what became known as the 'Gallipoli Legend'. I need hardly remind you about Charles Bean – quite the finest military correspondent and arguably one of the great military historians of the twentieth century. Bean landed with the Anzac forces and remained with them until the end of the campaign, meticulously recording everything that happened to them. He was to go on to do the same for two years on the Western Front, but it was Gallipoli that stuck in his mind and that he was determined to commemorate in a fashion worthy of the men who lived and died there. While the campaign was still in progress he collected the material for *The Anzac Book*, a popular compilation that was rushed out with government backing and had already sold 100,000 copies by September 1916. The success of this volume may in itself have done much to persuade the Australian government to institute Anzac Day when they did.

For Bean the Gallipoli campaign exhibited what, as a journalist, he had already identified as all the peculiar Australian virtues; self-reliance, scepticism towards authority, a sardonic and deprecatory sense of humour, and above all, 'mateship' – the comradeship of equals, especially (I am sorry to say) male equals. He saw in Australia an egalitarian society sharply different from the British class hierarchy embodied in the British armed forces and which he increasingly despised as archaic, humiliating, and above all *inefficient*. The Anzac contribution at Gallipoli was distinct and distinctive. It was possible to describe and celebrate their achievements with little or no reference to the contribution of the far larger British contingent – to say nothing of the French – which was also present and whose sufferings and achievements were at least as considerable. In the background there was certainly the Royal Navy, but in the background it stayed. In the background was also the British High Command and General Staff, whose performance was universally damned by the troops in the front line and whose staunchest defenders find it hard to say that they emerged from the campaign with any great credit. Behind them again were the British politicians who had blithely set in train an enterprise whose difficulties they had barely begun to assess, and whose utility was, to put it mildly, very questionable indeed. The men in Anzac Cove lived in an apparently isolated and self-contained world, ruled by unpredictable and capricious gods; much as the Homeric Greeks had seen themselves living when they landed a few miles further south to besiege Troy a few thousand years earlier. But this time there was no expectation that the right kind of sacrifice to the right kind of god or goddess would make things any better.

The reaction of the Anzac forces to their predicament was not to display 'heroism' of the classic kind – the kind still admired by the classically educated British officers with whom Bean had been educated at Clifton College. They rapidly found that heroism in modern war was not only selfish but suicidal: a machine-gun bullet rapidly put an end to it, if dysentery enabled them to display it at all. Courage – yes: there was no lack of courage, especially in the early days of desperate hand-to-hand fighting and such later encounters as Lone Pine. But on the whole the courage needed was of a different kind; the courage that enabled people just to 'stick it'; to be loyal to their mates, to do what they were told by officers whom they respected because they were their own sort and shared all their hardships, and to make the intolerable tolerable by a mixture of grumbling, humour and ingenuity in 'making do'. In fact British troops on the Western Front were developing exactly the same defence mechanisms, which were to prove equally effective in the Second World War; the stoical anthem 'We're here because we're here because we're here because we're here' was sung with equal relish by both armies in both wars. The virtues that Bean identified as being peculiarly Australian were more widespread than he was prepared to admit. But they were virtues none the less, and, combined with such identifiable Antipodean characteristics as self-reliance, skill at improvisation and a contempt for such superficialities as saluting or wearing clean or even recognisable uniforms, they were to be found in a state of high concentration in Anzac Cove in 1915.

Another peculiarity about the Anzac campaign was this. There was no 'generalship' of a traditional kind; or at least, none that anyone could observe. The generals were certainly there and highly visible: Birdwood, Bridges, Walker, Godley, Monash, White; and because they were there and highly visible they earned the respect, if not always the affection, of the troops they commanded. But the scope for exercising their talents was little more than that normally enjoyed by battalion commanders; planning small-scale actions and keeping up the morale of their men. They did as well as could be expected under the circumstances, and Bean gave them due credit. But the Anzac campaign consisted not of skilfully planned operations but of soldiers' battles, each of which was to be meticulously chronicled by Bean, for which credit must be shared almost equally among the hundreds – thousands – of officers and men who took part. The names that survive are those after whom, almost at random, physical features were named: Quinn, Russell, Courtney, Owen, Steele; together with a handful of quite exceptional commanders such as Leane and Malone. And this suited the Australian character as well. The British on the whole rather like generals, if they are any good; the Australian instinct is to cut them down to size. It was an egalitarian campaign, fought by an egalitarian army: history has not distributed credit for its achievements in proportion to rank.

A third and appropriate peculiarity was the *indecisiveness* of the campaign. Not that Australians are indecisive; far from it. But imagine two alternative scenarios. One is a catastrophe: the landings being decisively repulsed at the outset, or the Anzacs being later swept into the sea by a successful counter-attack. Neither was at all impossible. Gallipoli would then have been a disaster best forgotten, not even redeemed by the successful evacuation that enabled the British to forget the humiliation of Dunkirk and remember it as a miracle of deliverance. There would then have been no celebrations of 25 April; the effect on Australia's self-image, and indeed on the cohesion of the British Empire, would have been as disastrous as the capitulation of Singapore a generation later.

Alternatively, what if it had been a success? The Dardanelles would have been cleared in short order; Constantinople (perhaps) captured; but, whatever happened thereafter, the actual landings that opened the campaign would have been remembered as a mere incident preliminary to wider operations in which the Anzacs would have played their part as a subordinate corps on a British-led army – as they went on to do on the Western Front. Something equally memorable might have happened to provide an appropriate occasion for national celebration, but it is hard to visualise anything having the distinctive quality of Gallipoli. In that campaign the courage and endurance of those who took part cannot be considered simply as contributions to a final success that overshadowed all that had gone before. They were their own justification. Disaster might have made them tragic, while in triumph they might have been almost forgotten. As it was, the Anzacs would leave the Gallipoli peninsula eight months after landing there knowing that they had done all that they could. They had much to be proud and nothing to be ashamed about. If there was fault to be found, it was not with them. And it was in that mood that they would celebrate the first Anzac Day four months later.

And there is one final aspect of the campaign that gives us cause to be grateful. It was not a triumph, and provided no incentive for triumphalism. It is remembered, not as a victory over the Turks – which it certainly was not – but as a victory over circumstances; something that Anzacs and Turks could celebrate together, as they do. That has been the trouble about commemorating other wars as the 'birth of nations': what were, for some, memorable triumphs were for others equally memorable humiliations. The victories the French celebrate at the Arc de Triomphe were largely won at the expense of the Germans; the victory sealed by the proclamation of the German Empire at Versailles in January 1871 was not to be easily forgotten by the French. Anglo-French relations were not improved by the laying out of Trafalgar Square or the naming of Waterloo Station. And it is only thanks to the abysmally low level of history-teaching in British schools that few Englishmen understand what the Americans are on about when they sing 'The Star Spangled Banner' – though it is some consolation that probably very few Americans do either. Australia and New Zealand were born as nations without triumphing over anyone else in the process. That in itself may have done something to shape their self-image.

But it has to be admitted that few memorials of twentieth-century warfare are 'triumphalist'; I certainly know none commemorating the campaigns of the First World War. Victory came at too high a price, and it was the price that people remembered rather than the victory that it achieved. In London the Cenotaph and the tomb of the Unknown Soldier in Westminster Abbey – memorials to be imitated all over the world – were symbols of mourning, not of triumph, and the emotion annually renewed in remembrance ceremonials is still one of grief rather than of pride. This is as it should be. We have learned the hard way that war is not to be glorified, even if we still very properly wish to commemorate, with pride and gratitude, those who died in it. But it can be taken too far. In mourning the dead of the First World War the victorious democracies tended to forget what they had actually died for, and the possibility that they might have to fight for it again. 'Never Again' became the watchword, and it was very nearly a fatal one.

I don't think that this was the message of Gallipoli. Never again get involved in such a God-Almighty cock-up, perhaps; but the overriding sentiment of the celebrations – as it is of the Australian War Memorial – was pride in what Anzacs had accomplished, and at belonging to a nation – two nations – that could produce such men. And quite right too.

Charles Bean concludes his great work *The Story of Anzac* with the words: 'In no unreal sense it was on the 25th of April 1915 that the consciousness of Australian nationhood was born', and the same of course can be said of New Zealand. But it was consciousness not only in the minds of Australians and New Zealanders, but those of everyone else as well; those of their British and French allies, of their Turkish and German adversaries, and of all those, all over the world, who followed the press accounts of the campaign during those months when the Western Front was deadlocked and the Germans were winning huge victories on the Eastern Front at unpronounceable places of which nobody had ever heard. The men who fought at Anzac showed that they were no mere colonial levies, but the representatives of proud and independent peoples who had to be taken into account both in the waging of war and in the making of peace. Of course it suited the political book of that master-politician, David Lloyd George, that they should be represented in the Imperial War Cabinet that he created in 1917, and even more that they should appear as independent nations at the Paris Peace Conference in 1919; but it was universally admitted that they took their seats as of right: a right earned by the men who had suffered and died at Gallipoli four years earlier. The failure of the campaign was unimportant: it was the sacrifices made there that mattered. They have borne lasting fruit.

FOURTEEN

STRATEGIES AND AGONIES IN THE EASTERN MEDITERRANEAN

Michael Stürmer

23 April 1998

It is not an accident that the two great epics of western civilisation, the Bible and the Homeric tales, are played out in that geostrategic environment that today is known as the Greater Middle East. This is the ellipse, of vital strategic importance and rich in sources of energy, from the eastern shores of the Mediterranean to the Indian Ocean, from the Caucasus to the valley of the Nile.

When the children of Israel left Egypt, Moses, their leader, sent spies into the promised land, one from each of the twelve tribes. They brought back the fruits of the land but warned that it was also a land that eats its own people. The result was panic and rebellion among the children of Israel, and it was only after putting down the uprising that Moses, supported by God, marched his columns through the desert for another forty years so that all those above the age of twenty would die and only a new generation would see the promised land.

The story shows that it can be hazardous for analysts to tell the rulers what they do not want to hear, but it also indicates the very special quality of the Holy Land and its environment. Over today's troubled Greater Middle East the shadows of empires ancient and modern loom large; Babylon and the kingdoms of Egypt are not forgotten, nor Alexander and his warring successors. To this present day the most visible of all those ancient cultures is the Roman civlisation which was, by far, the most formative experience of the entire region until it fell apart, under Constantine, into an eastern, Greek, and a western, Latin, half. Byzantium, while Rome decayed under its military overstretch, under the assault of northern tribes and the weight of its own success, continued to flourish for another millennium. Arab conquerors, driven by the fire of Islam, swept the shores of the Mediterranean until they met resistance from the European heartlands at Tours and Poitiers in the early Middle Ages and, later, from the crusaders from Europe. After the fall of Byzantium in 1453 the Ottoman Turks carried on their conquering mission, fighting the navies and fortresses of the Serenissima and the Emperor until they reached the Adriatic Sea, the Carpathian Mountains and the gates of Vienna. It was only in 1699, 300 years ago, that the Peace of Karlowitz established the earliest model of a European balance of power, with Austria and the Emperor no longer under constant siege from the Turkish armies, Britain and the Netherlands in a continental alliance with Austria, and France's Roi Soleil on the losing side.

From then on, the issue dividing the major European powers was who would inherit the Ottoman lands and the power that went with them. Poland and Ukraine had dropped out of the race in the mid-seventeenth and early eighteenth century, respectively, while the Muscovite Czars were aiming for both the Imperium Maris Baltici in the north and the key to the Dardanelles to the south. The quest for control of the eastern Mediterranean has been a leitmotif of European power politics ever since and probably, if the recent past is any guide, well into the future.

Long before oil became a strategic resource, every European dream of empire sooner or later had to include those strategic lands between the Black Sea, the Caspian Sea, the Red Sea and Crete. When Napoleon concluded the peace treaty of Tilsit with Czar Alexander on a raft in the middle of the Niemen river in 1807, both rulers pursued the dream of unhinging the British Empire and taking its most precious possessions in the east. Napoleon had not forgotten how, ten years previously, he had fought the battle of the Pyramids only to lose the coveted prize of an Egyptian empire in the naval engagement of Aboukir against the Royal Navy, and how he had been humiliated by having to sneak through British defences back to France and his imperial destiny. Meanwhile, Czar Alexander understood that, in order to fulfil the dream of Peter the Great and of Catherine the Great, his predecessors, and open the gates to the Mediterranean for Russia, he had to aim for a wider strategy. Nothing came of that, as the Czar and the Emperor soon parted ways, Napoleon marching his armies to Moscow and defeat, Alexander marching his armies to Paris and victory. But the lure of the east was never forgotten, not in Paris and not in St Petersburg, and in London most certainly not. The rulers of the British Empire were keenly aware of the permanent geostrategic threat, on land or by sea, to the lifelines of the Empire and to their access to India.

In the 1830s, between Greek independence and the loss of Egypt, the rulers of the Ottoman Empire were beginning to look for help from Europe. After one and a half centuries of decline, in which Turkey had been reduced to a mere object of European power politics, it was high time to prepare for ultimate survival. Little did the rulers at Istanbul understand that after the French Revolution and the rise of revolutionary nationalism the days of multinational conglomerates like their ancient empire were numbered. It was forever beyond them to transform their vast land into a more modern system, centrally run and with a strong organising principle. The chief reason for the Empire's continuing existence was that it had been there for so long and that for the time being none of the great powers had the will or the liberty to overthrow it and take the best pieces. In fact, the Ottoman Empire continued to exist largely thanks to the rules, written and unwritten, of the European concert and the balance of power.

The Sultan, when looking for advice, could not possibly turn to Russia, as the Russians made no secret of their imperial appetites, nor could he turn to France, as French interests were all too obviously directed towards inheriting British imperial power. The Austrians had been the victors throughout the eighteenth century; the British were not a disinterested party, and the Turks, as their arrogance was easily surpassed by British assumptions of superiority, found the British difficult to deal with.

That is how the Prussians came in. Helmut von Moltke, a young General Staff captain, who was to be one of the great strategists of the nineteenth century, impressed the Sultan and was engaged for three years as an adviser to improve the Empire's defences and the army's training and organisation. This was the beginning of Turkey's German connection, long before Germany became united and rose to be a player on the world scene at the turn of the century. An exchange of officers and cadets took place, first between Turkey and Prussia, later on also with the Austrian General Staff. As Russia was the new common enemy, the Austrians were forgiven the fact that many of their military monuments showed Austrian generals on horseback and Turkish prisoners on their knees.

Captain von Moltke saw at once that the Turkish Empire lived in a pre-modern time-zone, its armies no match for European troops, its equipment ripe for a museum, its strategic communications not much improved since the time of the siege of Vienna. The whole structure cancerous through vast inequities, the heterogeneous character of the Empire and its constituent parts, the brutal treatment of soldiers, corruption in high places – in short, the very opposite of what the Prussian military reformers had effected under the shock of utter defeat at the time of Napoleon and against him. Moltke immediately recognised that without a system of strategic railways the vast country was doomed both in economic and military terms: too vast, too heterogeneous, too badly run.

He also saw that there was an avenue of expansion for German settlements serving, in a strategic alliance, both the cause of future Germany and the survival of the Sultans' rule. This obsession with strategic railways, by the way, proved to be the secret of success in the two wars Moltke had to conduct, first against Austria in 1866 and second against France in 1870.

Nothing, of course, came of those early ideas of a strategic alliance. Most Germans, when thinking about the Ottoman Empire, would let things rest with the famous lines that Goethe gave to the petit-bourgeois intellectual who dreamed of a beautiful day embellished by rumours of war 'wenn hinten fern in der Türkei die Völker aufeinander schlagen' (when far away in Turkish lands the nations rise in conflict). Moltke's advice notwithstanding, German popular emigration did not turn to Mesopotamia but continued to go massively across the Atlantic Ocean to North America and nowhere else. A few Christian and Jewish fundamentalists, however, went to Palestine not to conquer temporal power but in pursuit of their respective religious preoccupations. In 1848, in the German national parliament, the Paulskirche in Frankfurt, when the definition of the future Germany was on the agenda, some hotheads spoke of the Reich between the four seas, meaning the North Sea, the Baltic, the Adriatic and the Black Sea. All of this had no consequence, except as a dream of finally catching up with the more powerful nations of Europe: Britain, France, Russia, and also the Netherlands, Portugal and Spain.

The Crimean War in the 1850s, however, fought largely over control of the eastern Mediterranean, greatly helped the cause of German unification through Prussia. The powers that had the Vienna system under lock – Russia, Britain and France – fought each other at Balaclava and elsewhere. Russia was in need of an ally and found one in Prussia – but only halfway into neutrality – while Austria, notwithstanding the help the Habsburgs had received from Russian troops in 1849, was clearly in the western camp, reflecting the words of Count Schwarzenberg: 'The world will marvel at our lack of gratitude.' The two decades after Sebastopol opened a window of opportunity for Prussia and for Bismarck to take up the German cause and lead Prussian conservatism and German nationalism into a forced marriage. Thus Germany became, indirectly, the chief beneficiary of the power struggle that had engaged Russia, France and the British Empire in the eastern Mediterranean.

At the time of the 'Iron Chancellor', Germany was far from a steely foreign policy. Bismarck was out to forge an alliance system, above all with the key powers of Europe, Britain and Russia. On both counts he was only modestly successful. Meanwhile, he hoped that the Turkish inheritance could, for a long time to come, provide enough material for conflict among the other powers but also for compensation and thus help to secure Greater Prussia a peaceful existence and take away from a united Germany the perennial 'cauchemar des coalitions', inherited from time immemorial.

When, however, in the mid-1870s, Britain threatened war on Russia unless the Russians would let their recent Turkish conquests go, it was Bismarck who saw the sudden danger of a major European conflict, with

Germany inevitably drawn in. Therefore he convened the congress of Berlin in 1878, trying to be, after Russia had already conceded most British demands, the 'honest broker'. He did not heed the advice of Gerson Bleichröder, his banker, that there is no such thing as an honest broker. The result was a fundamental and, as it turned out, lasting alienation of Russia and the rise of the Franco-Russian alliance, with not much gratitude coming Bismarck's way from the British side. From then on, Bismarck was keenly aware of the fact that in the Balkans a mortal danger loomed. His ambiguous alliance with the Habsburg Empire and with Russia was meant to keep those two bulldogs from eating each other and to give Germany a pause in time of war. His often quoted dictum that the whole of the Balkans was not worth the healthy bones of a single Pomeranian grenadier was nothing but a warning to both St Petersburg and Vienna that in case of war they had better not count on Germany.

The Franco-Russian alliance of the early 1890s and the progressive decline of the Danube monarchy forced Germany into a more active role in the Balkans and vis-à-vis the Turkish Empire. This also appealed to the aspirations of the young Kaiser. Wilhelm II had inherited from Bismarck the conflict with France, and he had all but given up on Russia. With Great Britain this grandson of Queen Victoria entertained a very personal love–hate relationship that led him into the building of the German battle fleet. At the same time he embarked on an official visit to the Holy Land, going on shore at Haifa and riding into Jerusalem, claiming – a bit too much for Turkish taste – a protectorate over the Christians.

In today's Lebanon, at the glorious temple of Bacchus in Baal'bek in the middle of the strategic Beqa'a Valley, one can still see the plaque which the Sultan and the Kaiser put on the wall to commemorate their joint visit. With much support from the Emperor, German industry and banks secured vast orders for the railway lines that, six decades previously, Captain von Moltke had prescribed as a strategic remedy for the ailing Ottoman structure. The 'Baghdad-Bahn', as it was called, was to open much of the Balkans and the whole of the Ottoman dominions to German commerce, but also to link the strategic interests of both countries. In addition, the Germans were welcomed to bring the rotten Turkish armies to modern standards in equipment and training; but this was largely beyond the capacity of even the most devoted and dutiful Prussian officers. Of the latter there were *some* before the war and *many* after Turkey joined the Central Powers.

Why was Turkey unable to stay out of the war? Almost through a conditioned reflex, a war with Russia on one side and Germany on the other was bound to activate all the collective memories and every trauma of Turkish officers and diplomats. They pointed to the mortal danger to

Turkey's overstretched dominions should the Entente prevail. If, however, the Turks had taken the long view, they would probably have recognised that, come what may and despite the promises made to the Czar, Britain would not let the Dardanelles slip into Russian hands – much as the United States under President Truman in 1947 parted with Stalin rather than allow the Soviets control over the Turkish straits and a dominant role in the eastern Mediterranean.

By November 1914, the efforts of the Central Powers, notably Germany, had succeeded in bringing Turkey into the war. The British immediately reacted by landing an invasion force in Basra to secure oil supplies. With Turkey on the side of the Central Powers, the Balkan countries, though not under formal German control, came under pressure to conform. In addition, there was a Turkish army of 20,000 men ready to threaten the Suez canal, which in turn forced the British to station an army on the other side. Moreover, given the importance of petroleum, Turkey was doubly important for the Central Powers with regard both to Roumanian oil and to Caspian resources and supplies from Mesopotamia. The problem, however, was transport in both directions, troops to the south-east and oil to the north-west. This was never solved in spite of the vast efforts on the German side. The Germans may not have believed in Turkish efficiency, but they certainly knew the key value of a railway.

The war in Asia Minor was not central either to the Germans or to the Entente powers. In the official German records of the war, where every major battle of the Eastern or the Western Front is described in detail, this theatre is barely mentioned, reflecting the disdain Prussian army leaders felt for dare-devil operations in faraway countries. Even the much discussed revolutionary missions of some diplomats and explorers like Oppenheim, Wassmuth or Hentig, sent to light the fire of Jihad, were taken much more seriously by the British than by the Germans themselves. It was, even in the fiercest of wars, once again, a matter of 'hinten fern in der Türkei'.

The war in the Mediterranean was asymmetrical, though in essence it held a promise of strategic breakthrough for both sides. But there were weaknesses, too. On the British side the exposed position of the Suez Canal, with most of the oil having to go through a narrow waterway; on the German the backwardness and inefficiency of the Turkish army, poor in strategy and logistics but also overstretched and not well motivated. It is strange that the German High Command did not immediately recognise the British Empire's Achilles heel within easy reach of Turkish artillery. And it is equally strange that the British Navy, once it had chosen to attack the heart of the Turkish Empire, did not have the nerve to persevere. Strategic mistakes come in pairs and very often almost in symmetry, as if the generals followed, by hidden command, the same textbooks. While the

Germans sent a detachment led by Major Kress von Kressenstein to the canal and allowed the Turkish troops to stage a weak advance, botch the surprise factor and be beaten by British forces, the British recognised the vast consequences should these attacks succeed. The German Supreme Command was so preoccupied with the Western Front and the struggle in Poland that they thought the Middle East no more than a sideshow. There was no-one on Falkenhayn's staff who fully understood the strategic geography of the Greater Middle East and the decisive results it offered to a determined and well-oiled attack.

It should be noted in passing that, twenty-seven years later, Erwin Rommel's rapid advance in 1942 from Tunisia through Libya to El Alamein showed a much clearer understanding of the overriding importance of the Suez Canal. But, again, supplies did not follow, the British put up a formidable fight, and Rommel's small corps faced defeat. It should also be noted that in 1942 the Oberkommando der Wehrmacht issued road maps to the Southern Army Group advancing through Ukraine to the Caucasus, showing Beirut and Damascus and indicating the strategic pincer movement that Alexander and Napoleon had once planned to destroy the British position in the Middle East and beyond.

The Churchillian strategy of opening the Dardanelles to cut Turkey in two, take her out of the enemy alliance, supply Russia with arms, and receive food from the Ukraine was a grand design indeed. The Germans believed that the Russians had suggested the idea, and they suspected that Greece and Bulgaria would immediately join the fray. Moreover, as Turkey had no direct supply lines to Germany and munitions were scarce, it looked like a calculated and limited risk. If successful, it would have knocked out Turkey and would have taken important oil assets away from Germany and Austria. But as it turned out, it was a disaster, its long-term political repercussions for the British Empire even worse than its immediate military fall-out.

The Germans may not have seen Turkey as the most important theatre of war, and they may have grossly underestimated the strategic breakthrough possible at the Suez Canal. But once the Entente's navies showed up at the Dardanelles the Germans understood that Turkey's very existence was threatened and that Russia was promised an outlet. So they lost no time and spared no effort. The Turks, in turn, needed no prompting to understand that the attack on the Dardanelles and the subsequent landing at Gallipoli were a life or death struggle. Even so, it was only through German insistence that, in a last-minute effort, the fortifications had been put into good repair.

On 19 February 1915, British and French ships finally staged the show of force demanded by the Russians. They began to hammer the Turkish fortifications guarding the Dardanelles. One month later British and French naval forces attempted a breakthrough but ran into mines. The commanders decided to break off the offensive. The next step was the landing on both the European and the Asia Minor side by five divisions of British, French, Australian and New Zealand troops. On the barren rock of the coastal strip the 5th Turkish Army Corps, led by German General Liman von Sanders and reinforced by 500 German specialists both in the firing line and on the staff, defended the high ground and, in spite of its technical disadvantage and shortage of ammunition, did not give way. The invading forces were unable to gain sufficient ground or expand into enough of a bridgehead. The German Chancellor and Foreign Office insisted more than ever before that, now or never, the Germans had to secure the supply lines through the Balkans. But owing to the treaty with Italy, Austria could not move in the Balkans; and the Austrian General Staff, probably correctly, saw a decision on the Russian front as the overriding priority. Serbia and Roumania were in the way, Bulgaria caught in a precarious neutrality.

While the Gallipoli landing threatened Turkey's centre, the Germans and the Austrians were unable, in military and diplomatic terms, to overcome Turkey's geographic isolation. In June 1915 it was evident, unless fresh munitions could come, that the Turks could not hold out. Turkey had to be saved through an offensive on Serbia – as the German Foreign Office insisted – or through those victories on the Eastern Front that would persuade Roumania to open its railways – as General Falkenhayn expected.

Meanwhile, the Russians prepared a division in Odessa to be part of the future occupation force of Turkey. On 6 September, after the failure of the Suvla landing but while the Entente was still sending reinforcements into Gallipoli, Bulgaria signed a military convention with Vienna and Berlin, thus opening the way towards decisive action against Serbia while securing no small number of promises for compensation after victory. Turkey had ceded territory in Thrace to the Bulgarians. In late summer 1915, Field Marshal von der Goltz, head of the German military mission in Istanbul, assured Berlin that Turkey could hold out. By then, the Turks had sent more than half of their total fighting force into battle.

While the Gallipoli campaign failed to yield any military gains, it was through diplomacy, vast promises and a lot of cash that the Entente secured Italy's entry into the war. Although the Italians in the next three and a half years failed to make headway on their northern front, this was an important step in forming the great alliance that was to outgun and outnumber the Central Powers in the end. In the early autumn of 1915 German, Austrian and Bulgarian divisions started the offensive against Serbia. The Entente reacted through landing troops at Salonika – uninvited and in breach of Greek neutrality – on 5 October 1915. This was at the expense of the precarious operation in the Dardanelles. In late December 1915 and early January 1916 allied forces gave up the Gallipoli peninsula.

In Gallipoli nothing had been achieved except the wish of the Central Powers to establish a direct railway and supply link with Turkey and take Serbia out. In Salonika meanwhile the effort remained half-hearted, 200,000 men immobilised, the action not helping the beleaguered Serbs. Altogether, the strategic losses were on the Entente's side, the strategic gains on the side of the Central Powers. Gallipoli was a disaster not only in military terms, but also in the diplomatic dimension. Far from improving the overall Allied position in the Balkans, the attempt upon Gallipoli forced the Central Powers to establish that firm link with Turkey that had been absent so far. Bulgaria joined the Central Powers, and Serbia was defeated. On the Entente's side almost half a million troops, mostly British, Commonwealth and French, were engaged, and more than 50,000 lost their lives. Turkey's dead may have numbered as many as 160,000.

In the end Turkey had survived in one piece, the Balkan front had been consolidated, and half a million Entente soldiers were kept away from the Western Front. For Turkey Gallipoli was a strategic victory. It certainly gave the military élite, the backbone of the modern Turkish state, a boost of self-confidence and helped the leaders to forge modern secular Turkey out of the turmoil following the breakdown of the Central Powers in 1918. The Turkish nation-state managed to survive the fall of the Ottoman Empire – though one might ask whether the Allies succeeded in putting something better in its place. For modern Turkey Gallipoli was a cruel virility test, proving that the sick man on the Bosphorus had enough substance and resilience to define his own role – notably against the final dictate from the Entente.

Meanwhile, it should not be forgotten that Gallipoli, like Waterloo, was a close-run thing, and Field Marshal von der Goltz might well have echoed Wellington's words: 'The closest run thing I ever saw in my life.' History is not about the *what if*. But it is worth a thought whether the strategic rationale behind the campaign was merely a light-hearted wager or the tragic failure of a grand strategy. If the Allies had indeed broken through Turkish defences, Russia would probably have stumbled on and avoided the Bolshevik Revolution. Austria would soon have been forced out of the war, leaving Germany no choice but to conclude a peace halfway between victory and defeat. The United States would not have entered the European war. In short, the First World War would have ended sometime in early 1916, with Europe deeply shaken and changed, but not yet down the infernal grove to total war, crushing defeat, revolution and counter-revolution. Taking the long view, it is impossible to say who won and who lost.

Many of today's troubles in and around the Greater Middle East stem from the bitterness and destruction that the First World War left behind. Given the horrors that were to follow from Sarajevo to Basra and back to Sarajevo, Ottoman rule was, as much as Habsburg rule in Central Europe, the last way of life which tribes and nations who otherwise had nothing but hatred for each other could share. Nothing is in sight today to restore a measure of peace to the troubled lands of the Greater Middle East.

Today's Turkey is, now that the gross simplifications of the Cold War are ended, once again at the crossroads of history and geography, a land torn between incompatible traditions from inside and exposed to irreconcilable pressures from outside. At Gallipoli the question was who would control Turkey and her future. The question was decided at horrendous cost, in favour of Turkey. Today's question is how the Turks define themselves and where their country belongs, west or east, Asia or Europe, to a secular order or a religious destiny. In this, once again, the stakes are high and the outcome open. There is no end in sight to either strategies or agonies in the Greater Middle East.

FIFTEEN

GALLIPOLI:
A VIEW FROM SEAWARD

Julian Oswald

21 April 1999

In today's strategic parlance, power projection is usually thought of in terms of projecting a land force, or seaborne air-power, on to land from the sea. Originally it was seen more as the use of sea power alone, and it appears there was a serious misunderstanding of what sea power alone could achieve. This misunderstanding led to tragic and expensive consequences in the Dardanelles.

I believe a large part of the importance of Gallipoli is that it was the first major modern amphibious campaign – it was the first that did *not* depend to some extent on the wind for getting there! In 1807 Vice-Admiral Sir John Duckworth was detached by Admiralty Orders copied to his Commander-in-Chief, Lord Collingwood, to force the Turks to expel their French advisers and to ally themselves to Britain, whose Ambassador to the Porte had already had to quit his post. Duckworth was advised to give the Turks no more than half an hour before opening fire. He forced the Dardanelles under fire, destroying a Turkish squadron on his way – not a conciliatory approach to an ostensibly diplomatic task. Thereafter he was unable to execute his orders. Adverse currents and weak or adverse winds prevented him from getting nearer than 8 miles to the city. He had no troops to land; his Royal Marines were repulsed in a pointless landing. When a favourable wind allowed him to retreat, he had to repass the narrows under even heavier fire from the forts. Because Gallipoli was the first it was, understandably, the one in which a lot of mistakes were made – recognising and learning from these has done much to help us achieve success in, for example, Normandy and the Falkland Islands.

Control from London

I won't divide the cast I am about to introduce into goodies and baddies, but there is no doubt in my mind that the War Council, or as we would now say War Cabinet, presided over by the PM, Asquith, scored very badly. They should have demonstrated supreme strategic grip. They should have curbed the amateur enthusiasm of Churchill and modified the brooding opposition and grudging acquiescence of Kitchener. They did neither. Amazingly, they did not even meet between 19 March and 14 May 1915, an absolutely crucial period. With the total absence of advice from them, Churchill, Kitchener and others were free to plough their own preconceived furrows. In January 1915 Fisher wrote, 'Procrastination, Vacillation, Indecision are the watchwords of the War Council and all it directs. *I really don't think I can stand it!'*

All this is not to suggest that there were not good reasons for undertaking the Dardanelles campaign if it *could have been won*. Victory could have greatly reduced the threat to Egypt and the Suez Canal, eased the pressure on Russia, possibly brought Italy, Bulgaria and Roumania into the Allied camp, and provided an alternative to the trench warfare stalemate on the Western Front.

A small incident right at the beginning of the war demonstrated a lack of political judgement. The appropriation, at Churchill's insistence, of the two Turkish battleships being built in British shipyards caused violent resentment. A subtler way could surely have been found. In 1956 an Egyptian destroyer refitting in the UK was allowed to sail shortly before the outbreak of the Suez Canal hostilities. By a regrettable oversight she sailed with a full outfit of 4.5-inch ammunition for her 4.7-inch guns! It has to be said that Churchill's enthusiastic, intuitive methods were not suited to the direction of a complex distant campaign. This asp came back to bite us again in the Second World War, his great overall achievement notwithstanding.

In 1911 he said, 'It is no longer possible to force the Dardanelles and nobody would expose a modern fleet to such peril.' He had probably seen a very thorough 1906 analysis by the Director of Naval Intelligence and the General Staff, which concluded that – 'A naval (only) raid would be dangerous and ineffective'. But by 1915 his enthusiasm had totally reversed his earlier judgement and his almost paranoid anti-Turk feelings swept the War Council into accepting a naval-only attempt. In the event he didn't actually expose a *modern* fleet to this peril, but a largely very *ancient* one – which paid a terrible price. One cannot help wondering whether Churchill really appreciated that, at their narrowest point, the forts on the European and Asian sides are only 1,600 yards apart. Difficult to miss a battleship at 800 yards!

And what if, somehow, the Navy had got through the straits into the Sea of Marmara in strength and shelled Constantinople? Panic would probably have ensued. But if, as I can only presume was likely, the Turkish military had kept their heads and shown all the bravery they did at Gallipoli, surely their fixed and mobile shore batteries, on both sides of the straits, would have disrupted the essential supply chain of colliers, ammunition ships, victuallers, water carriers and more. Only if all batteries on both shores had been effectively silenced, and there had been no big guns in Constantinople itself, might a hostile naval force have been maintained there. Was this ever a possibility with naval forces alone? I very much doubt it.

Kitchener too stands accused of serious errors. Clearly his heart was never really with the Dardanelles initiative and his shilly-shallying over deployments, particularly 29 Division, was flabbergasting. Of the many qualities he did muster delegation was clearly not one. Most importantly, and fatally, he totally overawed Hamilton, a good fighting man, who could never bring himself to tell Kitchener what Kitchener might not like to hear.

I turn next to a representative of my own service who did his, until then, outstanding reputation considerable harm. Fisher, serving as Commander-in-Chief Mediterranean in the late nineteenth century, considered the possible forcing of the Dardanelles 'mighty hazardous'. In early 1915 he was opposed to the enterprise because of his own pretty hare-brained scheme for a descent in the Baltic. 'Damn the Dardanelles, they will be our grave', he wrote in a pretty prescient letter to Churchill. Cajoled by Churchill into the Dardanelles scheme, he gave lukewarm support, then got cold feet, resigned in a huff, hid in the Charing Cross Hotel and took flight to Scotland – a bizarre little story which would be quite funny were it not such a sad conclusion to a brilliant career.

All in all there was a dreadful lack of coherence in London and inevitably this rubbed off on the in-theatre commanders. I do not propose to consider these gentlemen individually because I want to turn now to specific aspects of the campaign, starting with naval ones, but I am afraid that command weaknesses (predominantly) and strengths (very occasionally) will show through in this, as any, examination of the events at Gallipoli.

Naval Aspects

It seems logical to start by considering some amphibious aspects of the campaign. It is interesting to note the time, in relation to daylight, chosen by commanders of amphibious landings for H (hit the beach) hour. The dreadful slaughter at V Beach in broad daylight immediately raises the question – why not land in the dark? But a night landing is not necessarily advantageous, especially on a very confined and well-defended beach, because the defenders will know where their guns are laid, while the attackers are groping in the dark. It is of interest that the D-Day landings commenced at 0800 hours because of the importance accorded to spotting and air attacks, both requiring daylight, while in the Falklands in 1982 the first wave hit the beach at 0200, a time chosen to disadvantage the Argentinian Air Force.

Soldiers depend on sailors to land them in the right place. In the case of the Anzac landings at Gaba Tepe, the evidence indicates that their trust was misplaced by about a kilometre, leading to them being landed into exceptionally difficult country. The argument is still not closed, but it does seem that a navy which prided itself on navigational skill fell short of expectations, with very serious consequences.

Better marks can be attributed to the inventiveness and enterprise used over the means of landing, even if it didn't quite match the bridge of boats with which Xerxes carried his troops across from Asia to Europe for the invasion of Greece. When one considers the years spent building the thousands of landing craft which were used for the Normandy landings, what was achieved at Gallipoli by steam pinnaces, ships' cutters and whalers and various makeshifts, including hastily constructed armoured barges and the use of ships taken up from trade, like the *River Clyde*, was very creditable.

In summary, the actual ship-to-shore movement wasn't very good but, with the exception of V Beach, it wasn't very bad either. All beaches had a defensible perimeter by D+2, but the Turks were not standing idly by, and it was the failure to regroup and especially to push inland quickly which was so damaging, eventually fatal. Turkish sources marvel at this lack of initiative and drive,particularly in relation to the successful and unopposed landing at Y Beach. Had these troops moved less than an hour's march to assist their beleaguered colleagues at V Beach, things could have been different.

Fire support to the troops ashore was both crucial and problematical. Not enough artillery, what there was not landed quickly enough, not enough ammunition and considerable technical difficulties for the large-calibre, high-muzzle velocity, flat-trajectory naval guns, attempting indirect fire into the central depressions in the peninsula. Amazingly, the destroyers with their 4-inch guns, well suited to close-range direct fire, were grossly under-utilised. Some commendable initiative was shown, perhaps particularly the arbitrary reduction of propellant charges which involved drawing up new range tables on the spot. Interestingly, Turkish accounts speak very highly of Allied direct fire support and aver that it caused very serious casualties in their trenches. They talk of its having saved the Anzacs.

Spotting was always a problem for indirect fire. The very courageous efforts of the Royal Naval Air Service were largely frustrated by communication difficulties and one can only marvel at the bravery, but unfortunately not the effectiveness, of the intrepid spotters who ascended by balloon. A small plus for the Allies was the deployment of the shallow draught monitors which did good work, especially when the battleships were withdrawn, but none of the sea-based fire power or the land-based artillery proved effective against the Turkish mobile howitzers which so cleverly employed tactics which we would nowadays somewhat inelegantly describe as 'shoot and scoot'.

It would be unfair not to recognise that the Gallipoli peninsula posed special difficulties in respect of airborne reconnaissance, considering the very basic equipment available. In the parlance of those days, aircraft didn't fly – machines ascended! Most of those involved were Royal Naval Air Service, as Kitchener refused to deploy the Royal Flying Corps.

Considerable doubts are raised in my mind as to whether the best, or in some cases any, use was made of the reconnaissance results available. Quite small details of the Turkish trenches are clearly visible in some of the original reconnaissance photographs taken in 1915. Yet, weeks after submitting their reports, RNAS pilots realised that, almost without exception, those beaches described by them as the best defended were chosen for the landings.

Just as aerial reconnaissance was a first at Gallipoli, minesweeping found itself catapulted into the twentieth century in far from happy circumstances. Initially, very slow converted trawlers were used to tow the cumbersome A Sweeps – a wire secured at the stern of each of a pair of ships which greatly limited their ability to manoeuvre. The pressed civilian crews found the lack of manoeuvrability, the fire from shore batteries and the strong Dardanelles current too much for them and the initial efforts resulted in almost complete failure. Stiffening the crews with RN personnel did little to solve the overall difficulties. The scene was transformed when much faster, more powerful destroyers arrived with improved minesweeping gear, but the way in which they were utilised, or not utilised, seems extraordinary. On 18 March, when several battleships were mined and sunk, HMS *Scorpion* (under the command of the future Admiral Andrew Cunningham) and seven other destroyers of the Beagle Class were not involved. *Scorpion* was at anchor off Tenedos. It is extraordinary how often powerful navies are caught napping by a relatively primitive minelay. The US Navy's experience off Inchon in the Korean War comes to mind.

A much better school report would be accorded to the RN and Royal Australian Navy submarines. Not only did they account for two Turkish battleships but, more importantly, they virtually brought to a halt Turkish re-supply of the peninsula by sea, forcing the Turks to use the much slower and more difficult land route. The conditions for these primitive early submersibles were exceptionally difficult, but the perseverance and courage of their crews is legendary, marred only by their own heavy losses. They represent one of the proudest and most successful aspects of the Dardanelles campaign and, as I shall relate, this praise should certainly be shared with the German submarines and their crews who were also particularly valiant and very successful.

One of the many difficulties for the naval command was that no anti-submarine capability really existed. ASDIC had not been invented and there were no depth charges. Visual spotting and gunfire were all that was available and they were almost completely ineffective.

I will not paint in at any length the wider naval scene, in the Mediterranean as a whole, as my time canvas is not large enough. Suffice to say that the passage of the *Goeben* and the *Breslau*, right at the start of the war, through the entire length of the Mediterranean, generously populated with British warships, was a disgrace which ruined several reputations, and their arrival at Constantinople was a factor of immense importance in determining Turkish attitudes. Quite frankly it should never have happened. It was more difficult to stop the German submarines arriving in the Dardanelles. For reasons already explained, there was little capability to range against them, but in theatre terms the fact that two enemy capital ships and a number of submarines penetrated into an area of major Allied naval operations was a very serious setback. In the later stages of Gallipoli, even the threat of German submarines seriously disrupted onward transit from Mudros, and all the larger transports were withdrawn.

In brutal summary, the Navy at Gallipoli was in a classic Catch 22 situation. Naval forces had to destroy the shore batteries and sweep the mines. But the existence of each threat precluded dealing with the other. Only a totally different approach involving land forces as well was likely to succeed. This in turn failed because it was not pursued early enough or in a sufficiently vigorous or determined manner, great bravery and sacrifice notwithstanding.

The Principles of War

The principles of war have been discussed by military men since classical times or even earlier. There has been a remarkable degree of agreement between totally different cultures in widely spaced centuries as to what broad precepts should be considered to maximise a miltiary commander's chances of success. I would like to review the extent to which the conduct of the campaign in the Dardanelles conformed to the principles of war used by British forces today. I will look at this largely from the Allied side, but in many cases the Turkish position was clearly the reverse of the coin.

The first and overriding principle is the *Selection and Maintenance of the Aim*. At the grand strategic level the ultimate aim is usually to break the enemy's will to continue fighting. Clearly at Gallipoli the Turks met this aim; the Allies did not. For the Allied side it would be idle to suggest that this principle of war was observed. In fact the Allies found themselves prisoners of events and almost throughout were very slow to make reassessments and to put in place the necessary changes. While some of the blame for this must be laid on the shoulders of Hamilton, de Robeck, Hunter-Weston and other on-scene commanders, a great deal more is attributable to the higher direction in London. What was meant by such vague phrases as 'Knock Turkey out of the War'? Did the government really believe that if they had been able to open up the route to Odessa the Allies would have had arms and ammunition which could be spared to send to the Russians? Could the Russians have distributed and used them? Incidentally, what an interesting parallel with the North Russian convoys of the Second World War. At the highest level, the War Cabinet never really sorted out clear priorities as between Gallipoli and the Western Front. Subsequently the Salonika initiative introduced further obfuscation of their strategic aims.

Perhaps the second most important principle is that of *Offensive Action*. This is often the chief means open to a commander to influence the outcome of a campaign. It confers the initiative. The Allies started offensively, but possession of the ball was ceded to the Turks by slowness, mistakes and hesitation. Most obviously, the naval failure to press ahead after the relatively successful bombardment of the forts in March, when the Turkish defenders were almost out of ammunition, the failure to expand the perimeters after many relatively successful landings, and the unnecessary evacuation of Y Beach, were sad examples of the neglect of this principle.

On the positive side, as already mentioned, the submarine operations on both sides were fine examples, as in general was the way in which Liman von Sanders deployed his assets.

The principle of *Security* covers both the physical protection of important assets and the denial of valuable information to the enemy. Regrettably, the loss of both HMS *Triumph* and HMS *Majestic* demonstrated lamentable lapses in regard to physical security. When torpedoed, *Majestic* was preparing to open up her protective torpedo nets because the Admiral wished his steam pinnace to be hoisted out. Many of the hands were involved in this major evolution and others were scrubbing out messdecks. Scuttles had been opened for ventilation. The ship sank in a matter of minutes and virtually no damage control was possible. It is not a breach of security to take risks, but it is an egregious breach not to realise they are being taken.

Closely allied to *Security* is *Surprise* – a potent psychological weapon. It can cause confusion and paralysis in an enemy's chain of command. On the whole, little strategic or tactical surprise was achieved by either side, but at least some opportunities were open to the Allies. However, most punches were signalled. The landings at Suvla are perhaps an honourable exception, but the value of surprise was lost by the failure to follow up swiftly.

On the naval side, the Fleet bombardment of the forts in November 1914 served mainly to alert the Turks to the need to strengthen them — which they did, just as they strengthened the land defences on the peninsula after the naval attacks in early 1915. A nice example of tactical surprise was the very effective minelaying by the Turkish minelayer *Nousret*. The Allies were caught out because the main line of mines was laid parallel to the shore, not as had been expected across the line of advance of the attacking ships.

Flexibility is the ability of commanders at all levels to change their plans to meet unexpected developments. It requires flexibility of mind and rapidity of decision. Ashore there were some good examples of this principle being exploited by General Liman and particularly by Mustafa Kemal. Unfortunately, Allied troop commanders were completely without reliable maps and many lacked an understanding even of the tasks assigned to their own troops, so there was little basis for imaginative, flexible decisions at lower levels. At Suvla, Commodore Keyes located a better landing site on the north side of the bay, but General Stopford refused to change the orders. Flexibility forgone.

Another important principle of war is *cooperation*. This involves coordination of all assets to achieve the maximum combined effort from the whole, albeit with a clear division of responsibilities for element commanders. We must be careful not to judge by today's standards, when the services naturally and normally work with each other on almost all operations. At Gallipoli the difficulty started at the top: in Whitehall there was no machinery for coordinating a major operation involving the two services. The War Cabinet handed a poisoned chalice to General Hamilton and Admiral de Robeck by appointing neither in overall command, and by the shameful lack of proper briefing given to General Hamilton in particular. One slightly brighter aspect, probably because of the personalities involved, was that Anglo-French cooperation was generally good.

The principle of *Sustainability* clearly requires that the commander be given the tools necessary to accomplish his task, even if it takes much longer than planned. But it also suggests that the commander in the field requires at least a degree of control over the logistic plan, corresponding to the scope of his responsibilities. Clearly at Gallipoli the commanders did not have this. An important aspect of sustainability is medical support. This was dreadful, and many lives were lost unnecessarily. It was bad from the start when the Adjutant General, the Quartermaster General and the Chief Medical Adviser of the force were left behind! Hamilton's skeleton staff estimated there might be 3,000 casualties. The eventual Allied total was 50,000 killed or died, 219,000 wounded or sick. Before being critical of the gross underestimates of the hard-pressed, and very small, staff, we should recall that casualty estimates for Operation Desert Storm, conducted over many months by professionals, were wrong by two orders of magnitude. Luckily they were wrong in the right direction.

Concentration of Force means not just the massing of forces, but their concentration in time and place to deliver the decisive blow. In general, at Gallipoli, at the strategic level, there was drip-feeding following reverses, which does not amount to observance of this principle. At the tactical level, I think land forces were so forced to concentrate by the terrain that in terms of position a very high degree of concentration was, of necessity, achieved by both sides.

Finally I turn to *Economy of Effort*. This is the corollary of *Concentration of Force* and requires that the best possible use be made of all the resources available. Clearly when it came to the evacuations this was done, and done supremely well. At most earlier stages of the campaign a great deal of effort was wasted. One Allied failing under this heading was not making anything like full use of the close-range direct-fire capability of the destroyers and other smaller ships, which was quite effective against the Turkish trenches. Cunningham, CO of *Scorpion*, commented, 'We and other destroyers were 500 yards off V Beach ready to do anything required of us. We could see into the Turkish trenches, full of troops, but were strictly forbidden to fire at them.' Further examples, both from the Allied side, are the waste of naval gunfire support effort due to poor spotting and ill-coordinated fire plans and, on the medical side, the ghastly tale of wounded soldiers being brought off to hospital ships, from which they were turned away on the grounds that there was no room for them, only to be returned to the beach whence they came and as a result receiving no food or real medical attention for 20 hours. Inevitably, lives were wasted.

Believe It or Not

Examples in the 'incredible' category are rife: some astounding, some worrying, some just bizarre; like the naval officer who landed at Anzac Cove and asked to be directed to the Officers' Mess. How can one explain how Colonel Matthews of the Royal Naval Division after landing at Y Beach had neither acknowledgement nor answer to his increasingly desperate signals for 29 hours? We know they were received.

Two British officers serving in Turkey before the war had detailed up-to-date knowledge of the terrain and of Turkish forces. Yet Admiral Limpus was sent to Malta and played no part in the campaign and Colonel Cunliffe-Owen's detailed report was never shown to General Hamilton, who was not even made aware of its existence. Instead, he was furnished with an out-of-date textbook on the Turkish Army and two guide books to western Turkey.

An officer serving in the battleship *Agamemnon* wrote that when bombarding at anchor, quite close to the coast, with Turkish shells falling around them, the Commander was trying to get the ship's side painted and the sailors were not very willing!

I have mentioned the complete lack of anti-submarine capability: one desperate suggestion was that a naval whaler, under sail or oars, be sent on patrol carrying a small canvas bag which could be slipped over an enemy submarine's periscope and secured – thus blinding them. When *Goeben* and *Breslau* were transferred to the Turkish navy, the German crew remained in place but were provided with fezes!

Considering the perfectly ghastly privations of the soldiers in the field, and the fairly uncomfortable situation of many sailors afloat, the mind can only marvel at the insensitivity of those who arranged a banquet for all senior commanders on the arrival of Lord Kitchener.

Conclusion

It is not easy to summarise the Dardanelles campaign. Clearly Allied strategy was fundamentally flawed and they were always on the wrong side of the drag curve – feeding in more forces after reverses. Very occasionally, success was not *perhaps* impossible; if a combined assault had been launched initially it could just have succeeded, but Churchill torpedoed that idea – so success got more and more difficult. For the Allies it was a cruel accident that one junior Turkish commander of genius should have been on top of Chunuk Bair, almost alone, when the first somewhat confused Anzacs reached the hill. But Mustafa Kemal quickly rallied the defenders, the Anzac soldiers were thrown back and Chunuk Bair, critically, remained in Turkish hands. Tactically, the hills were the key to success at Gallipoli. For success, total strategic support by the War Council with full commitment of resources would have been essential, and it never came. Half-hearted support and less-than-honest prevarication were the order of the day; this made failure inevitable. There was much individual heroism and some aspects were well, some brilliantly, conducted (on the Allied side the evacuations for example) but the mountain was too steep. For Turkey, horrifying loss of life was involved in maintaining the status quo, but maintained it was and all the invaders were pushed out.

More importantly, for Turkey, Gallipoli saw the planting of the seed of national liberation, renewal and modernisation,which gave us the fine independent, democratic country with whom, today, we proudly share NATO membership, and have much else in common including very special bonds of friendship.

Gallipoli has been described as a classic example of defeat snatched from the jaws of victory. I beg to differ. I am persuaded that the appalling, vacillating strategic direction of the campaign, poor tactical command, totally inadequate logistic support and some clearly defective equipment, offset by little more than some outstanding bravery, and not even much luck, leave it better described as a nearly impossible feat – not achieved.

Final Thoughts

All war is bad. Gallipoli was very bad. In terms of killed, wounded, sickness, degradation, misery, disease, deprivation and hopelessness, it was about as bad as war can get. Walking quietly through the beautifully kept cemetery above V Beach, reading the inscriptions on the headstones, I was brought up with a round turn when I noticed that among many others lay the graves of three brothers, Royal Dublin Fusiliers, who had all been killed within two days. Just think of the shocking impact of those three telegrams, perhaps on a poor family in the back streets of Dublin. For me it is so sad as to be almost unimaginable.

Despite sinking morale, acts of bravery on both sides abounded. And many of them were almost unbelievably chivalrous and unselfish. Even the somewhat case-hardened and slightly cynical war correspondent Ashmead-Bartlett commented, 'I have never seen anything like those wounded Australians in war before. Though they were shot to bits, without hope of recovery, their cheers resounded throughout the night.' In a totally different way, one can only marvel at the bravery of the submarine crews, whose frail craft were hardly safe on the surface and were, too often, quite literally a death trap when submerged.

Turkish bravery is legendary, but in the Dardanelles they won yet further laurels. For all the hype of war, British soldiers never really disliked their Turkish opponents; in fact they deeply admired them. Ecclesiasticus enjoins us to praise famous men, our ancestors in their successive generations, and notes that their bodies have been buried in peace and that their names will live on for all generations.

But for me perhaps the most beautiful words of all on the subject were written many centuries later by a very distinguished and successful commander in the campaign, who later went on to lead his country, almost literally, into the modern world:

Heroes that shed their blood and lost their lives. . . . You are now lying in the soil of a friendly country. Therefore rest in peace. There is no difference between the Johnnies and Mehmets to us where they lie side by side here in this country of ours. You, the mothers, who sent their sons from far-away countries, wipe away your tears; your sons are now lying in our bosom and are in peace. After having lost their lives on this land, they have become our sons as well.

Mustafa Kemal Atatürk, 1934

SIXTEEN

THE DE-ROMANTICISATION OF WAR AND THE STRUGGLE FOR FAITH

Richard Harries

13 April 2000

The Gallipoli campaign highlights major strategic issues and crucial tactical ones. But it was particular individuals who fought and feared and died. So I begin with short extracts from the letters which William Wilson, a young chaplain with the 8th Scottish Rifles, wrote to his mother.[1]

On board SS Ballarat, *Sat 22 May [1915], 6.30 p.m.*
By the way we are still ignorant of our destination, but presume it to be Alexandria. The officers have all got an official textbook about Turkey. It is the most wonderfully complete thing I have seen . . . It even goes so far as to give instructions as to billetting our men in Constantinople, – what houses and classes of people are to be billetted upon and what is to be avoided!

On board HM Troopship Ballarat, *Saturday 12 June 1915*
On this campaign we have to travel light. I have got a tommy's pack. . . . The pack holds quite a lot, and as a matter of fact we will have to do with what we can each *carry* for three or four days after we land, which means sleeping in our clothes upon a waterproof groundsheet, which is the only article of bedding we can carry. It will be quite exciting won't it, and I expect I shall quite enjoy it! Our valises will follow us when convenient.

8th Scottish Rifles, 16 June 1915
I have had plenty of experiences to talk about these last two days, but you will have to accept my apologies if I am neither interesting nor

coherent in this epistle! – there are one or two disturbing features about the atmosphere, but for all that I am really and truly enjoying it!

I will say at once that we are on the Gallipoli peninsula, and under fire . . . I am in a trench with four company officers and we are really very snug. A trench is rather a narrow place to live in, but we only retire to it when they bombard us. You must understand that we are in reserve at present and out of rifle range; we occasionally get a few shells but they are very local in their effect. The only gun we don't like is 'Asiatic Annie', and so far she has only had one go in our direction and it was rather terrifying at first and cost us two killed and one badly wounded, which is quite an exceptional occurrence I believe and rather bad luck on us. . . .

We are quite old hands at the game now, though I must confess that I had the 'Jumps' yesterday and so did we all – but it is perfectly wonderful how soon one gets used to it; we only duck now when we actually hear the whiz of a shell coming, and are getting to know the sound where they will burst. The trenches are absolutely safe unless a shell lands plump into one which isn't a frequent occurrence, thank goodness! I had a topping bathe in the sea yesterday evening, and it only takes ten minutes to get there and I hope to continue the practice. Our rations are jolly good, plenty of army biscuits of course (exactly like dog biscuits).

Friday 18 June
The open air life is agreeing with me, I sleep out in front of my trench every night. . . . The noise of rifle firing goes on all night from the front line trenches and acts as a lullaby!

Sunday 20 June/15
You can imagine us lying out in trenches on an absolutely bare plain, in the blazing sun, and with the dust everywhere, and flies galore. (By the way you would be conferring a tremendous boon if you could send me a bag of mosquito gauze to put over my head – with a string to gather it round my neck.)

Sunday 27 June/15
We expect to have some hard fighting, and really I feel that I shall not see a good many of my friends again. It is perfectly wonderful what good fellows both officers and men are when they know they are going into danger. Several officers (whom I know very well by now) came up to me this morning quite quietly and asked me to recommend a passage of scripture for them to read (I suggested Psalm XCI and parts of NT). I know that a good many of the men have taken NTs with them in their pockets.

This is really quite a pleasant spot, if it wasn't for the dust and heat and flies. The sunsets over Imbros are simply magnificent from the top of the cliffs; and in fact very often in the early mornings and at dusk when there is usually no firing it would be difficult to imagine a more peaceful scene! I always bathe before breakfast at 6.30 a.m. and very frequently about 6.30 p.m. as well and there could be nothing more heavenly to ask for here.

1/8 Sco Rifs BME7 Sunday 4 July 1915

By the time this reaches you, you will have heard of our smash up. I think I said in my last letter that I felt I wouldn't see many of my pals again. It was only too true. There was a big attack next day, and only *one* of our officers came back unhurt. The rest are mostly wounded, two are definitely known to be killed and about ten are missing and probably killed. The men lost heavily too. It is awfully sad, isn't it? But we have got to face these things out here. . . . I am the only one left of our mess and now occupy the whole of the dug out in solitary state.

8th Scottish Rifles, British Mediterranean Exped. Force, Sunday 11 July 1915

I have had to write to a good many relatives of dead and missing, enclosing money and inventories of kit etc and it hasn't been a pleasant job. . . . It was an awful wiping out. But they died gallantly, and that is all that is to be said about it. . . . There has been a good deal of 'Hate' today (i.e. Turkish shellfire) but nothing near us. They seem to be anxious to keep our fatigue party at the main beach on the hop!

1/8th Scottish Rifles, BR Mediterranean Ex. Force, Sunday 18 July 1915

The fifth week of our sojourn here has not been marked by anything very special. The Scottish Rifle Battalion went up to support the trenches last Sunday night and were moved up into the firing line during another big attack on the 12th/13th. There was another big casualty list. . . . We lost Major Bird (killed) the CO of our composite battalion; and my *fourth* Commanding Officer is now a young captain. It is appalling! . . . In the meantime we have just got to peg away at our respective jobs.

We have managed to have porridge two days this week, with *cream* (tinned) but I fear that all these little luxuries will soon come to an end, as our five mess baskets are almost depleted.

Same old place, Saturday 24 July 1915

Our new CO Captain Davenport is a 'nailer' – he has been in the Egyptian army for several years (he's a regular). . . . All the same it was rather amusing watching a regular officer with his experience when the Turks plugged some shells in our direction: we knew from the sound that they were going to land way beyond us, but for a newcomer the whiz is rather terrifying! I speak like a veteran – but six weeks of it has certainly taught us something!

Plague spot as before! Sunday 1 August 1915

Our men are not the least bitter against the Turks – it is only the German officers they swear about – the Turks (so far) have been fighting like gents and although we always carry gas respirators about with us wherever we go, I don't think we will ever have to use them. I hope not – it's too hot to wear extra clothes out here!

1/8 Sco Rifs BME7, Sunday 8 August '15

We have had three days of terrific bombardment from land and sea and the place has been a regular inferno. The Turks opposed to us were by no means subdued and have been counter attacking and shelling us like mad. The din is still going on. I expect we shall keep hammering away until somebody or other cracks. I wish I could tell you what I know, but probably the public at home will soon be enlightened. It's a great show this! But the casualties are terrific.

8th Scottish Rifles BME7, Sunday 29 August

The one surviving 8th combatant officer (Macklay) retired from the peninsula last week – broken down. . . . Poor fellow he lost his brother on June 28th and the strain of acting adjutant since then has been rather too much for him.

8th Scottish Rifles ME7, Sunday 12 Sept 1915

We get much amusement at times from newspaper descriptions and pictures of this show here, a good many of them are exaggerated and a few of them positively false! One picture in the *Daily Sketch* was a photo of a field ambulance (about 400 yards behind our 'Rest' camp) with a Turkish shell bursting away behind and it was entitled 'The Turks abuse the Red Cross flag' or some such words – absolute bosh! The Turks do not fire on the Red Cross, they are a jolly sight cleaner in their fighting than the Germans; and the shell in question was bursting on one of our gun positions; their marksmanship is generally accurate – even if their shells don't always explode.

More and more chaplains are crocking up, or getting 'cold feet'. . . . I breakfasted this morning with a jolly old colonel who gave me tinned prawns and boiled sausages! The one Presbyterian chaplain left in my brigade has been in bed for three days, but I think he will recover all right. I am in great spirits and in A1 health.

Helles, Sunday 3 October 1915

We had great sport on Monday night September 27th. A type-written message was sent round to all units quoting a wire from Kitchener about the splendid general advance in France. At 7.00 p.m. we celebrated the event in the following manner. Precisely on time all troops were formed up (it was dark) and all along the firing line, rockets and parachute star lights were sent up – all the guns on the peninsula blazed away hard at the Turks and the men from the firing line down to the beach cheered like mad. The Turks got quite a shock and must have wasted millions of rounds of small arms ammunition in a panic fear that we were going to attack. We enlightened them, however, by shooting notes in Turkish into their trenches from catapults, informing them that their game was nearly up as Germany was being pushed back!

8th Scottish Rifles ME7, Sunday 10 October 1915

I am still extraordinarily fit and happy. By the way, my servant considers that I have a pair of boots worth polishing! Could you send out a tin of polish – but I don't want any unless you can get some *dark* stain – polish – mahogany or dark red!

These are of course only short extracts, in letters that are full of jaunty descriptions of the food they are eating, the weather, responses to letters from home and requests for film for the camera, cigarettes and so on.

That was one soldier's perspective, of one lucky enough to survive. The wider picture of the 8th Scottish Rifles, to which he belonged, which was part of 156th Brigade, which itself was part of 52nd (Lowland) Division is described by Michael Hickey in his chapter 'The Battle of Gully Ravine':

Considering the adverse conditions under which they had been thrown into battle the territorials had done remarkably well, charging into the enemy position with tremendous dash and inflicting many casualties on the Turks. . . . All suffered terrible losses as the morning wore on. The 4th and 7th Royal Scots got into the Turkish line, but on the right, where there was virtually no artillery support to keep the Turks' heads down, the 8th Scottish Rifles were massacred. In the first five minutes of the attack they had lost 25 out of 26 officers killed or wounded, and more than 400 men. In the words of the divisional history: 'All ranks were slaughtered, literally by platoons. . . . In a few minutes nothing was left of the battalion but one officer and a few men who dribbled back to their own front line.'[2]

The men had advanced after being told that there were 300 guns trained on the Turkish position. In fact their attack was virtually without any fire support. It now appears that the artillery commander of 29th Division was not even made aware of the attack by 156th Brigade. In relation to a further attack, in Hickey's chapter entitled 'The Destruction of the 52nd Division', he wrote:

> As night fell on the 12th, the 52nd Division was all but broken, despite the remarkable heroism of its officers and men. . . . Out of the 7500 men of the Lowland Division who had gone into the attack on the 12th, 2500 had fallen. . . . Such was the faulty state of the intelligence available to Hunter-Weston that he did not realise that despite the eccentricity of the operational plans and poor staff work, the sheer gallantry of the Division in whom he had clearly had no confidence had won him a battle; but there were now no reserves capable of exploiting it.[3]

How did all this come about? How was it that the 52nd (Lowland) Division, of which the 156th Brigade was a part, the brigade including the 8th Scottish Rifles of which the young Scottish chaplain was a member, experienced such terrible casualties?

The Gallipoli Memorial Lectures have explored this question from a variety of complementary perspectives. Some have considered the wider historical background, Professor Stürmer taking into account the whole sweep of European relationships with the Ottoman empire and John Grigg the war as a whole in contrast to the Second World War. Others like Prince Philip have concentrated on the grand strategy, with Martin Gilbert focusing particularly on the role of Churchill. We have had a naval perspective from Sir Julian Oswald and a military one from Sir Nigel Bagnall, as well as French, New Zealand and Turkish views of the events. Out of them, as we know, came the birth of Australia, New Zealand and Turkey as nations with a clear and proud identity, as Sir Michael Howard highlighted. Some have sought quite specifically to draw out lessons for today, Sir Edward Heath in relation to defence and Professor O'Neill in relation to both strategy and tactics. All have emphasised the terrible conditions, the suffering, the casualties and, not least, the heroism on both sides. Those of us who have walked over the scene will never forget those opposing trenches, sometimes barely 20 yards apart. Above all, lecturers have been conscious of what Sir Hugh Beach called the 'cybernetic failure', the murderous responsibility at a political and senior military level for the tragedy that ensued.

There is no need to go over the history of the conflict again. I will simply sum up the main failures that lecturers and other writers on the subject have identified.

First, the lack of any real unity in London about the desirability of the strategic plan in the first place. The Admiral of the Fleet, Fisher, who was called out of retirement at the age of seventy-three, had a close, mutually fascinated relationship with Churchill, but was always sceptical. His words 'Damn the Dardanelles – they will be our grave!' have gone into history. Understandably, there were a good number who argued that the first priority for troops and supplies should be France, not Gallipoli, and who were not convinced by Churchill.

Secondly, there was no joint command of the army and naval forces. It was never entirely clear how the two should act together.

Thirdly, only the vaguest plans were drawn up at the outset, with no attempt to think through the force levels that were required and the necessary back-up in the way of transport, supplies and landing craft. Fighting a major campaign 3000 miles from Britain and hundreds of miles from headquarters in Alexandria and Malta would have been a logistical challenge even if people had realised what was involved. But they didn't. In our own time the conflicts over Suez, in the Falklands, in Kuwait and former Yugoslavia have made us aware of the sheer feat of organisation and meticulous planning that is required to mount an action miles from home. The troops in Gallipoli had, in the early stages, no intelligence to go on, out-of-date maps, no reserves, an inadequate estimation of the casualties, very poor communications, and so on. Lessons were subsequently learnt, thank God. As Lord Runcie put it in his lecture:

> Those of us who fought in the Normandy campaign were aware of the preparations made for it and could not fail to be heartened by the thought that Winston Churchill – at 40, the daring architect of the 1915 adventure – was determined that close on 30 years later the mistakes would not be repeated. Perhaps those of us who survived owe a strange debt to the shadow of Gallipoli.[4]

These terrible failures should not of course be seen apart from the strengths on the other side: mobile howitzers which, as we discovered with the conflict with Saddam Hussein and in Bosnia, are extremely difficult to locate and eliminate; the skilful mining by the Turkish navy; and the professionalism and bravery of the Turkish soldiers, who took full advantage of the delays among the Allies to reinforce positions and prepare well for the landings and subsequent attacks. They also had a number of highly competent German officers who trained the men well, and above all, of course, there was the leadership of the one whom we have come to know as Atatürk, who inspired his men to die rather than give an inch.

There are also the wider political questions. For why was Turkey on the opposite side anyway? There was a large British business community in Turkey and a great deal of pro-British feeling. As we know, it had a very great deal to do with the fact that the British government had taken possession of two ships that had been ordered by the Turks for delivery in the autumn of 1914, paid for by collecting boxes in the streets of Constantinople. In contrast, there was an able German ambassador in Constantinople who ensured that the Germans gave Turkey two German warships to replace the British ones.

Others, better qualified than I, have drawn the political, strategic and tactical lessons and no doubt will continue to do so. I want to do something rather different: to examine the attempts made to evaluate what happened in Gallipoli in moral and spiritual terms. First there was the interpretation of Gallipoli as heroic, and then, in reaction, the tendency to see it all as waste and futility. I will suggest that neither response is fully adequate and that, from a Christian perspective, the initial response, however dangerously romantic, has a seed of truth that we cannot relinquish.

I began this lecture with extracts from the letters of a young chaplain with the 8th Scottish Rifles. Those letters told it how it was, albeit in a tone that sought to reassure his loving mother and with the characteristic public school 'cool' of the period. After the war, however, others wrote about what happened in a larger, consolatory context. In particular there was Ernest Raymond, who had himself been a chaplain at Gallipoli. His best-selling novel *Tell England*[5] was published in February 1922; it was reprinted fourteen times in that year, six times in the year after and many times subsequently.

The novel traces the story of a group of public schoolboys from school to Gallipoli, especially two, Edgar Doe and Rupert Ray, through whose eyes the scene unfolds. But the authorial stance comes across above all in the chaplain, Padre Monty, who befriended the young men. On the boat going out as the champagne corks pop and the boisterous subalterns shout 'Take cover' Padre Monty initiates the two into the glories of Catholic Anglicanism. He expounds the nature of the mass and the importance of confession. First Rupert and then Edgar are won over. Rupert wrote:

He gave me the very thing that my opening manhood was craving; one clear and lofty ideal . . . I was to see three ideals, Goodness, Truth and Beauty, and merge them all in one vision – Beauty. For Goodness was only beauty in morals and Truth was only beauty in knowledge . . . 'Pursue beauty' he said, 'Like the Holy Grail.'[6]

Rupert makes his confession and goes out on the submarine watch on deck where a sense of the beauty of nature and the beauty of character and the beauty of life coalesce within him in one moment of exultation.

When they get to Gallipoli, however, it begins to dawn on them that the campaign is already lost. Rupert becomes depressed and begins to doubt whether there is more beauty than horror in life. Then a friend is killed. Rupert goes into action and finds himself killing others. Then Edgar, his old schoolmate, gets killed. Rupert grieves bitterly but Padre Monty looks at his death very differently. He argues that when Edgar set out to neutralise an enemy gun he did his duty without thinking of his personal glory.

> 'And, Rupert, this afternoon he told me, that when he went forward to put out that gun, he felt quite alone. He seemed surrounded with smoke and flying dust. And he thought he would do one big deed unseen. . . . He did his perfect thing at the last.'
> 'There's no beauty' I repeated dully.
> 'Rupert, Edgar is dead . . . and there is only one unbeautiful thing about his death, and that is the way his friend is taking it.'[7]

Padre Monty then expounds the theme of beauty in death and the beauty of the friendship of the two young men. If it was not for the war they would not have been brought together again: 'But, as it is, the war has held you in a deepening intimacy till – till the end. It's – it's perfect'.[8]

Rupert survives Gallipoli and in 1918 goes out to France. There he receives a letter from his mother who had been to a Gallipoli memorial service at which Monty had preached, likening the sacrifice of fathers and mothers of their sons at Gallipoli to the sacrifice of God the Father and Mary the Mother of Christ. 'All you who have suffered, you fathers and mothers, remember this: only by turning your sufferings into the seeds of God-like things will you make their memory beautiful.'

Rupert is killed in France and before he died he wrote: 'In the Mediterranean on a summer day, I learned I was to pursue beauty like the Holy Grail. And I see it now in everything. I know that, just as there is far more beauty in nature than ugliness, so there is more goodness in humanity than evil. There is more happiness in life than pain. Yes, there is.'[9]

For Ernest Raymond himself it was not so certain as that. He lost his faith, gave up his orders and made his living for the rest of his life as a novelist. I was privileged to know him when I was curate at Hampstead parish church from 1963 to 1969. During that period his faith flared up again and he returned to the church, a pilgrimage he again reflected in his writings. But our concern now is with the consolatory framework within which he set the tragedy of Gallipoli as expressed through Padre Monty.

There are a number of reasons why we would find it difficult today to write in those terms.

First, after nearly a century soaked in Freud, we are responsive to the words of Iris Murdoch that 'All that consoles is fake'.[10] Closely connected to this view, we believe it is important to face the harsh realities, however bleak, and not try to gloss or romanticise them. Talking to Rupert after the death of his close friend Edgar we would acknowledge his grief and bitterness, not suggest that it was somehow inappropriate and spoiling a beautiful death. And perhaps even more seriously still the kind of language used by Padre Monty cannot only blind us to the actual horrors of war but can be used to justify its most terrible happenings. Father King, a Mirfield Father, was also a chaplain at Gallipoli. On board ship before storming the beaches, a thousand men were called to prayer and, as he put it, 'A deep and solemn silence passed along both decks'. He told his men 'This is a holy war'. But he did not glorify it. It was also 'Hell'. Yet at the same time it was 'Instrumental in drawing from men deeds of unparalleled heroism and self-sacrifice'.[11]

One of the important points made by Alan Wilkinson in his seminal study of the Church of England in the First World War was the development of a deep conviction in the British populace that those young men killed in battle would go to heaven. All previous teaching that there was a severe judgement and a sifting of the good and the evil was set aside. Those young men who had fought so bravely were thought to go straight into the better life of the world to come. That was the only way people could cope with their loss, the only way they could make sense of the terrible waste and heroic courage. A lieutenant writing to his family from Gallipoli in May 1915 told how a badly wounded soldier asked him 'Shall I go to heaven or hell, Sir?' He replied with perfect confidence 'To heaven'.[12] All this worries us. Millions of unarmed or scarcely armed Iranian youths were pitched into battle against Iraq on the basis of a paradise that awaited them just ahead. That indeed was part of the motivation of Turkish soldiers at Gallipoli. Hans Kannengiesser, one of the most influential of the 500 Germans serving with the Turks in Gallipoli, wrote that they were brave and trustworthy. 'It was the will of Allah that he should follow his leader without question. He is deeply religious and believes that his life is only a prelude to a yet better one.'[13] We are disquieted by this because the last four decades have been shaped by the poets of the First World War, especially Wilfred Owen, who among other things referred to *Dulce et decorum est pro patria mori* as 'The Old Lie'.

Ernest Raymond, looking back at Gallipoli at the end of his life, had come to a similar conclusion. He describes first how as a young curate he asked his vicar if he could go into the army. When the vicar said yes, Raymond writes, 'You can scarcely imagine my joy'.[14] Then, as he read Sir Ian Hamilton's first despatch from Gallipoli to Kitchener, his reaction was 'This was the battlefield

I would long to go to'.[15] It was 'My heart's desire, the Gallipoli campaign'.[16] On the way there he sees it through the eyes of Greek myth and the neighbouring battleground of Troy. This romantic enthusiasm for war in general and Gallipoli in particular, as seen in the light of ancient Greece, was not unusual. Rupert Brooke wrote to Violet Asquith in February 1915 to say

> I've never been quite so happy in my life, I think. Not quite so *pervasively* happy; like a stream flowing entirely to one end. I suddenly realise that the ambition in my life has been – since I was two – to go on a military expedition against Constantinople. And when I *thought* I was hungry, or sleepy, or falling in love, or aching to write a poem – *that* was what I really, blindly wanted.[17]

Brooke did have the sense and self-knowledge to add 'This is nonsense', but there is no disguising the feeling. A.P. Herbert's *The Secret Battle*[18] provides a remarkable account of that romantic enthusiasm and how it turned into disgust at Gallipoli, describing well all the terror of being constantly sniped at, the weaking effect of dysentery and the horror of smelling the dead bodies of his men.

At the same time, there was a surprisingly positive attitude towards the Turkish enemy. William Wilson recorded his lack of hatred towards 'Johnny Turk'. Geoffrey Dearmer, whose brother was killed at Gallipoli, wrote a number of poems about the campaign, including one about a Turkish trenchdog that licked his face. Most remarkable however is his short poem entitled 'The Dead Turk':

> Dead, dead, and dumbly chill. He seemed to lie
> Carved from the earth, in beauty without stain.
> And suddenly
> Day turned to night, and I beheld again
> A still Centurion with eyes ablaze:
> And Calvary re-echoed with his cry –
> His cry of stark amaze.[19]

The dead body of the Turk brings to mind the cry of the centurion at Christ's death, 'Truly this man was the Son of God.' (Mark 15, 39, in the Authorised Version with which Dearmer would have been familiar.) It is an extraordinary juxtaposition to bring together a Christian confession of faith in Jesus as the Son of God and the body of a dead Turkish soldier so that the latter is seen in the light of the former. The dead enemy soldier is also a son of God.

Ernest Raymond too wrote that after the first raging battles the Turk 'Became popular with us, and everything suggested that our amiability toward him was reciprocated',[20] but at the end of his life Raymond's feelings about Gallipoli in general are very different. 'The naive romanticism, the pieties, the too facile heroics and too uncritical patriotism – of these I can almost cry aloud in distress',[21] though he did note that he could understand the overspill of pieties and 'spiritual uplift' because he was then in religious orders. Some of this later reaction was clearly felt by some immediately after the Gallipoli campaign because Raymond's novel *Tell England*, although it met vociferous acclaim in some quarters, also experienced violent criticism from people like Rose Macaulay. I doubt whether that reaction was entirely a literary one, and in any case the literary cannot be dissociated from questions of sensibility and morality.

The reaction against the romanticism with which the First World War was seen, at least in its early stages and by people who were not actually involved in the fighting, led to a very different attitude in the second. At this point we can distinguish between a crusade mentality, in which people believe they are fighting God's enemies in God's name, and the Christian Just War tradition which sees war as a tragic necessity that might sometimes have to be fought, if certain criteria are met. With a few notable exceptions those who went into the First World War tended towards the former outlook. In the Second World War it was the much more sombre and sober latter attitude that prevailed. We see an example of this in the prayers composed during that war by Reinhold Niebuhr, one of which reads:

Look with mercy, O Lord, upon the peoples of the world, so full both of pride and confusion, so sure of their righteousness and so deeply involved in unrighteousness . . . have mercy upon our own nation, called to such high responsibilities in the affairs of mankind. Purge us of the vain glory which confuses our counsels, and give our leaders and our people the wisdom of humility and charity. Help us to recognise our own affinity with whatever truculence or malice is confronting us that we may not add to the world's woe by the fury of our own resentments. Give your Church the grace in this time to be as a saving remnant among the nations, reminding all peoples of the divine majesty under whose judgement they stand, and of the divine mercy of which they and we have a common need.[22]

In these and other prayers there is an implacable sense that the war has to be fought but no sense of self-righteousness and a profound underlying assumption that there are wider and higher truths, in the light of which even war might not be seen as the ultimate evil.

Yet looking back on that war as we look back on Gallipoli, the courage and willingness to sacrifice life itself for a higher cause is still to be identified, affirmed and not forgotten. Les Murray in his poem 'Visiting Anzac in the Year of Metrication'[23] explores something of the tension. There is pathos and sadness in the human bones that still come out of the clay at Gallipoli. There is a sense that those who fought there were 'misemployed, undone by courage'. Yet also a sense that there was brotherhood and incomparable friends which also needs to be taken into account and fully weighed in an age when all is measured. For, in full awareness of the terrible mistakes and waste, the tragedy and futility, and despite all the acute difficulties and dangers of which we are conscious in a consolatory framework, there is a truth that we cannot let slip away. For, on a Christian view of things, it remains true that sin and suffering, tragedy and death, do not have the last word. It remains true that while there are terrible physical battles, there are no less important moral and spiritual ones. It remains true that the purpose of human existence cannot simply be grasped as a calculus of pain and pleasure. Even in the midst of battle people make choices that have eternal significance. We find it difficult, perhaps almost impossible, to talk about this today. But we cannot give up on this way of seeing things, not least because on this occasion we remember still those thousands of young men cut off in their prime.

I am concerned above all with the tension between seeing Gallipoli as a tragic waste (which it was for the Allies, though not of course for Turkey) and celebrating the courage that was shown there by so many. It is difficult for the human spirit to face failure and loss, total loss. There is an instinct to try to see some ennobling feature. As Lord Runcie put it, 'The conviction that war on such a scale must have a meaning on the same grand scale has been doggedly clung to by many'.[24] The Anzac nations found the meaning of Gallipoli by relating it to the birth of their confident, independent identity. Michael Howard pointed out that if Gallipoli had been won the losses would have been subsumed in the euphoria of a larger victory. If on the other hand there had not been that dramatic and highly successful withdrawal, there would be nothing to celebrate at all.

> In that campaign the courage and endurance of those who took part cannot be considered simply as a contribution to a final success that overshadowed all that had gone before. They were their own justification. Disaster might have made them tragic, while in triumph they might have been almost forgotten . . . it is remembered, not as a victory over the Turks – but as a victory over circumstances.[25]

As it was, the Anzacs had much of which to be proud and nothing to be ashamed about. This was the mood that led to the celebration of the first Anzac Day a few months later.

What happened for the Anzac nations raises questions about what it is possible to say in a larger context unrelated to the birth of a particular national self-identity. For in Britain and France there was not that justification.

The men who returned from Gallipoli did not dwell on the errors and terrors they had experienced. This was not the way then, and besides there was a campaign still to be engaged in, many battles still to be won. So they kept silence and the glorious legend of Gallipoli was established. As General Thornton put it, 'The loss of life had been so great that it was necessary to find justification in the heroic rather than admitting tragic failure'. A.P. Herbert, continuing in service in France in 1916, noted that 'All the men from Gallipoli talk of it with something like reverence'.[26] It is this sense that is reflected in Ernest Raymond's *Tell England*. The beaches of Gallipoli had come to be sacred ground in the minds of the young officers from England. They think of them with bated breath and cannot wait to have the privilege of walking upon the hallowed shore.

In all this there is a very human, though totally understandable, motivation. But what justification does it have? Here a Christian is drawn once again to the paradox of the Cross. Here was one of the worst tortures that the world has ever known, utterly horrific. Yet Christians see here the culmination of a life lived in total trust and faithfulness, a life that brought the redemption of humanity. We see it through the Resurrection, in the light of which Christ's death is seen as a triumphant victory, a view reflected in the Fourth Gospel. Such a life can only be seen as a victory and the lives of those who died bravely at Gallipoli in the light of that victory, on the basis of two convictions that the modern world finds difficult to believe.

First, life is not about avoiding pain and maximising pleasure. It is not about money, power or prestige. It is about growing more and more like God, who is love. That love is not sentimentality. It is self-giving for the well-being of others. It certainly includes courage. On this perspective there is no circumstance in which it is not possible to reflect, in one way or another, the love of God that undergirds and fills all things and to grow in that love through love of family, friends, and even nation.

Secondly, this life opens up beyond space and time to a future that, though unimaginable, is as real as the present, more real in fact.

To go further than this would be to go beyond the scope of this lecture, into theodicy. But here in brief are the two reasons why, however much we might react against the romanticisation and easy pieties of the early post-Gallipoli period, and however difficult we find it to talk about such things today, we cannot let go the kernel of truth which saw in the courage of those who fought something to celebrate in the darkness of a tragically suffering world.

The best novels and poems cannot be summed up in a slogan. They contain a proper ambiguity, a sense of the unresolved, which reflects the character of life itself. We are uneasy about easy words of hope and consolation. Yet, from a Christian point of view, we should be equally uneasy about easy words of scepticism and despair. If there are lessons to be learned from Gallipoli and the First World War generally about how not to deploy religious rhetoric, it may be that in a post-Wilfred Owen world there are also lessons to be learnt of a more positive kind.

Owen wrote a poem called 'Last Words':

> 'O Jesus Christ!' one fellow sighed.
> And kneels, and bowed tho' not in prayer, and died
> And the bullet sang 'In Vain',
> Machine guns chuckled 'Vain',
> Big guns guffawed 'In Vain'.[27]

But the funeral service of many of those who died at Gallipoli will have contained the words: 'Therefore, my beloved brethren, be steadfast, immovable, always abounding in the work of the Lord, knowing that in the Lord your labour is not in vain'.[28]

'Not in vain.' That is our hope even though the way in which that hope is fulfilled goes out in mystery.

Notes

1. Unpublished letters of the Reverend William Skinner Wilson reprinted by permission of his son, Lord Wilson of Tillyorn.
2. Michael Hickey, *Gallipoli*, Murray, 1995, pp. 220–1.
3. *Gallipoli*, p. 231.
4. The Rt Revd Lord Runcie, 'The God of Battles and the Fight for Faith'.
5. Ernest Raymond, *Tell England*, Cassell, 1922.
6. *Tell England*, p. 216.
7. *Tell England*, p. 299.
8. *Tell England*, p. 317.
9. *Tell England*, p. 319.
10. Iris Murdoch, 'The Sovereignty of Good'.
11. Alan Wilkinson, *The Church of England and the First World War*, SPCK, 1978, pp. 148–9.
12. Quoted by Sir Nigel Bagnall, 'The Human Story', pp. 91–103.
13. *War Letters of Fallen Englishmen*, ed. Laurence Housman, Gollancz, 1930, p. 27.
14. Ernest Raymond, *The Story of My Days: an Autobiography 1882–1922*, Cassell, 1968, p. 120.
15. *The Story of My Days*, p. 123.
16. *The Story of My Days*, p. 126.
17. *The Letters of Rupert Brooke*, ed. G.L. Keynes, p. 662.
18. A.P. Herbert, *The Secret Battle*, Oxford University Press, 1980.

19. Geoffrey Dearmer, *A Pilgrim's Song*, foreword by John Stallworthy, Murray, 1993, p. 7.
20. *The Story of My Days*, p. 128.
21. *The Story of My Days*, p. 179.
22. Quoted in Richard Harries, *Praying Round the Clock*, Mowbray, 1983, p. 195.
23. Les Murray, 'Visiting Anzac in the Year of Metrication', *Collected Poems*, Carcanet, 1998, p. 119.
24. 'The God of Battles and the Fight for Faith', pp. 37–48.
25. Michael Howard, 'War and the Making of Nations', pp. 152–7.
26. Leonard Thornton, 'Echoes of Gallipoli', pp. 109–21.
27. Wilfred Owen, 'Last Words', *War Poems and Others*, ed. Dominic Hibberd, Chatto and Windus, 1975, p. 88.
28. I Corinthians 15, 58 (RSV).

Two other books that should be mentioned for the light they shed on the reaction of the church to Gallipoli are *Almost Like a Dream: A Parish at War 1914–18*, ed. M. Austin, Merton Priory Press and *Hell's Foundations: A Town, its Myths and Gallipoli*, Geoffrey Moorhouse, Hodder & Stoughton, 1992. The latter describes the effect of Gallipoli on a town closely connected with the Lancashire Fusiliers, Bury, which suffered grievous loss of its young men. The rector at the time, Charles Hill, preached sermons of unabashed patriotism. Even when he lost his only son in the Gallipoli campaign his patriotism remained undaunted. His successor, Hugh Hornby, who had served as a chaplain through the First World War took a more nuanced view. The theme of his sermons on the annual commemoration of Gallipoli was 'What we commemorate and idealise today is not war – far from it – but the unequalled self-sacrifice and devotion that was shown in the war. . . . With the resolve that, God helping us, we will harness that same spirit of self-sacrifice and devotion to the tasks and the deeds of peace.' (p. 152)

AFTERWORD

MARTIN GILBERT

Every soldier, sailor and airman, every politician, every historian, each of those whose lecture is printed above, has a personal perspective with relation to the Dardanelles and Gallipoli. In 1961, Sir Clifford Norton, a British diplomat whom I got to know while writing about pre-1939 British foreign policy, told me of when he was fleeing Poland in September 1939, pushing towards the Roumanian frontier in the hope of crossing it before German troops arrived. As he looked across the border from a blacked-out Polish village to the lights of the first Roumanian town in the distance, he was reminded of the lights of hospital ships off Cape Helles as he looked back from the darkness of his trench on the Gallipoli peninsula. What safety and comfort there seemed to be there.

A year later, in 1962, my first employer told me how he had never fully overcome the trauma of having been told, when he was a young schoolboy: 'Your father killed my father at the Dardanelles.' That schoolboy was Randolph Churchill, whose hope of writing the definitive, and honest, account of his father and Gallipoli was dashed by his premature death at the age of fifty-seven. That biographical task then fell to me. My first volume of the Churchill biography, Volume 3, entitled *The Challenge of War*, contains more than two hundred pages on the Dardanelles and Gallipoli. Its two companion volumes of documents contain more than six hundred pages devoted to the origins and aftermath of the Dardanelles. In preparation for these books I made three visits to the peninsula, the first in 1969. I also spent time in Atatürk's house in Ankara, where his collection of books on the campaign was comprehensive. He had re-read Churchill's own account in *The World Crisis* on the eve of what was to have been Churchill's own visit to the peninsula, and meeting with Atatürk, in 1937. But, because of a political crisis in Britain, Churchill had to postpone his visit, and before he could rearrange it, Atatürk was dead.

Like every visitor to Gallipoli, I was struck by the enormous care being taken over the cemeteries. During the period of my visits, the Commonwealth War Graves representative there was Norman Pemberton. My last visit coincided with the visit which Prince Philip mentions, of The

Queen, Princess Anne and himself to Cape Helles. To be present at the ceremony, I had to rise before dawn from one of the fishermen's huts near Anzac Cove, walk across the peninsula (using the low terrain that the soldiers would have used had they been landed at the correct spot, according to the original plan), and then on to the Cape, through several villages that were decked out in their finery to welcome the royal visitors. At Cape Helles, after the royal party – and the coach full of journalists – had gone, I looked across the fields to the summit of Achi Baba, the objective, so near, that eluded repeated assaults. The soft beauty of the landscape belied the savage fighting that had taken place all around me. The sea was calm. The land was quiet. Yet everywhere one walked there were reminders of what had taken place: scraps of metal, fragments of shell cases, broken bottles, rusting tins.

The twenty-first century will see new research and new writing on the Dardanelles and Gallipoli. The campaign will not lose its fascination, even when a century will have passed since the guns were firing. Just as we still read and relish fresh accounts of the Crimean War or the Napoleonic Wars, so this small spit of land will retain its ability to draw future scholars and visitors to it. It is not only a question of different perspectives and evaluations, but of the lives, and deaths, of so many tens of thousands of individuals, each one of whom, whatever his rank or station, had a story to tell, and was part of the wider human story of war.

INDEX